FOR AND AGAINST THE STATE

FOR AND AGAINST THE STATE

New Philosophical Readings

edited by
John T. Sanders
and
Jan Narveson

ROWMAN & LITTLEFIELD PUBLISHERS, INC.

ROWMAN & LITTLEFIELD PUBLISHERS, INC.

Published in the United States of America
by Rowman & Littlefield Publishers, Inc.
4720 Boston Way, Lanham, Maryland 20706

3 Henrietta Street
London WC2E 8LU, England

British Cataloging in Publication Information Available

Library of Congress Cataloging-in-Publication Data
For and against the state : new philosophical readings / edited by
John T. Sanders and Jan Narveson.
p.   cm.—(Studies in social, political, and legal
philosophy)
Includes bibliographical references and index.
1. State, The.   2. Anarchism.   I. Sanders, John T.   II. Narveson,
Jan, 1936–   .   III. Series.
JC11.F67   1996   320.1—dc20   95-26486   CIP

ISBN 0-8476-8164-5 (cloth: alk. paper)
ISBN 0-8476-8165-3 (pbk.: alk. paper)

Printed in the United States of America

⊗ ™ The paper used in this publication meets the minimum requirements of
American National Standard for Information Sciences—Permanence of Paper
for Printed Library Materials, ANSI Z39.48—1984.

Contents

Preface

The idea for this collection came to the editors on the occasion of a panel discussion on anarchism at the Helsinki meetings of the International Society for Value Inquiry in 1993. It seemed to us that for many years philosophers in particular and students of politics in general were busy looking at trees when they might have another go at the forest. This collection addresses the central issue of political philosophy or, in a couple of cases, issues very close to the heart of that question: Is government justified? This ancient question has never been more alive than at the present time, in the midst of continuing political and social upheaval in virtually every part of the world. It seems high time for a volume that addresses questions of political authority in light of recent work in political theory as well as new experience of worldly political convulsion.

Only two of the pieces collected here—those by Gregory Kavka and David Schmidtz—have been published previously. All the other contributions were, at the time of the inception of the volume, fresh from the pens—or still to emerge from the pens—of their authors. The collection is thus about as up to the minute as one gets in the realm of academic philosophy.

Since each of these essays is self-contained, and their writers can speak very well indeed for themselves, it remains only (1) to express our gratitude to the writers for being astonishingly prompt with the drafts and, in a few cases, reworked drafts of essays; and (2) to express our pleasure at what we have found to be the extremely high level of discussion sustained by them. Of course, that is what we had hoped, but such hopes are not always fulfilled. We think we have gotten considerably more than we bargained for.

Vital time and funding were provided at various stages of the project by the University of Waterloo and the Social Sciences and Humanities Research Council of Canada, by Fulbright Scholar Award #95-65079, by a Rotary International Grant, by the Rochester Institute of Technology, and by the Graduate School for Social Research at the Polish Academy of Sciences.

We also owe thanks, finally, to the editors at Cambridge University Press and the University of Chicago Press for permission to reprint the essays by Kavka and Schmidtz, and to our editors at Rowman & Littlefield, especially Jennifer Ruark and Julie Kuzneski, for their very efficient and able attention to our project.

1

Who Believes in Political Obligation?[1]

Leslie Green

Is there a general obligation to obey the law, at least in a reasonably just state? Increasingly, political theorists deny that proposition. Of course, anarchists, marxists, and many theologians have denied it all along—their allegiance is to things higher than, or at any rate different from, the state. Now, however, a number of writers within the liberal tradition are denying it too.[2] To call this an emerging consensus would be more performative than descriptive; but it is, shall we say, a significant coalescence of opinion. Here, I want to explore one particular reaction to this skeptical thrust.

The issue arises this way. Theorists are denying the existence of an obligation to obey the law while most other people are said to endorse such an obligation. The skeptical position thus appears to be at variance with what most people in fact believe; so, quite apart from any internal difficulties in the skeptical argument itself, it fails to meet an external test: reasonable correspondence with our considered judgments. George Klosko, for instance, calls the belief in political obligation one of "our deepest intuitions about political matters": "[T]he existence of strong general feelings that we have political obligations . . . is supported by our most basic feelings about politics. I take it as obviously true that most people believe they have obligations to their governments."[3]

Is the claim that most people believe this, as Klosko supposes, "obviously true," and, if it is, does it matter? Those are the questions I try to answer here, taking the second first.

1

Coherence and Common Opinion

Whether it is significant that there is a widespread belief in political obligation depends on one's account of the nature of justificatory argument in political theory. One popular view, advocated by Klosko, is that we should strive for a certain kind of coherence, or what Rawls calls a "reflective equilibrium," between our considered judgments about cases and a systematizing normative theory.[4] An acceptable theory should therefore normally account for our most basic pretheoretical judgments, what Rawls calls our "provisional fixed points" in argument: fixed because we are not to abandon them lightly, but provisional because they might, in principle, yield to a compelling theory that had enough other merits.

Is the method of coherence circular, or does it involve some other kind of cheating? That is a common enough charge, and one often brought by those whose model of justification is patterned after one view of natural science: data are to be explained, not altered. It is in fact, however, the naive view of scientific justification that is wrong: the theory-ladenness of observation statements means that a recalcitrant observation can always be explained away. The process should be quite familiar to empirical social scientists who regularly remove "outliers" from their data plots before drawing a regression line through the remainder. It is only confidence in an attractive theory that lets us identify outliers in the first place. Because all data may include outliers, our fixed points are always provisional.

In moral and political theory, it is true, there is often more willingness to mess with the data, but even here there are points that most would agree must be explained and not just explained away. Consider a familiar example. Utilitarianism offers a coherent and elegant justification for punishment. It says that punishment is justified when, but only when, it brings about the greatest social good. The difficulty for the theory is notorious. It needs somehow to explain our view that the innocent ought never to be punished; yet one can construct a variety of scenarios in which it would be optimal to do just that. Very few utilitarians are willing simply to bite the bullet and say, "Well, that just proves that we may sometimes punish the innocent." On the contrary, they go to great lengths to show that their theory does not commit them to the repugnant conclusion. As much as their opponents, they regard the case of punishing the innocent as a fixed point.

Some political theorists treat the belief in political obligation that way. Klosko, for example, is willing to reject consent theory because it cannot explain the general belief in an obligation to obey.

> If legitimate political power can be derived only from the consent of (a
> high but oftentimes unspecified percentage of) the governed, then most,
> if not all, existing governments are illegitimate. Moreover, if we were to
> argue that individuals—including those who have consented—can be
> obligated to obey only legitimate governments, then the implication would
> be that very few citizens have political obligations.[5]

His point is that consent theory is incompatible with one of our deeply
entrenched judgments. And this is just a special case of the general
complaint against skepticism: it gives insufficient weight to one of the
provisionally fixed points of political consciousness.

Is this a good argument? I do not wish to challenge the coherence
method in the example of theories of punishment, but I do want to
examine the putative analogy with those arguments. I think that a
Klosko-type response ignores an important distinction. In the case of
punishing the innocent, the conflict is between a general theory of
punishment and our "intuitive" judgment about a particular case. The
problem is one of casuistry: can the utilitarian get the right answer in
this circumstance? The objection to skeptical theories of obligation is
not like that, however. It is not a conflict between a theory and a
judgment about a *case*, but between a theory and another *theory*,
namely, the "theory of political obligation." The claim is that the
skeptics' theory is not widely held, not that the skeptic has failed to
deliver the correct judgment about a certain case, for instance, a case
in which a useless or unjust law should nonetheless be obeyed. What
is claimed to need explanation is not such a judgment, but rather the
fact that a competing theory, the doctrine of political obligation, is
widely accepted.

The distinction between particular casuistic judgments and theoretical beliefs at a high level of abstraction is an important one. To get a
good analogy with the dispute about punishment, we need to consider
instead the conflict between utilitarianism and the popular view that
the guilty deserve to suffer or that offenders should always be paid
back. In philosophical argument about punishment, however, antiutili-
tarian theorists rarely appeal directly to the supposed popularity of
retributivism. The method of coherence does not take as its provisional
fixed points popular theories—and for good reason, for in this case
they recognize a need to distinguish retributive sentiments from mere
vengeance. That is why, against the utilitarians, the retributivists
appeal to our judgment about a particular case. They recognize that
that case has more probative force than does the abstract statement of
their theory.

The belief in political obligation, however, is more like the belief in the propriety of retribution than it is like the belief that a particular innocent person ought not to be punished. Political obligation is not a fixed point of moral consciousness, but a popular though controversial theory. That it is widely held might be relevant to its credibility, but if it is, it cannot be for the reason suggested by coherentist justifications.

There is, however, a different argument to which one might turn, one found in Hume's criticism of Locke. This is the argument from the authority of common opinion in moral matters.

The distinction between the two is this. In the argument from coherence we draw on the authority of a deeply held, intuitive belief about the morally correct disposition of a certain case. To know that this belief is among our considered judgments, we do not normally need to survey opinion. The armchair reflection of a single, fair-minded person will do. In this respect, casuistic judgments claim an authority analogous to the judgments of grammaticality that a single native speaker is competent to make about his or her mother tongue. In the case of punishment of the innocent, the fixity of that judgment rests not on its certification by social science, but in the security of our armchair. The argument from common opinion is different. It inherently relies on knowledge of public opinion. To know whether some theoretical proposition is widely held, we need to go and find out. It is not part of the surface grammar of our judgments; we must put it to people and see how they react.

I thus want to draw a distinction between the nature and methods of the casuistic argument from coherence and the more general argument from common opinion. The distinction is not specific to political theory. Do people believe that they have bodies? Armchair reflection about the logical grammar of terms such as "my hand" will suffice to tell us the answer. Do they generally believe that comet impact was responsible for the extinction of the dinosaurs? We would need to find out.

Hume does not clearly distinguish this second form of argument from the first, though he relies on its distinctive power whenever he contends that historical evidence refutes consent theory.[6] Whether the argument from common opinion is a sound justificatory procedure in political theory is a matter I have disputed elsewhere.[7] I think the strongest case that might be made for it is the one that Hume invokes, namely, that to the extent that morality rests on sentiment, there can be no higher court than public opinion, and that competing, more rationalistic, theories are philosophically suspect. The cogency of these arguments cannot be addressed here. Suffice it to say that the significance of the common belief in political obligation would have to rest on something like this, rather than on the standing of "provisional fixed points" of casuistry that figure in the argument from coherence.

Explaining Away

Interpreted in this second way, as an appeal to common opinion, a widespread belief in political obligation may or may not be threatening to skeptical theories. The argument from common opinion must always allow for the possibility that some opinions are formed in circumstances that make them likely to be false or misleading. In some cases it is therefore proper to explain away a consensus.

A belief, however well entrenched, might nonetheless be false. John Mackie introduces the idea of an "error theory" in ethics to describe the deeply ingrained but (he thinks) false view that moral judgments are objective.[8] Ordinary moral thought, he concedes, incorporates the belief in objective values, so subjectivism cannot be sustained on the strength of any sort of "linguistic" or "conceptual" analysis of moral discourse. But the belief is nonetheless a false one, and Mackie thinks that its falsity can be adequately established by empirical and theoretical considerations.

We might, in a similar way, adopt an error theory of political obligation. We might concede that the theory is ingrained in ordinary political discourse but reject it as false or even incoherent. It is true that this will involve refuting or at least weakening the argument from common opinion, but perhaps that can be done. An error theory depends on the positive strength of the skeptical argument.

A different, though overlapping, approach is to reject the widespread belief in political obligation as being ideological, or grounded in false consciousness.[9] Antonio Gramsci properly recognized that the deliverances of "common sense," our everyday theoretical beliefs, are often deeply ideological. Here, one emphasizes the negative case by calling into question the grounds on which the belief is held. In particular, beliefs that result from manipulation or indoctrination or which would be abandoned if their causal origins were known are suspect. If one is to avoid the genetic fallacy, specifying the conditions under which such beliefs may be dismissed will be a delicate matter; but if the argument from common opinion is attractive, the counterargument from ideology may be too.

This is, in part, John Simmons's move in addressing the consequences of his own skeptical position:

> If it [skepticism] runs counter to normal feelings about the citizen-state
> relationship, I think there are better explanations for this fact than the
> falsity of my conclusion. For what belief can better serve the interests of
> one's political leaders than the belief that all are specially bound to
> support their government and obey the law?[10]

Of course, this is a very compressed statement of the argument.
Practically all interesting political beliefs serve someone's interests.
The important point is that this particular belief is, in most political
societies, the normal outcome of a complex system of formal and
informal processes that foster such beliefs. This means not merely that
it is unsurprising that many people believe in political obligation, but
also—and this is a different point—that many people will avow the
belief who do not in fact hold it, because it is both socially expected
and often advantageous to do so.

Klosko objects to Simmons's argument. He says that Simmons
proceeds on the basis of the coherence method, relying freely on our
considered judgments about cases, but then, when he gets to the
feeling that we have special bonds to our own states, he inexplicably
shifts gears and becomes more rationalistic. Klosko objects:

> Unless Simmons can distinguish aspects of our consciousness that result
> from indoctrination from aspects that do not, his appeal to indoctrination
> in regard to this one aspect of our political beliefs undermines his use of
> the coherence method throughout his book.[11]

This is an objection targeted at someone thought to endorse the
method of coherence in justification; it would have no purchase against
a more thorough-going rationalist. That is not, however, the most
important point; rather, it is this: the belief in political obligation is
not, as I have said, a provisional fixed point in judgment; it is not a
particular judgment at all. It is a piece of low-level, commonsense
political theory like, for example, the widely held view that majority
rule is democratic. A coherentist thus can distinguish our commonsense theories from our casuistic judgments and with good reason set
a higher threshold for the credibility of the former than for the
latter. Commonsense theories are at one remove from our practical
experience. Being taught as doctrines, insisted on by officials, incul-
cated in schools, and so on, they are more susceptible to ideological

distortion than are casuistic judgments thrown up by the unstructured experiences of life.

This particular theory is, moreover, right at the center of the power structures of the modern state. Historically, its career has paralleled that of the state. It emerged in the conflict between the normative order of the state and the claims of a universal church. Now, as the state transforms itself under the pressure of the globalization of market economies, the doctrine of political obligation is losing some of its appeal. The idea that we are all, first and foremost, citizens of particular states to which we owe particular duties of allegiance is under strain, just at the moment those states are themselves under strain. Political obligation is thus a doctrine that is peculiarly sensitive to the ideological context in which it functions.

This is not, of course, a decisive argument in favor of explaining away political obligation as a piece of ideological detritus. It is not decisive, in part because ideological beliefs should be self-effacing under the scrutiny of reason. Once their social roots are exposed, the weed should wither away; yet that does not seem to be the case here. The belief in political obligation has proved remarkably resilient; it is endorsed even by those who are perfectly aware of its ideological functions. That suggests that the case against it is not proven, but at the same time I do not see how one can doubt that there is a serious case here to answer.

The Content of the Belief

I turn now from the question of the significance and standing of the claim to its truth. Klosko says that it is "obviously true" that there is a widespread belief in political obligation. I want to begin with some general reasons for doubting that and then, in the next section, consider briefly some empirical evidence that purports to bear on it.

What does one have to believe before one can properly be said to believe in political obligation? This is the crux of the issue. Let me begin with an analogy. Suppose that an adherent of the Roman Catholic church says that he believes in the authority of the pope. What would make it correct to say that he has this belief? To begin, we need to distinguish the claim that he has the belief from the claim that he avows the belief. All sorts of Catholics avow this belief who do not in fact accept it. They avow it because, theology aside, it is part of

Roman Catholic religious culture to do so; thus, there are reasons for Catholics to avow it whether or not they actually hold it.

To get behind the avowals, one therefore needs to know more. Because it is papal authority that is in issue, one needs to know what that amounts to before one knows whether our subject believes in it. How do we identify the character of such authority? By recourse to the authoritative sources and traditions of Catholic theology. Suppose we find, to simplify things, that one essential element of papal authority is the claim to infallibility in certain matters of faith when the pope speaks ex cathedra. Believing in that is thus part of what it is to believe in papal authority. If, like many North American Catholics, our subject avows the belief in papal authority but wholly rejects the doctrine of infallibility, then it would be wrong, in fact, to say that he believes in the authority of the pope. What he believes just does not amount to that.

Political obligation is similar. One believes in an obligation to obey the law only if one accepts, on certain terms, the authority of the state. How does one determine what the terms are? We may consult the tradition of argument within political theory to see what it is that people are arguing about when they dispute political obligation, and we may consult the authoritative voices of the state to see what it is that the state actually claims for itself. These are, of course, matters for discussion, and they do implicate, indirectly, a variety of different evaluative standards, but they are not matters for first-order moral or political argument; they are part of the abstract but descriptive part of political theory.[12]

By either route, one comes to the following conclusion.[13] Political obligation is the doctrine that everyone has a moral reason to obey all the laws of his or her own state and that this reason binds independently of the content of the law. This does not imply that the obligation to obey is absolute, nor that it applies in fundamentally unjust circumstances. The doctrine of political obligation is supposed to explain the character of allegiance, prima facie, in reasonably just states. One believes in political obligation only if one thinks that states have the authority they claim, and what they claim is supreme power to determine our rights, obligations, and powers and to have our compliance with their requirements independent of our assessment of the merits of what is required.

Like any other descriptive proposition, this one is disputable; but it is not in fact much disputed. It is the image of the state that is presented in the Western tradition of political theory as well as in the works of contemporary writers.[14] Most important, it is also what the officials of states have in mind as they issue orders and expect compliance.

Although it is fairly general, this characterization of the authority of the state nonetheless has theoretical bite, for it entails that a belief in political obligation differs from a variety of other beliefs that people may hold. For example:

(1) We ought never lightly to disobey the law.

This is not political obligation. One who believes this need not concede the authority of the state at all. This belief can be supported just by the (important) truism that the state regulates matters of vital concern in which the moral stakes are high. In a reasonably just state, officials act in good faith to promote the public interest, and citizens make plans based on the expectation that people will give serious weight to what the law requires.

(2) We ought, most of the time, to comply with most of the laws.

This is entailed by a belief in political obligation, but it is not equivalent to it. It is not equivalent because, for one thing, it acknowledges a commitment to comply only most of the time and, for another, it says nothing about the nature of the reason for complying. It might, for instance, have nothing to do with the fact that the requirements are laws or are the laws of our own states. After all, (2) is, on plausible factual assumptions, entailed also by (3).

(3) There is an obligation to do what the law requires, but not because the law requires it. The only reason for compliance is that there is normally a coincidence of moral and political obligations.

This is not political obligation, because the fact that the behavior in question is required by law is immaterial to the duty to comply. This duty rests instead on a content-dependent reason for compliance. Even an anarchist can believe that it is wrong to murder people and thus that there is a moral reason for complying with the law against murder. In a reasonably just state, most of the laws will be coincident with, or at least not objectionably discordant with, what we ought to do anyway.

(4) With respect to some laws there is a strict obligation of obedience; here, we ought to take the law at its word. There are other laws, however, with respect to which it is appropriate to assess one's compliance on a case-by-case basis.

This is not political obligation, though it is on the margins of it. This view allows that there is a certain range over which the appropriate attitude to the law is to regard it as authoritative, and another range where this is inappropriate, and that it is a matter of individual discretion where to draw the line. This is not political obligation because the state does not itself share this view: it claims authority wherever it purports to regulate.

I think the four statements above are fairly common attitudes toward law, and there are many other similar examples; moreover, they are politically important attitudes, for they help support valuable institutions such as governments and they contribute to a shared conception of justice and so on. What is relevant here, however, is that they all stop short of acknowledging the authority that a reasonably just state claims. They do not amount, severally or jointly, to the belief in an obligation to obey the law as it claims to be obeyed.

Which of these or other related attitudes are most prevalent in our societies is a factual question. I am not sure of the answer, but bearing in mind these distinctions, it does seem hasty, to say the least, to claim that it is "obviously true" that most people believe in political obligation. All that is obviously true is that most people have proattitudes toward their own governments—but that truth is no threat at all to the skeptical position about political obligation.

Some Empirical Evidence

To the best of my knowledge, no one has yet designed a satisfactory study to test the extent to which people believe in the theory of political obligation. There are, however, a number of studies that bear on it indirectly, studies of things such as compliance with law, support for governments, willingness to pay taxes, and so forth. One of the very few to make an explicit effort to estimate the popularity of belief in political obligation is Tom R. Tyler's *Why People Obey the Law*.[15] A brief review of its methods and findings shows how hard it is to come to firm conclusions even here.

Tyler surveyed people in Chicago to investigate the extent to which compliance with law is based on normative as opposed to instrumental reasons. He finds, unsurprisingly, that people obey because they think it is proper to do so and that this belief has roots in things other than the consequences of compliance, such as the perceived legitimacy of the system. In particular, he claims, "The extent to which respondents endorsed the obligation to obey is striking."[16]

His account of the normative grounds of compliance draws an important distinction between what he calls "personal morality"—the view that the law corresponds with what the agents regard as right behavior—and "legitimacy"—the view that the legal system has a right to dictate their behavior whether or not it corresponds with their own view of what is right. The theoretical significance of legitimacy is evident, for personal morality may require resistance as well as compliance.

Tyler is rightly critical of those social scientists who, following David Easton, have assimilated a belief in the legitimacy of the system to a diffuse sort of support for it. Merely feeling positive about one's state does not amount to accepting its authority.[17] Tyler writes:

> The fundamental difference between obligation and support lies in the clarity of the motivation underlying compliance. Theories that measure legitimacy assume that support for the government leads to the type of discretionary authority directly tapped by measuring the perceived obligation to obey.[18]

That assumption is plainly a fragile one. If a person agrees with the laws, he or she will be supportive of the government but need not feel any obligation at all, and might even withdraw support following a policy change. What is needed, then, is a direct measure of the perceived obligation to obey. In service of this, Tyler asked respondents whether they agreed with the following statements and got the following results:[19]

(1) People should obey the law even if it goes against what they think is right. (82 percent agreement)
(2) I always try to follow the law even if I think it is wrong. (82 percent agreement)
(3) Disobeying the law is seldom justified. (79 percent agreement)
(4) It is difficult to break the law and keep one's self-respect. (69 percent agreement)
(5) If a person is doing something and a police officer tells them to stop,

they should stop even if they feel that what they are doing is legal. (84 percent agreement)

(6) If a person goes to court because of a dispute with another person, and the judge orders them to pay the other person money, they should pay that person money, even if they think that the judge is wrong. (74 percent agreement)

(7) A person who refuses to obey the law is a menace to society. (74 percent agreement)

(8) Obedience and respect for authority are the most important virtues children should learn. (82 percent agreement)

Items (5) and (6) were ultimately dropped from the scale, since a first test suggested that some respondents had trouble understanding the questions, and items (7) and (8) were introduced because there was little variance in the other answers and thus not much to explain.

A number of methodological questions are worth pursuing here, but I want instead to focus on the conceptual ones, and here I am reminded of Wittgenstein's remark about psychology enjoying both experimental methods and conceptual confusions.

Do these questions, in the first place, accurately track the distinction between obligation and support? They do not. Items (3), (4), (7), and (8) may all elicit agreement from a person who rejects the obligation to obey the law and complies instead on grounds of prudence or personal morality. I, for example, do not believe that there is an obligation to obey the law, but I do think that those who make a point of refusing to obey it are generally a menace, and I think that disobeying it, at least in a reasonably just state, is seldom justified. All those questions are thus just irrelevant to the perceived obligation to obey.

The only items that might capture the attitude in question are (1), (2), (5), and (6). These do probe the binding and content-independent character that political obligation purports to have, though none of them conclusively eliminates the possibility of a purely prudential attitude. (Consider (5): Most people are aware that even a cop in the wrong can cause them big trouble.) Still, it is true that only these items ask whether a person would comply even in cases where he or she feels that compliance is wrong, and thus only they measure a noncoincidental connection between legal requirements and obedience, one that does not depend on the content of what is required.

How then should we interpret the overwhelmingly affirmative (and nearly invariant) responses to these items? Does it indicate a broad consensus, or is it perhaps a warning that respondents know what they are expected to say? Is it significant that items (5) and (6), the two that give the clearest test, are also the questions that gave some respondents trouble? They do not seem conceptually or linguistically challenging. Could it be that, in a concrete application, people become more hesitant about avowing an obligation to obey when it is made plain that this means obeying even when the police and judges are wrong?

All this is so much speculation; the difficulties in assessing the sincerity of sample survey responses are well known. There is, however, a more urgent, conceptual point. Even if sincere, these avowals are insufficient to establish the belief in an obligation to obey. The point is simply that they do not reveal why these avowals were made. They do not tell us enough about the structure of the views they express.

Let us return to the religion analogy, this time in more general form. If we ask respondents, "Do you believe in God?" we will find, particularly in America, an overwhelming majority who say yes. Can we therefore conclude that Americans overwhelmingly believe in God? Well, some of those who agree to that question might, if asked to elaborate what their belief in God amounts to, say things such as, "Well, I believe there really is meaning to life," or, "I believe there is a basic principle of order in the universe," or "There are truths about the universe we cannot explain." Some of these may or may not fall within the margins of religious belief, and, of course, just what one has to believe in order to be said properly to believe in God is a controversial matter, but many of these avowals extend well beyond the hazy boundaries of that controversy, and some of them are compatible with atheism. If all one means by "God" is "some principle of order in the universe," then any atheistic naturalist believes in God.

This is not a fanciful analogy. Many people who say they believe in God do not really do so, and the fact that they do not can be shown by investigating what their supposed belief commits them to. They may nonetheless avow the belief because they believe it is socially acceptable to do so or because they are unsure about the most appropriate terms of denial (am I an atheist? an agnostic?) or just because they want to avoid argument.

What then of people who are willing to agree with the proposition, "People should obey the law even if it goes against what they think is right"? Might they be committed to something other than a belief in political obligation and yet honestly make such an avowal? Plainly, they might. The question does not ask them whether this is something people should always or even normally do. It does not ask whether it makes any difference to them if the law in question is the law of their own state or whether they owe similar allegiance to any state that exercises de facto control over their behavior. It does not even ask whether the "should" is a moral "should" as opposed to a purely conventional or prudential "should." (One valid reason for obeying the law, especially in a foreign country, is that it is rude not to.) As it stands, we have no evidence about what the eighty-two percent who agreed with this proposition thought they were agreeing to, nor even whether they all took it in the same way.

The same objections apply also to the other relevant items. I am not saying that it is impossible to design a survey instrument that could tell us who believes in political obligation, and I am certainly not saying that no one believes in it—some citizens, many officials, most judges, and certain political theorists plainly do. My only point is that complex, abstract beliefs such as the belief in God or the belief in political obligation need to be approached in a more subtle way than is normally done and that the casual empiricism on which the argument from common opinion rests is in fact too lax for the confidence that theorists place in it. To isolate the true believers we will need a tighter marriage of normative and empirical political theory than we have yet had.

Conclusion

Theorists are inclined to believe that abstract philosophical ideas are more influential than they are. This is usually a harmless enough piece of self-deception. It is frequently said, for example, that Western liberal culture is founded epistemologically on a Cartesian notion of reason or morally on a Kantian notion of the person. These ideas, however, are difficult—in the case of Cartesian reason, probably unintelligible—and they are certainly not as deeply entrenched as some suppose. To the extent that nonphilosophers have any view about reason or the person, what they believe is usually indecisive among competing accounts.

Some political theorists hold that there is a belief in political obligation that is of wide enough currency and deep enough root to be taken as a datum that any competent theory of allegiance needs to explain. I have argued to the contrary: first, that even if there is such a belief, its importance cannot be certified by the method of coherence and that it requires instead confidence in the authority of common opinion. Even if such confidence is in general well placed, I have claimed also that with respect to this particular theory there are reasons to want to explain away the opinion. Second, I suggested that it is far from obvious how widely held the belief in political obligation actually is and that the best empirical evidence we have is deeply equivocal. The skeptics' positive case remains unanswered, and its incompatibility with common beliefs remains unestablished. The doctrine of political obligation is an implausible view of what we owe the state.

Notes

1. An earlier version of this paper was presented to the North American Society for Social Philosophy panel at the American Philosophical Association, Eastern Division Meeting, Washington, D.C., December 1992. I am grateful to the participants and especially to George Klosko, John T. Sanders, John Simmons, and Jeremy Waldron for their helpful comments.

2. See M. B. E. Smith, "Is There a Prima Facie Obligation to Obey the Law?" *Yale Law Journal* 82 (1973): 950–76; J. Raz, *The Authority of Law* (Oxford: Clarendon Press, 1979); A. J. Simmons, *Moral Principles and Political Obligations* (Princeton, N.J.: Princeton University Press, 1979); J. Feinberg, "Civil Disobedience in the Modern World," *Humanities in Society* 2 (1979): 37–60; R. Sartorius, "Political Authority and Political Obligation," *Virginia Law Review* 67 (1981): 3–17; L. Green, *The Authority of the State* (Oxford: Clarendon Press, 1990).

3. George Klosko, *The Principle of Fairness and Political Obligation* (Lanham, Md.: Rowman & Littlefield, 1992), 22. See also p. 68: "I take it as intuitively obvious that most individuals believe they have political obligations. As a corollary of this belief, most individuals believe that their governments are legitimate and so, by implication, acceptably fair."

4. See J. Rawls, *A Theory of Justice* (Cambridge, Mass.: Harvard University Press, 1971), 19–21, 46–53, 578–86. *Cf.* N. Daniels, "Wide Reflective Equilibrium and Theory Acceptance in Ethics," *Journal of Philosophy* 76 (1979): 256–82.

5. Klosko, 142–43.

6. For example, I take this passage in the *Treatise* as an appeal to the argument from common opinion: "[A] man living under an absolute government, wou'd owe it no allegiance; since, by its very nature, it depends not on consent. But as that is as natural and common a government as any, it must certainly occasion some obligation; and 'tis plain from experience, that men, who are subjected to it, do always think so" (L. A. Selby-Bigge, ed., *A Treatise of Human Nature* [Oxford: Clarendon Press, 1967], 529). In contrast,

Edmund Burke's remark is an appeal to our judgment about a case: "[I]f popular representation, or choice, is necessary to the legitimacy of all government, the house of lords is, at one stroke, bastardized and corrupted in blood. That house is no representative of the people at all. . . ." (C. C. O'Brien, ed., *Reflections on the Revolution in France* [Harmondsworth, Middlesex: Penguin, 1969], 147).

7. L. Green, "Against Hume on Allegiance," a paper delivered at the 1991 Annual Meeting of the American Political Science Association, Washington, D.C.

8. J. L. Mackie, *Ethics: Inventing Right and Wrong* (Harmondsworth, Middlesex: Penguin, 1977), 35, 48–49.

9. For a good account, see R. Geuss, *The Idea of a Critical Theory: Habermas and the Frankfurt School* (Cambridge: Cambridge University Press, 1981).

10. Simmons, 195. For my own, slightly different, response, see Green, *The Authority of the State*, 263–67.

11. Klosko, 25–26.

12. I should reiterate that I am *not* arguing that this is a matter of value-free science. I am claiming that it is a descriptive rather than a moral question. For the distinction I have in mind, see L. Green, "The Political Content of Legal Theory," *Philosophy of the Social Sciences* 17 (1987): 1–20.

13. Green, *The Authority of the State*, 220–34.

14. Simmons endorses a similar view in *Moral Principles and Political Obligations*, 7–38, as does Klosko in *The Principle of Fairness and Political Obligation*, 2–16. It may be that Ronald Dworkin rejects parts of the view; see his *Law's Empire* (Cambridge, Mass.: Harvard University Press, 1986), 190–215, and especially 429–30 n. 3. For criticism of Dworkin on obligation, see L. Green, "Associative Obligations and the State," in A. Hutchinson and L. Green, eds., *Law and the Community: The End of Individualism?* (Toronto: Carswell, 1989), 93–118. Apparently, Bikhu Parekh also disputes what political obligation amounts to in his "A Misconceived Discourse on Political Obligation," *Political Studies* 41 (1993): 236–51. He says that I and other skeptics confuse the narrow duty to obey the law with a wider sense of political obligation that also includes things such as an obligation to participate in politics, take an interest in public affairs, and so on. If this is true, it is irrelevant, for the skeptical argument shows that there is no narrow obligation to obey the law; it follows therefore that there is also no combination of this and wider, more exigent obligations—if p is false, then the conjunction of p and q is also false, and nothing substantial turns on whether we call p or $(p \& q)$ "political obligation."

15. T. R. Tyler, *Why People Obey the Law* (New Haven: Yale University Press, 1990).

16. Tyler, *Why People Obey the Law*, 45.

17. I have argued the same point against Easton in my "Support for the System," *British Journal of Political Science* 15 (1985): 127–42.

18. Tyler, 28.

19. Combining Table 4.3 and 4.4, Tyler, 46–47.

2

Philosophical Anarchism[1]

A. John Simmons

Anarchist political philosophers normally include in their theories (or implicitly rely on) a vision of a social life very different from the life experienced by most persons today. Theirs is a vision of autonomous, noncoercive, productive interaction among equals, liberated from and without need for distinctively political institutions, such as formal legal systems or governments or the state. This positive part of anarchist theories, this vision of the good social life, is discussed only indirectly in this essay. Rather, I focus here on the negative side of anarchism, on its general critique of the state or its more limited critique of the specific kinds of political arrangements within which most residents of modern political societies live. Even more specifically, I center my discussion on one particular version of this anarchist critique—the version that is part of the theory now commonly referred to as philosophical anarchism. Philosophical anarchism has been much discussed by political philosophers in recent years,[2] but it has not, I think, been very carefully defined or adequately understood. My object here is to clear the ground for a fair evaluation of philosophical anarchism by offering a more systematic account of the nature of the theory and of possible variants of the theory and by responding to the most frequent objections to the theory. I hope by this effort to present philosophical anarchism as a more attractive, or at least a less obviously flawed, political philosophy.

The Illegitimacy of States

Commitment to one central claim unites all forms of anarchist political philosophy: all existing states are illegitimate. I take this thesis to be

19

an essential, if not the defining, element of anarchism.[3] Anarchist commitments to this thesis are usually motivated by prior commitments to voluntarism (to the great moral importance of autonomy or free choice or self-determination, etc.), with existing states then characterized as fundamentally nonvoluntary or coercive;[4] to egalitarianism (to equal rights or equal opportunities or equal access to basic goods, etc.), with existing states then characterized as fundamentally hierarchical, sexist, classist, or otherwise inegalitarian;[5] to the values of community (to the great moral importance of shared ends or feelings of solidarity or sympathy, etc.), with existing states then characterized as alienating or divisive;[6] or to some combination of these positions. Anarchist theories may also be motivated by the perception of inadequacies in all purported defenses of state legitimacy without the necessity of their making any prior commitment to particular values (which the state is seen as frustrating). That is, some anarchisms are driven by a general skepticism about the possibility of providing any argument that shows some or all existing states to be legitimate—a skepticism perhaps taken to be justified simply by the systematic failure of political philosophy to this point to produce any good argument of this sort.

Philosophical anarchism, as a form of anarchism, is of course committed to the central anarchist thesis of state illegitimacy, and, like other kinds of anarchism, philosophical anarchism generally is motivated either by the kinds of commitments or by the kind of skepticism I have just summarized. What is distinctive about philosophical anarchism, I suggest, is its stance with respect to the moral content (or practical force) of judgments about state illegitimacy. Philosophical anarchists do not take the illegitimacy of states to entail a strong moral imperative to oppose or eliminate states; rather, they typically take state illegitimacy simply to remove any strong moral presumption in favor of obedience to, compliance with, or support for our own or other existing states. To make plain the structure of this position, I propose to provide a reasonably general view of the possible range of anarchist positions by specifying certain distinctions along which anarchist positions divide. I do not pretend that the divisions I describe are exhaustive, but I do think that they are the most salient and important divisions.

Perhaps the most basic division between anarchist theories (and also between philosophical anarchist theories) is that between what I call a priori anarchism and a posteriori anarchism. A priori anarchism maintains that all possible states are morally illegitimate. Some essential feature of the state or some necessary condition for statehood—say, the state's coercive character or its hierarchical nature—makes it impossible for there to be something that is both a state and legitimate.[7] A posteriori anarchism, by contrast, maintains that while all existing states are illegitimate, this is not because it is impossible for there to be a legitimate state. Nothing in the definition of the state precludes its legitimacy;[8] rather, existing states are condemned as illegitimate by virtue of their contingent characters. A posteriori anarchists may defend an ideal of legitimacy that existing states simply fail to live up to or approximate—for instance, a voluntarist or egalitarian or communitarian ideal of the state—or they simply may be unconvinced by purported a priori arguments for the impossibility of the legitimate state.[9]

Within the class of a posteriori anarchisms we can distinguish theories most fundamentally according to the ideals of legitimacy, if any, that they profess and also according to the optimism that they display about the possibility of realizing the ideal in the actual political world and the distance of the ideal from the actual state of affairs in some or all political societies. Most a posteriori anarchists, of course, are not very optimistic about soon realizing their ideals (if they defend any), nor are their ideals very close to any existing modern political society; indeed, anarchists who are either very optimistic about soon realizing their ideals or who regard the real political world as a reasonably close approximation of their ideals of political legitimacy should be thought of as anarchists in only the most nominal or technical sense.

Whether anarchists defend their central thesis of state illegitimacy as an a priori or an a posteriori judgment, they must defend as well some analysis of the idea of illegitimacy, that is, some position on the moral content of judgments of state illegitimacy. What, for instance, does a judgment of state illegitimacy imply about our rights and obligations with respect to the state? While there are, of course, many senses of *legitimate* and *illegitimate* that we employ in discussing states and governments,[10] the view that probably deserves to be called the traditional view of state or governmental legitimacy holds that legitimacy consists in a certain, normally limited kind of authority or right to make binding law and state policy. State legitimacy or authority is viewed as the logical correlate of the obligation of citizens to obey the law and to in other ways support the state, that is, to the obligation that is usually referred to as political obligation.[11] Most anarchists have embraced something like this traditional conception of state legitimacy, with the consequence that anarchist judgments of state illegitimacy typically are taken to entail that subjects of those illegitimate states have no political obligations. These subjects are, of course, still bound by their nonpolitical moral obligations and duties, and these nonpolitical duties will sometimes have the same substance as the subjects' legal requirements. Subjects have no political obligation, however, to obey the law because it is law or to support the political leaders or institutions that try to compel their allegiance.

This, we may say, is the minimum moral content of anarchist judgments of state illegitimacy: the subjects of illegitimate states have no political obligations. We can then define weak anarchism as the position that asserts no more than this minimum content. Weak anarchism is the view that there are no general political obligations, that all (or, at least, virtually all) subjects of all states are at moral liberty to (i.e., possess a privilege or permission right to) treat laws as nonbinding and governments as nonauthoritative. What we can call strong anarchism also accepts this minimum moral content of judgments of state illegitimacy, but strong anarchists hold in addition that a state's illegitimacy further entails a moral obligation or duty to oppose and, so far as it is within our power, eliminate the state.[12] This obligation can be taken to bind either the subjects of the illegitimate state or persons generally; so where weak anarchism says that we may regard the state as one more powerful bully whose commands and actions we may ignore where we can, strong anarchism argues that all such bullies must be deprived of their power to coerce. Weak anarchists, of course, may also hold that on independent grounds some or all states should be opposed and eliminated, but for the weak anarchist, any such obligation is grounded in factors beyond the mere illegitimacy of the states in question. How strong a strong anarchist position is will depend on how weighty or imperative the obligation to oppose the state is taken to be.[13]

This last point plainly raises a second kind of question about the moral content of anarchist judgments of state illegitimacy: how are we to understand the weight of the rights and obligations said to be entailed by such judgments? Here there seems to be nothing distinctive about anarchist views. Anarchists treat questions of moral weight or finality in the same range of ways that other moral and political philosophers do. At least two clearly opposed positions on these questions need to be distinguished. An anarchist can treat the relevant obligations to oppose the state and rights to treat law as nonbinding as immediately implying final or absolute moral judgments, or the anarchist may treat these obligations and rights as possibly defeasible moral reasons, understood as these would be within what I will call a balance-of-reasons view.

On the first approach, to say that there is an obligation to oppose the state is to say that there is a final, conclusive moral reason so to act. The obligation's weight is overriding or absolute with respect to competing considerations (i.e., those supporting nonopposition, if any). To say also that there is a right to treat the law as nonbinding is to say that no further justification for so treating the law need ever be given. One's rights trump competing considerations (i.e., those supporting compliance, if any).

On the second, balance-of-reasons approach, obligations and rights are treated as strong but variably weighted and certainly not conclusive reasons for action. Obligations and rights may on this view conflict with and possibly be outweighed by other obligations or rights, or they may conflict with and be outweighed by reasons for action of other sorts. Strong enough prudential reasons for action, for instance, may override weak obligations, just as strong enough reasons grounded in the happiness of others may render unjustifiable our acting on the weak rights that we possess. In short, the finality or imperativeness of rights or obligations is, on the balance-of-reasons approach, very much a function of the context within which the rights or obligations are exercised.[14]

Defining Philosophical Anarchism

We are now, I think, in a position to see more clearly what is and what is not distinctive about philosophical anarchism. Like other anarchists, philosophical anarchists can defend their central judgments about state illegitimacy on either a priori or a posteriori grounds and, like others, they take this judgment to entail the nonexistence of general political obligations—that is, the removal of any moral presumption in favor of compliance with and support for the state. What is distinctive about philosophical anarchism is that its judgment of state illegitimacy (even of necessary state illegitimacy) does not translate into any immediate requirement of opposition to illegitimate states. This is what leads many to contrast philosophical anarchism to political anarchism.

Philosophical anarchists hold that there may be good moral reasons not to oppose or disrupt at least some kinds of illegitimate states, reasons that outweigh any right or obligation of opposition. The practical stance with respect to the state, the philosophical anarchist maintains, should be one of careful consideration and thoughtful weighting of all of the reasons that bear on action in a particular set of political circumstances. The illegitimacy of a state (and the absence of binding political obligations that it entails) is just one moral factor among many bearing on how persons in that state should (or are permitted to) act. Even illegitimate states, for instance, may have virtues, unaffected by the defects that undermine their legitimacy, that are relevant considerations in determining how we ought to act with respect to those states, and the refusal to do what the law requires is, at least in most (even illegitimate) states, often wrong on independent moral grounds (i.e., the conduct would be wrong even were it not legally forbidden). So there may be a variety of sound moral reasons not to oppose or not to act contrary to the laws of even some illegitimate states.

What does this mean in terms of the distinctions drawn in the first section of this essay? It means, first, that philosophical anarchists must reject the view of obligations and rights as final moral reasons and accept some version of the balance-of-reasons approach, for if the permission right entailed by the absence of political obligations is seen as providing a final justification for disregarding or opposing law and government, no moral reason for supporting a government or complying with a law could ever outweigh our permission right—and this, I am claiming, is one thing philosophical anarchists wish to deny. Second, philosophical anarchists must embrace either what I call weak anarchism or else a version of strong anarchism that takes the obligation to oppose the state to be a relatively weak obligation. Otherwise, of course, they will be committed to a moral obligation of opposition to illegitimate states that will be likely to outweigh any competing reasons for nonopposition or compliance, even within the best illegitimate states. This, again, is a position that philosophical anarchists wish to avoid. What is distinctive about philosophical anarchism, then, is chiefly its position on the weight or finality of the moral obligations and rights entailed by judgments of state illegitimacy.

Can philosophical anarchism intelligibly deny in this way the connection between, on the one hand, the illegitimacy of the state and the absence of political obligation and, on the other hand, a strong obligation or right to oppose and try to eliminate the state? I think it is clear that it can. A state's being illegitimate means that it lacks the general right to make binding law and policy for its subjects (it lacks political authority), and it means that the state's subjects lack the correlative general political obligation to support and comply with it. This by itself, however, entails neither that the state could have no right to command (and citizens no obligation to obey) on some particular occasion nor that the state could have no moral justification for its actions in particular cases (based on moral reasons unrelated to any strict right to act), nor does it entail that citizens, simply because they lack general political obligations, have strong or conclusive rights to oppose the state or act contrary to its legal requirements. Our general duties to our fellow citizens qua persons, our general duties to promote justice and other values, and our other, nonduty moral reasons to treat others well will all often be good reasons not to disrupt the state's functioning or to act contrary to its laws.[15] Within many decent, but still illegitimate, states, serious (e.g., revolutionary) opposition to the state or regular conduct contrary to its laws simply will not be morally justifiable on balance.

To this point, I have been concerned primarily to clarify what philosophical anarchists must say if their position is to be distinctive in the way its primary defenders have wished it to be and if their position is to be at all plausible. Let me add now a few words about what philosophical anarchists should say if they wish their position to be not just distinctive and initially plausible, but also correct. Philosophical anarchists should, in my view, defend their theory, first, as a form of a posteriori anarchism and, second, as a form of weak anarchism.

While it is not possible to show (without presenting a complete defense of an ideal of state legitimacy) that no form of a priori anarchism could be successful, it is hard on the face of things to see how a convincing a priori case could be made by the anarchist. If the anarchist values autonomy or free choice, for instance, it is hard to see why a possible ideal state that promotes or respects these values could not be described. A fully voluntary, genuinely contractual democracy could be rejected as an ideal on such voluntarist grounds, it seems, only if the voluntarist anarchist was also prepared to deny the legitimacy of the ordinary practice of promising—on the ground, say, that promissory obligations objectionably constrain freedom, despite their being freely undertaken. This seems too high a price to pay, as R. P. Wolff's failed attempt to defend a voluntarist a priori anarchism clearly shows.[16] Similarly, if the anarchist values equality or community, say, it is hard to believe that a strict egalitarian state, or the kind of state favored by strict communitarians, could not be defended in those terms as an ideal of political legitimacy. If the anarchist argument is only that actual states have never even approximated (and likely never will approximate) these voluntarist, egalitarian, or communitarian ideals, the argument seems persuasive, but that argument is perfectly consistent with a posteriori anarchism. The a priori anarchist must argue not just that there never has been and never will be a legitimate state, but also for the more dramatic and less plausible claim that such a state is not even possible. In anarchist writings such claims have often (mistakenly, in my view) had to be based on assuming that the forms that all modern states have taken provide us with the proper definitional content of the term *state*.[17]

As for my preference for weak over strong anarchism, I have argued already that even if philosophical anarchism is defended as a strong theory, it still must accept that the obligation to oppose the state is a relatively weak obligation; but there are good reasons to believe further that the mere illegitimacy of a state entails no such obligations (weak or strong) to oppose it. Only if illegitimacy is taken to be a far more inclusive failing in a state than traditional philosophical analyses of legitimacy imply will it entail a moral obligation to oppose the state, for a state can clearly lack the general right to make binding law and policy without being sufficiently evil that it must be opposed and, if possible, eliminated. This is why the idea of, say, a benevolent dictatorship makes sense; there are at least two conflicting moral characteristics of such a state (benevolence, dictatorship), which makes our assessment of it complex.

I take the legitimacy of a state with respect to me and the other moral qualities of a state to be independent variables, just as I take the right of a business to, say, bill me and the charitableness or efficiency of a business to be independent variables. In both cases, the legitimacy or right is a function of its transactions or relations with me, while its other general qualities need have nothing to do with me at all. The fact that a state or a business has virtues appropriate to it cannot, by itself, argue for its having special rights over me or for my owing it special obligations, nor, of course, do these special rights and obligations, where they exist, necessarily override moral duties to oppose a vicious state. Only if the state also has special relations to me will special rights or obligations of that sort follow. Indeed, even if I had quite general duties to promote states or businesses that exemplified the appropriate virtues, these duties would be owed equally to all such exemplary objects, not specially to any particular one,[18] but insofar as even equally illegitimate states will exemplify the stately virtues in different ways and to different extents, if at all, it cannot be supposed that all illegitimate states should be treated in the same ways by their subjects or by others simply by virtue of their common illegitimacy. Some illegitimate states may be hopelessly evil; others, decent and benevolent (though not, for that, necessarily legitimate with respect to all or any particular citizens).

Three Objections to Philosophical Anarchism

Suppose the philosophical anarchist defends, as I have recommended, a weak, a posteriori anarchism, understanding the weight of the rights this entails from a balance-of-reasons perspective. Are there obvious objections to which the resulting position would be liable? There are none, I think, that are convincing. As a start to showing this, I want to mention here and indicate appropriate responses to the three objections that have been raised in the most prominent recent criticisms of philosophical anarchism.

There are two general lines of attack on philosophical anarchism that may be sensibly pursued by its critics. One, of course, is simply to defend a systematic theory of political obligation and state legitimacy and show that it applies to existing states. In my view, efforts along these lines have uniformly failed, but I will not pursue such questions here. The alternative approach is to try to directly discredit the philosophical anarchist's position—for instance, by showing it to be internally inconsistent or to have unacceptable implications. It is criticisms of this latter sort that I will discuss here.

Objection 1: The Hypocrisy of Philosophical Anarchism

Perhaps the most fully developed of these attacks is that mounted by Chaim Gans in his recent book *Philosophical Anarchism and Political Disobedience*. Gans, like many others, argues, in effect, that philosophical anarchism is not really anarchism at all, that it is a "toothless" theory with an "embarrassing gap" between its "radical look" and its quite "tame" practical implications.[19] Further, Gans maintains that philosophical anarchists draw the intuitive support for their view from focusing "on trivial and esoteric contexts, jaywalking at three o'clock in the morning," while simply conforming to common opinion about the need for obedience in more familiar, everyday contexts.[20] More damning still, Gans's analysis of this move by philosophical anarchists is that while they officially reject the well-known arguments for political obligation (and, on the strength of this rejection, proclaim state illegitimacy), they then implicitly rely on these very same arguments (they "resurrect" them) to maintain that even illegitimate states need not always be disobeyed or disrupted. It would be more honest simply to accept the familiar arguments for obedience to law, Gans suggests, especially once we recognize that accepting political obligation does not mean that obedience to law is always morally required.[21]

Gans's critique of what he calls "critical anarchism" seems to me to miss almost entirely the point of defending weak, a posteriori philosophical anarchism. It does this in several ways. First, and most obviously, it neglects to mention that only by embracing either a radical moral skepticism, or nihilism, or an unconvincing prioritization of moral concerns could a philosophical anarchist give his theory the "teeth" that Gans thinks a true anarchist theory should have. Second, Gans's critique completely—and mistakenly—collapses the very distinction between political obligations and general moral reasons for acting on which philosophical anarchism relies.

On the first point: it is, of course, a matter of only terminological interest whether we call philosophical anarchism a form of true anarchism or instead argue that it is misnamed. I have located the essence of anarchism in its thesis of state illegitimacy; others might argue that its essence is rather advocacy of active opposition to and elimination of the state[22]—in which case, "philosophical anarchism" would be an unhappy name for a still perfectly defensible political philosophy. What it is important to see, however, is what would be required for anarchism to defend the radical practical stance Gans seem to associate with real anarchism. All anarchists—with the exception only of moral skeptics (nihilists) and those embracing extremely eccentric moral theories—must allow that in virtually all modern states, including even those that are deeply unjust and otherwise illegitimate, a significant body of the law's requirements, both criminal and civil, constitutes a formalization, with the backing of coercive sanctions, of independently binding moral requirements. Even, then, if the law has no moral standing, the conduct required by law is often morally obligatory. Similarly, the fact that our illegal actions would cause widespread suffering, unhappiness, and frustrated reasonable expectations surely makes these actions morally suspect, even if their being merely illegal does not.

We should not, then, be very surprised or troubled—as Gans seems to be—to find that both defenders and opponents of political obligation argue for similar practical stances with respect to many of the law's requirements and with respect to revolutionary political activities. That both the anarchist and the defender of state legitimacy find murder, assault, and acts aimed at producing massive and violent social upheaval to be morally indefensible in no way suggests that their theories are really indistinguishable, for the theories clearly differ importantly both on the source of these moral worries—independent moral concerns versus violation of general political obligations—and on the issue of to whom the relevant moral duties and moral consideration are owed—our fellow citizens qua persons versus our government or our fellow citizens qua citizens.

Radicalness of practical implications is hardly the only measure of substantive difference in political philosophies. Indeed, to acquire the radical "teeth" that Gans wants anarchist theories to brandish, these theories have to either deny the existence of independent moral concerns about murder, assault, and causing widespread misery or else argue that the evil represented by the existence of the (i.e., every) state is sufficiently great to justify or require violence and rending the social fabric in an effort to remove that evil. I, along with many anarchist philosophers, find neither of these moves compelling. Philosophical anarchism's less radical "teeth" will be found rather in its assertions that many distinctively political legal requirements—such as payment of certain taxes or military service—along with many paternalistic and moralistic laws and laws creating victimless crimes may be disobeyed without moral impropriety.[23] This is no revolutionary stance, but neither is it addressed to or motivated by only trivial and esoteric contexts.

To turn now to my second concern about Gans's critique, does this anarchist reasoning not just amount to reintroducing, after the official denial of political obligation, the very same moral considerations that are usually and properly employed in defending accounts of political obligation? No, it does not. Anarchists allow for justifiable disobedience in many cases (such as those noted above) where Gans does not; and, as we will see, anarchists typically reject most of the lines of argument on which Gans relies heavily, rather than implicitly reintroducing them, as Gans suggests they do. Indeed, it is not the philosophical anarchist who has implicitly given up the game to the defender of political obligation, as Gans suggests, but Gans himself who has unwittingly given up the game to the philosophical anarchist.

Gans's own defense of political obligation (or, as he usually prefers, of "the duty to obey the law") is in fact cobbled together from four different familiar, purported justifications of political obligation—justifications appealing to consequences, fairness, the duty to support just institutions, and communal obligations.[24] Not only, however, does Gans never bother to argue that these varied justifications can all be motivated by one consistent moral theory (let alone give us any hint of what such a theory would look like), but he also accepts many of the well-known shortcomings of these styles of justification, moving on to new arguments in the face of the acknowledged weaknesses of the ones under consideration.[25] The cumulative force of the many arguments is supposed somehow to make up for their individual defects, and then the resulting political obligation is weakened to make its affirmation consistent with substantial levels of disobedience.[26] What Gans then succeeds in presenting (insofar as the argument is successful at all) is less a case for a general political obligation than a list of often, though by no means always, operative reasons—of distinctly variable weight—for refraining from actively disrupting political life in just societies. As we have seen, however, anarchists can of course embrace a similar list without committing themselves to the legitimacy of the state.

Gans's project in effect just ignores the distinction between moral reasons for acting (of variable weight and application) and grounds for a general political obligation. Anarchists can happily allow, for instance, that acting contrary to law will often have profoundly negative consequences for others. It will also often have no such consequences. Where these consequences are at issue, they may constitute moral reasons for doing as the law requires, but this would in most cases be true independent of the law's formalized requirements. It is also true that negative consequences for others often give us some reason to refrain from causing them, even where there is nothing like a strict duty, moral or legal, to refrain. (It is not my duty, moral or legal, to tell a stranger the time of day when she politely requests it.) The moral weight of negative consequences can, for philosophical anarchists, both range far beyond the realm of duty and be regarded as largely independent of the institutional facts of legal requirement. It is very hard to see how anyone could take such a stance to amount to an implicit acceptance of a general political duty to obey the law.

Anarchists also often just reject, rather than deceptively "resurrecting," the other lines of justification for political obligation that Gans defends.[27] Gans's attempt to piece together a general political obligation from a wide variety of variable moral considerations both fails in its own right, I think, and in effect amounts to admitting that the

proper political stance is the one that philosophical anarchism pre-
scribes—namely, the careful weighing of a range of moral considerations that are at issue in some, but not even nearly all, cases of legal
disobedience, even within just political societies. No general moral
presumption in favor of obedience can ever be defended in this way,
nor do Gans's efforts succeed in showing how this might be done.

Objection 2: The Radicalism of Philosophical Anarchism

The other two recent criticisms of anarchism that are intended to
apply to the kind of weak, a posteriori philosophical anarchism I am
defending can, I think, be answered more quickly now that we have a
better sense of the extent of philosophical anarchism's commitments.
The first of these remaining criticisms, for instance, claims (directly
contrary to Gans) that philosophical anarchism's implications are too
radical to be intuitively acceptable. Embracing philosophical anarchism, it has been said, will "encourage general disobedience to
critical laws" and prove "a tragedy for liberal regimes";[28] it will have
"extreme" and "startling" consequences.[29] We can see now, however,
that these claims are far too strong. Philosophical anarchism will not
argue for mindless obedience to law, but neither, of course, will
most defenders of general political obligations, nor will philosophical
anarchists argue for mindless disobedience to law. It argues rather that
the simple fact that conduct is required or forbidden by law is irrelevant
to that conduct's moral status, even within decent states; we should
decide how best to act on independent moral grounds.[30]

The practical recommendations of philosophical anarchism will converge with those of defenders of political obligation wherever legally
required conduct is independently required or recommended by moral
considerations. The two views will diverge principally where the law
prohibits harmless conduct, where it imposes specifically political
duties, and where disobedience has no dramatic negative consequences for individuals or for those aspects of their social structure on
which they may reasonably rely. The claim that selective, thoughtful
disobedience in these latter areas would be "a tragedy for liberal
regimes" seems to me, however, most implausible. If the recommendations of philosophical anarchists were generally followed, subjects
would regard themselves (within this range of cases) as free to either
obey or disobey as their tastes and interests dictated—though, of
course, social pressure to conform and the threat of legal sanctions
would typically push in the direction of obedience. Even if the choice

was uniformly one of disobedience, such actions might very well push states to be more open, cooperative, and voluntary, less coercive in the name of contested moral and religious doctrines, less free with the money and with the lives of their subjects, and so on—in short, to become less statelike. It would presumably be the most liberal states that would have the least trouble with disobedient anarchists, since the most liberal states would have the smallest body of laws whose content could not be independently (i.e., independently of any appeal to general obligations to obey) defended on uncontested moral grounds.

Objection 3: Denying Political Obligation

The last criticism of philosophical anarchism that I will consider here might be said to bridge the two I have discussed already. The argument here concerns not the practical implications of philosophical anarchism (on which the two previous criticisms take opposed positions), but the higher order denial of political obligation itself. Philosophical anarchism, the argument goes, is "out of keeping with our general considered judgments," for "the idea that we have obligations to particular countries is a basic feature of our political consciousness."[31] Insofar as we think, as many moral and political philosophers do, that coherence with our considered judgments is an important part of the justification of moral principles (or general moral judgments), and insofar as we agree that general political obligations are a firmly fixed point in our set of basic judgments about political morality, then it may well seem that the anarchist's denial of political obligation must be unjustifiable—unless he can show that these particular judgments (i.e., that we are politically obligated) are suspect in a way that our other basic moral judgments are not.[32]

The philosophical anarchist can avoid the force of this criticism in a variety of reasonably obvious fashions. Most generally, he can of course simply deny that coherence with considered judgments has any (or, at least, such a privileged) place in the justification of moral principles or general judgments. Let us leave that possible response aside, though, and assume for the sake of argument that some version of this coherence method (the Rawlsian version, say) is correct.

There are still at least three convincing avenues of response available to the philosophical anarchist.[33] First, the philosophical anarchist can argue that the alleged considered judgments of general political obligation against which our theoretical judgments are supposed to be measured are not in fact the kind of particular moral judgments that coherence theories can appeal to in their accounts of justification. A judgment of general political obligation is itself a general theoretical judgment, not a provisional fixed point in our pretheoretical moral sensibility (such as, to use Rawls's examples, the particular judgments that slavery and religious intolerance are unjust). As a theoretical judgment, the judgment of general political obligation is either affirmed with the appropriate supporting body of theory or it is not. In the latter case it can be discounted as clearly irrational; and, if the reasons for the theoretical belief offered within the theory do not support the belief, it can again be discounted as irrational. The philosophical anarchist, of course, affirms precisely that the reasons offered do not support the belief; and he may affirm as well that if ordinary persons are in fact committed to this theoretical judgment of general political obligation, they are probably for the most part irrationally committed to a theoretical judgment that requires support that they are unable to provide or even understand.

Second, philosophical anarchists can simply deny that political obligation is for all or even most of us "a basic feature of our political consciousness." While most of us clearly believe that it is wrong, at least most of the time, to do what law forbids, many of us do not believe that it is, for example, wrong to break the law where it harms no one, wrong to use marijuana, engage in oral sex, or refuse military induction on moral grounds, even where such actions are proscribed by law and even within a basically just society. The principles of anarchist political philosophy may square with this set of considered judgments at least as well as do the principles of political obligation.

Finally, philosophical anarchists can offer reasons why judgments of political obligation are more suspect than our basic moral judgments are generally. Where beliefs in political obligation (and the habits of obedience, subjection, or loyalty such beliefs engender) clearly serve the interests of particular powerful classes of persons—those possessing (or actively aspiring to possess) political power, those endeavoring to coercively impose their favored moral or religious vision, and so on—our more basic moral beliefs (e.g., in the wrongness of murder or the injustice of slavery) quite plainly do not (marxist claims to the contrary notwithstanding). Suggestions of manipulation and inculcation as the source of our beliefs are thus far more convincing in the former case (of beliefs about political obligation) than in the latter. Beliefs about political obligation—insofar as we actually have any— are, I think, "suspect" as a kind of "false consciousness" that it serves the interests of powerful others to induce in us.[34] Compared to our more basic moral beliefs, beliefs in political obligation have less compelling justifications and more insidious implications, and they more obviously and constantly advance the interests of some over others.

If I am right in this, then there are ample grounds for rejecting as well this last recent criticism of philosophical anarchism. And if, as I have argued, these recent criticisms all fail to establish any substantial defects in the weak, a posteriori anarchism we have been considering, then we have good reason to be confident about the plausibility of such a political philosophy. Only a quite new and unanticipated theory of political obligation and state legitimacy should shake this confidence.

Notes

1. I would like to thank Nancy Schauber for her insightful comments on earlier drafts of this paper.

2. See, for example, R. P. Wolff, *In Defense of Anarchism* (New York: Harper & Row, 1970); Chaim Gans, *Philosophical Anarchism and Political Disobedience* (Cambridge: Cambridge University Press, 1992), especially chaps. 1 and 2; and John Horton, *Political Obligation* (Atlantic Highlands, N. J.: Humanities Press, 1992), chap. 5. I discuss the sort of philosophical anarchism that I wish to defend in *Moral Principles and Political Obligations* (Princeton: Princeton University Press, 1979), especially chap. 8; "The Anarchist Position," *Philosophy & Public Affairs* 16 (Spring 1987); and *On the Edge of Anarchy* (Princeton: Princeton University Press, 1993), especially section 8.4. Others, besides Wolff and myself, who are frequently identified as defenders of some form of philosophical anarchism (though almost none of them describe their positions in that language) include M. B. E. Smith, "Is There a Prima Facie Obligation to Obey the Law?" *Yale Law Journal* 82 (1973); Joseph Raz, "The Obligation to Obey the Law," in *The Authority of Law* (New York: Oxford University Press, 1979); Leslie Green, *The Authority of the State* (Oxford: Oxford University Press, 1988); Donald Regan, "Law's Halo," *Social Philosophy & Policy* (Autumn 1986); A. D. Woozley, *Law and Disobedience* (London: Duckworth, 1979); David Lyons, "Need, Necessity, and Political Obligation," *Virginia Law Review* (February 1981); and Joel Feinberg, "Civil Disobedience in the Modern World," *Humanities in Society* 2 (1979). Other general discussions and/or defenses of philosophical anarchism can be found in Jeffrey Reiman, *In Defense of Political Philosophy* (New York: Harper & Row, 1972); M. B. E. Smith, "The Obligation to Obey the Law: Revision or Explanation?" *Criminal Justice Ethics* (Summer/Fall 1989): 60–70; Vicente Medina, *Social Contract Theories* (Lanham, Md.: Rowman & Littlefield, 1990), 150–52; and Michael Menlowe, "Political Obligation," in R.

Bellamy, ed., *Theories and Concepts of Politics* (Manchester, U. K.: Manchester University Press, 1993), 174–96.

3. Four qualifications need to be added here: (1) As we will see shortly, anarchists agree on the truth of this thesis but differ about whether the thesis is necessarily or only contingently true. (2) Some theories that probably should be called anarchist by association hold only that virtually all states are illegitimate. (3) How one defines *state* here is obviously a matter of great controversy, especially within anarchist theory. Some prefer to substitute *governments* or *political societies* in their versions of this thesis. Others think that governments or political authorities of certain sorts may be acceptable where *the state* is not. The vagueness on these scores of the thesis, as I have presented it here, should not affect the force of the discussion that follows, and a certain amount of vagueness is necessary, in any event, to give any very general account of the range of theories usually called *anarchist*. (4) Some prefer to describe anarchism as a view about political obligation. Horton, for instance, characterizes anarchism as "a theory or doctrine which rejects the possibility of any morally persuasive general theory of political obligation" (*Political Obligation*, 109). Gans does the same (*Philosophical Anarchism*, 2). I suspect that Horton, at least, intends this account not so much as a generally adequate account of anarchism, but rather only as one adequate for the limited aims of his discussion. I suggest in the text below that while anarchism's denial of state legitimacy entails the denial of political obligation, this former denial is taken by many anarchists to have more far-reaching moral consequences than the mere denial of political obligation.

4. See, e.g., Wolff, *In Defense of Anarchism*, chap. 1.

5. See, e.g., Kai Nielsen, "State Authority and Legitimation," in P. Harris, ed., *On Political Obligation* (London: Routledge, 1990).

6. See, e.g., Peter Kropotkin, *Mutual Aid* (London: Heinemann, 1910), and *The Conquest of Bread* (New York: Vanguard, 1926).

7. Wolff's version of philosophical anarchism is a good example of a priori anarchism. Wolff sometimes maintains that the authority that states must exercise in order to be states is inconsistent with the autonomy of individuals that any legitimate state would have to respect. "Hence, the concept of a *de jure* legitimate state would appear to be vacuous" (*In Defense of Anarchism*, 19). Some authors seem mistakenly to identify philosophical anarchism (or anarchism generally) with a priori versions of it. Stephen Nathanson, for instance, characterizes anarchism as the view that "governmental authority is always illegitimate" (*Should We Consent to be Governed?* [Belmont: Wadsworth, 1992], 57); and David Miller's arguments against what he calls philosophical anarchism are really only arguments against those, like Wolff, who find "the very idea of legitimate authority incoherent" (*Anarchism* [London: J. M. Dent & Sons, 1984], 15–16, 29).

8. With the exception of Wolff, all of the defenders of philosophical anarchism listed in note 2 (myself included) seem to defend its central thesis as an a posteriori judgment.

9. Other recent discussions of philosophical anarchism gesture at this distinction between a priori and a posteriori anarchism, sometimes in unfortunate ways. Gans, for instance, distinguishes "autonomy-based" anarchism (according to which "it follows from the very meaning of [the duty to obey the law], that its acknowledgement entails a surrender of moral autonomy") from "critical" anarchism ("the denial of the duty to obey the law which is based on a rejection of its grounds") (*Philosophical Anarchism*, 2), but autonomy-based arguments are, as we have seen, only one kind of a priori anarchist approach with appeals to equality or community, for instance, as clear and familiar alternatives; so these latter approaches are simply excluded by Gans's classifications. Also, Gans's characterization of critical anarchism is sufficiently general to cover any kind of anarchism (every anarchist denies political obligation by denying its grounds). Horton employs a different and more useful distinction between "positive" philosophical anarchism (which "offers a positive argument of its own as to why there are not, and could not be, any political obligations") and "negative" philosophical anarchism (which "simply concludes from the failure of all positive attempts to justify political obligation that there is no such obligation") (*Political Obligation*, 124). Horton's "positive" anarchism appears to be more or less what I have called a priori anarchism, but his "negative" anarchism plainly needs more careful definition, after which it will approach my a posteriori anarchism. "The failure of all positive attempts" is only a reason (let alone a good reason) to reject political obligation if one also believes that these positive attempts add up to a complete or comprehensive attempt (refuting a handful of miserable, silly, half-hearted, or obviously incomplete positive efforts to show that X clearly gives one no reason to believe not-X). "Negative" anarchist arguments thus need to be based either in an ideal of legitimacy (which existing states can be shown not to exemplify) or in some account of what an acceptably complete positive attempt would look like.

10. See, e.g., my *Moral Principles and Political Obligations*, 40–41, 58, 197.

11. It is, of course, now reasonably common for theorists to attempt to deny this traditional (and, I think, perfectly acceptable) correlativity doctrine, defending judgments of state legitimacy and judgments of citizens' political obligations by means of quite different kinds of arguments. For one particularly clear example of such a strategy, see Jeffrey Reiman, *In Defense of Political Philosophy*, xxv, 18, 23, 42–44 (though even Reiman allows that the traditional correlativity doctrine captures "common usage" of the language of legitimacy [pp. 53–54]).

12. Strong anarchists may treat this obligation as a uniform threshold obligation or as an obligation that varies in content with the extent of illegitimacy. In the former case, any state that crossed over the threshold of illegitimacy would thereby impose on us an obligation with uniform content to oppose it, regardless of how extensively illegitimate it was. In the latter case, the extent or nature of our obligation to oppose the state would be taken to

vary with the extent of its illegitimacy. Illegitimate states are not necessarily equally illegitimate; some may be worse than others and so may require us to more actively (or in some other way differently) oppose them.

13. Some moral obligations—such as the obligation to keep a relatively insignificant promise to meet a friend for coffee—are obviously quite trivial; others—such as the promissory or contractual obligation of a paid nurse to care for a critically ill patient—are clearly not at all trivial. Strong anarchists who nonetheless regard the obligation to oppose the state as relatively trivial weaken their position to the point where it becomes in practice indistinguishable from weak anarchism.

14. For further discussion of these two views of the weight or finality of judgments of obligation, or right, see my *Moral Principles and Political Obligations*, 7–11, and *The Lockean Theory of Rights* (Princeton: Princeton University Press, 1992), 93–95, 111–12.

15. For a fuller presentation of these lines of argument, see my "The Anarchist Position," especially pp. 275–79.

16. Wolff, it seems, cannot bring himself to deny that promises or contracts are morally binding, with the result that in the end he concedes that "a contractual democracy is legitimate, to be sure, for it is founded upon the citizens' promise to obey its commands. Indeed, any state is legitimate which is founded upon such a promise" (*In Defense of Anarchism*, 69), but this, of course, directly contradicts his earlier a priori claim that "the concept of a *de jure* legitimate state would appear to be vacuous" (p. 19). Contractual democracies, on Wolff's view, are legitimate states, but they gain their legitimacy through their citizens' sacrifice of their autonomy. Perhaps this introduces a second notion of "legitimacy*" in Wolff ("legitimate*" states would be those that reconcile citizen autonomy and state authority), and perhaps it is only the concept of the "legitimate*" state that is vacuous, but it is hard to understand how a theorist committed to the importance of autonomy could intelligibly claim both that all promises are morally binding *and* that some promises (i.e., political ones) objectionably sacrifice autonomy. For further difficulties in Wolff's arguments, see Reiman, *In Defense of Political Philosophy*; Keith Graham, "Democracy and the Autonomous Moral Agent," in K. Graham, ed., *Political Philosophy: Radical Studies* (Cambridge: Cambridge University Press, 1982), 113–37; Gans, *Philosophical Anarchism*, 10–41; and Horton, *Political Obligation*, 124–31.

17. The anarchist argument often then proceeds by maintaining that while no legitimate state is possible, it is possible to have a legitimate large-scale, cooperative, rule-governed association that incorporates positions of rightful authority. To me it seems reasonable to call such an association a state, but nothing of substance turns on the language we choose to use.

18. They would thus not satisfy what I have elsewhere called the "particularity requirement" for accounts of political obligation (*Moral Principles and Political Obligations*, 31–35, 143–56).

19. *Philosophical Anarchism*, 90, xi. See also, e.g., Miller, *Anarchism*, 15 (where philosophical anarchism is described as "bloodless"), or Reiman, *In Defense of Political Philosophy*, xvi, xxiii–xxiv (where philosophical anarchism is described as "chasing its tail").

20. *Philosophical Anarchism*, 90.

21. *Philosophical Anarchism*, 90–91. These claims are undoubtedly related to Horton's assertion that "most denials of political obligation . . . are more or less disingenuous" (*Political Obligation*, 160). R. George Wright also seems to accept this line of argument in *Legal and Political Obligation* (Lanham, Md.: University Press of America, 1992), 280. One recent denial of a general obligation to obey the law that probably is vulnerable to Gans's analysis is in Kent Greenawalt, *Conflicts of Law and Morality* (New York: Oxford University Press, 1989), part 2.

22. See, e.g., Miller, *Anarchism*, 6–7; Reiman, *In Defense of Political Philosophy*, xxii, 48; and Nathanson, *Should We Consent to be Governed?* 54, 57, 86.

23. I discuss these claims more fully in "The Anarchist Position," 276–79, and *On the Edge of Anarchy*, 262–69.

24. *Philosophical Anarchism*, 89.

25. See, e.g., *Philosophical Anarchism*, 71–78, 82–83, 87.

26. Ibid., chaps. 1 and 4.

27. They may reject arguments from a duty of justice because (a) this would bind us to no particular state (but only to all just states) and (b) the justice or injustice of a state varies independently of its legitimacy with respect to particular persons. They may reject arguments from fairness because (a) it is not unfair to benefit incidentally from schemes in which one has not willingly included oneself and (b) modern states do not sufficiently resemble the voluntary cooperative schemes (in civil society) from application to which the principle of fairness derives its intuitive force. They also may reject arguments from communal obligations because (a) there are no political communities in any strict sense of *community* in the modern political world and (b) communal obligations are not self-justifying, but themselves require some external justification of a sort similar to that required by the very political obligations these communal obligations are invoked to justify.

28. Steven DeLue, *Political Obligation in a Liberal State* (Albany: State University of New York Press, 1989), x, 1.

29. Thomas Senor, "What If There Are No Political Obligations? A Reply to A. J. Simmons," *Philosophy & Public Affairs* 16 (Summer 1987), 260. For similar criticisms, see Tony Honore, "Must We Obey? Necessity as a Ground of Obligation," *Virginia Law Review* (February 1981), 42–44, and George Klosko, "Political Obligation and the Natural Duties of Justice," *Philosophy & Public Affairs* (Summer 1994), 269–70.

30. Obedience to law thus stands as much in need of justification as does disobedience. Mark Murphy has argued that philosophical anarchism (by

which he means the view that "there is no reason to obey the law as such") does not in fact imply, as I have claimed, that obedience is as much in need of justification as disobedience ("Philosophical Anarchism and Legal Indifference," *American Philosophical Quarterly* [April 1995], 195–98). His argument, however, without his appearing to see it, actually attacks not the implication in question, but the truth of philosophical anarchism—that is, Murphy in effect asserts that there is a reason to obey the law as such, by appealing to MacIntyre's (in my view unjustified) privileging of the status quo. Since the actual, not the believed, reason-giving force of existing laws or conventions is precisely what is at issue in the debate over philosophical anarchism, an argument that simply appeals to our ordinary acceptance of actions conforming to existing rules (and our questioning of those that fail to conform) is hardly likely to have much force in deciding the debate.

31. George Klosko, *The Principle of Fairness and Political Obligation* (Lanham, Md.: Rowman & Littlefield, 1992), 26, 24.

32. Ibid., 25.

33. Variants of all of these kinds of arguments are advanced in Leslie Green, "Who Believes in Political Obligation?" in this volume, pp. 1–17.

34. *Moral Principles and Political Obligations*, 195.

3

Why Even Morally Perfect People Would Need Government[1]

Gregory S. Kavka

Why do we need government? A common view is that government is necessary to constrain people's conduct toward one another, because people are not sufficiently virtuous to exercise the requisite degree of control on their own. This view was expressed perspicuously and artfully by liberal thinker James Madison in *The Federalist*, number 51, where he wrote: "If men were angels, no government would be necessary."[2] Madison's idea is shared by writers ranging across the political spectrum. It finds clear expression in the marxist view that the state will gradually wither away after a communist revolution, as unalienated "communist man" emerges,[3] and it is implied by the libertarian view that government's only legitimate function is to control the unfortunate and immoral tendency of some individuals to violate the moral rights of others.[4]

I call this common view the Simple Account of our need for government—simple because it identifies a single factor, our lack of virtue, as the entire explanation of that need. Its basis is the belief that if people were sufficiently virtuous, they would either agree on all significant practical matters or could effectively work out any remaining disagreements without resorting to governmental mechanisms. While initially attractive, this belief is seriously mistaken and leads to an overly simple and misleading account of our need for government. In its place, I will suggest a more satisfactory Complex Account that attributes our need for government to a number of factors.

Showing what is wrong with the Simple Account of our need for

41

government is neither a short nor an easy task; thus, this essay is largely a programmatic one that offers a promissory note that I hope to make good on in later work.[5] Here I only sketch my approach in arguing against the Simple Account, and for the Complex Account, without providing the necessary details. I will have some substantive things to say, however, in response to the three most important general objections to my project that might be raised by supporters of the Simple Account.

Method

To determine whether morally perfect people would need government, we must have some working conception of what government is and what moral perfection consists in. For present purposes, we may regard the government of a society located within a territory as a subsystem of that society which possesses sufficient power to settle significant disputes among that society's members (and others in the territory), forcibly if necessary, and which claims unique legitimacy in exercising that power.[6] This account captures the key descriptive and normative elements in the idea of government. Descriptively, government is an authoritative mechanism that can impose settlements on disputing parties without necessarily obtaining their consent to the terms of the settlement, and it has, or at least claims to have, the normative property of being the unique agency in the territory with legitimate justification for carrying out this coercive activity.

What is a morally perfect person like? Or, to use Madison's wonderfully evocative terminology, as I often will in what follows, what is an "angel" like? I propose a three-part characterization. First, a morally perfect person has a system of moral beliefs that is without flaw. That is, his is a consistent, coherent, and reasonably complete moral belief system that contains whatever true (or objectively justified) moral beliefs there are and contains no false (or objectively falsified) moral beliefs.[7] Second, the morally perfect person always acts conscientiously on his moral beliefs. He is not subject to weakness of will or similar motivational defects that cause people sometimes to act against their best moral judgment. Third, morally perfect persons are like ordinary people in every other respect. They are, that is, as like us as they could be while always acting conscientiously on flawless moral belief systems. In particular, they are embodied mortal creatures of considerable but limited mental capacity who have lives, loves, hopes, plans, fears, and desires just as you and I do.

Given these characterizations, our central question boils down to whether people who always act on flawless moral belief systems would need a forcible mechanism—claiming unique legitimacy—to authoritatively settle practical disagreements that might arise among them. Posed in this form, the question is still too abstract and general for us to be able to arrive here at a fully determinate answer. To do that, we would need to know or assume more about the functions government can serve and about the substantive content of flawless moral belief systems,[8] but these definitions of government and moral perfection are sufficient to allow us to consider—and respond in general terms to—some of the most serious objections to the claim that even morally perfect people would need government. This will be done following a brief explanation of why significant practical disagreements would arise even among morally perfect people.

Disputes among the Morally Perfect

There are at least four kinds of reasons why morally perfect people might have disagreements with each other about practical matters.[9] The first and most obvious of these is their cognitive limitations. Given human beings' finite, limited, and differing intellectual capacities and their differing experiences and information, different morally perfect people would have different factual beliefs about the world and the causal processes characterizing it. These factual disagreements would inevitably lead to serious practical disputes, even among those who qualify as angels according to the same moral theory.

This is most evident in the case of utilitarian or other consequentialist moral theories. Where rightness or wrongness is determined in a straightforward way by the value of the consequences of alternative courses of action, disagreement on what those consequences would be leads directly to disagreement about what it is right and wrong to do.

The same holds true of the other types of moral theories, however, since they too allow that facts about actual or hypothetical consequences are relevant to determining right and wrong in many contexts. On Robert Nozick's libertarian theory, for example, whether a present distribution of property is just depends on whether that distribution sufficiently resembles what would have come about if neither force nor fraud had ever been exercised in determining property holdings in the past.[10] Even libertarians agreeing exactly about what constitutes force and fraud could hardly be expected to agree on the implications of this counterfactual test of distributive justice, given the enormous cognitive complexity involved in applying the test. A similar point holds with respect to communitarian rights theories, liberal pluralism, and other moral doctrines that attach importance to the notion of moral rights. Whether a right of mine has been violated or infringed will often depend, among other things, on whether any of my interests have been damaged, but this opens up a whole range of practical disputes among perfect rights-respecters, based on their differing factual beliefs. Angel *A* may disagree with angel *B*, for example, about whether smoking in public violates others' rights to life and well-being, because they have different beliefs about the health effects of breathing the fumes of other people's cigarettes.

A second source of practical disagreement among the morally perfect is the truth of the philosophical doctrine of moral pluralism or, as it might more accurately be labeled, *incomplete objectivism*. This doctrine allows that while there may be *some* objective moral truths (e.g., that torturing young children to death simply for the fun of it is wrong), there are also substantial issues (e.g., the morality of abortion) about which different people may hold differing views without any of them being guilty of any sort of error. Persons living in the same society holding opposing, but nonerroneous, beliefs on such matters may well need a government to ameliorate the practical conflicts that arise from these opposing beliefs.

These practical disagreements are also not necessarily linked to commitment to different types of moral theories. Equally irresolvable disputes may arise among angels adhering to the same general moral theory. This can happen in several ways. There may be irresolvable differences about the scope of a moral theory; thus, one utilitarian angel may disagree with another about the ethics of animal experimentation or factory farming because one seeks to maximize human happiness while the other aims to maximize the happiness of all sentient creatures. Moreover, the key terms of a moral theory (e.g., "utility," "liberty," or "rights") may be open to a variety of nonerroneous interpretations, each having its own policy implications. For example, pluralist angels may differ among themselves over whether the important right to liberty requires others to actively assist you in your exercise of certain options or only requires others not to actively interfere with your exercise of those options. Further, even when there is theoretical agreement about the meaning of key terms, the application of theoretical principles to particular situations may involve matters of judgment about which people may differ without any of them being in error. We would not, for instance, expect every perfect libertarian to draw the line between fraud and legitimate salesmanship in precisely the same place. In particular, we would expect some to endorse the principle of caveat emptor, while others do not.

A third source of practical disagreement among the morally perfect is the structure of certain of their interactions. Given moral pluralism and/or cognitive limitations, even angels believing in the same type of moral theory will often disagree in their value rankings of outcomes that may be brought about by their joint actions. As a result, they will find themselves facing interaction situations—such as Prisoners' Dilemmas or public goods problems[11]—in which each person's moral aims will be better achieved if all are mutually coerced by government than if they act independently in the light of their flawless moral beliefs.

Suppose, for example, that you and I are angels believing in moral theories of the same general type, but because of different factual or moral beliefs,[12] I believe that act X (which only you can do) is morally quite valuable, while act Y (which only I can do) is morally slightly undesirable. You have opposite beliefs about the moral value of these two acts, but we share the belief that promises to do what is immoral are not binding. We exchange promises: you agree to do X in your faraway location at the same time I do Y. Without enforcement, neither of us will keep the agreement, for neither will pointlessly do what is morally undesirable, and neither can affect the other's act, but if we have a government to enforce compliance (by imposing sanctions that we regard as morally overriding), we will both comply and bring about an outcome that is better from each of our points of view: production of the quite valuable at the cost of the slightly undesirable.

Before leaving the topic of interaction structures, it is worth noting briefly that government can also help alleviate interaction problems that are not the result of disagreement. Such problems of *coordination* involve independent agents combining their actions in ways that will produce mutually valued outcomes. Since such problems do not presuppose divergent evaluations, angels would be subject to them just like the rest of us. Typical examples of coordination problems include what side of the street we should drive on, what items should be used for currency, which of our offices you and I should meet at, and what time it is (or should be called) now. Coordination problems can be quite complex, and they may be difficult to solve efficiently without some enforcement mechanism, especially if they are not problems of pure coordination, but involve some elements of conflict. (Consider Southern California traffic flow as a salient example.)

Motivated belief—the fourth and final cause of angelic disagreement—may be viewed as a special case of our first cause: factual disagreement due to cognitive limitations; but it is a sufficiently important, and controversial, source of factual disagreement to deserve to be separated out for comment. Motivated beliefs are beliefs that are not determined solely by evidence but are instead influenced by motivational states of the agent.[13] This category is intended to include such familiar phenomena as wishful thinking (believing something because one wants it to be true), sour grapes (believing some object lacks desirable features simply because the object is unattainable), and various forms of self-deception (including holding beliefs because they are convenient or psychologically comfortable rather than because they are supported by evidence).

Since motivated beliefs may allow us to do what we want while believing it morally right (whether it is or not), they are an important potential source of disagreement among the conscientious—including angels, who are, by definition, perfectly conscientious. It might be objected that to hold motivated beliefs always constitutes a moral failing and, hence, that angels could never have such beliefs. I doubt that this is so. Whether holding a given motivated belief constitutes a moral failing, a cognitive error, both, or something else, depends on the details of the particular case. Indeed, motivated beliefs may sometimes be the result of cognitive-simplifying or motivational processes that are rational at the metalevel. It may, for example, help us get on with life in a difficult world if we often engage in wishful thinking or have excessive confidence in our judgments about facts.[14] Otherwise, we might have more serious morale problems or waste time and energy trying to resolve uncertainties that cannot be resolved.

Without going further into the ethics of belief, we may say this much: if, as I believe to be the case, having motivated beliefs is not always a moral failing, it can constitute a significant source of practical disagreement among the morally perfect. Together with factual disagreements derived from other cognitive limitations, moral pluralism, and the structure of some interactions, it provides us with ample grounds for expecting even a community of angels to suffer from a considerable degree of conflict and discord in the absence of an authoritative procedure for settling disputes.

The Conceptual Objection

In the last section, I offered some general reasons for thinking that the Complex Account of our need for government is superior to the Simple Account. In this section, I will sketch and answer the first of three main lines of objection to my position. I call this the "conceptual objection," because it attempts to argue for the correctness of the Simple Account on purely conceptual grounds.

The conceptual objection can take various forms. It may be argued that moral perfection requires correct judgment down to the level of picking out the right act or policy in all specific circumstances, for disagreement on such a matter would imply adherence to a mistaken moral principle or misapplication of some moral principle by at least one party to the dispute—and either error constitutes a moral failing.

Alternatively, the point may be expressed in terms of what it means to be a moral person. This implies, among other things, working in harmony with others (at least those who are also moral), but then being morally perfect must involve working in perfect harmony with others (at least those who are also morally perfect); hence, morally perfect people would never disagree with one another in practice.

However it is expressed, the core idea of the conceptual objection is that whatever powers, faculties, or dispositions are necessary to ensure practical agreement, these should be included in our conception of moral perfection. The nature of this objection is further clarified by looking at how it deals with the considerations advanced in the previous section—the four purported sources of practical disagreement among angels. The conceptual objector must deny moral pluralism in favor of complete moral objectivism. He will classify all cases of motivated belief as instances of moral imperfection and will regard cognitive errors and limitations as incompatible with an agent's moral perfection, at least when these beliefs, errors, and limitations have practical implications. To deal with potential interaction problems, the conceptual objector must ascribe to morally perfect agents whatever capacities are needed to ensure that these problems will not arise. Agreement on values at all levels, together with cognitive perfection, might be thought to preclude Prisoners' Dilemmas and public goods problems, and it could be argued that the morally perfect would know (or make known) each other's minds well enough to avoid coordination problems as well.

One may view the conceptual objection as offering a doctrine of the unity of practical perfections that is analogous to the ancient doctrine of the unity of the virtues. The latter doctrine says that, despite their apparent distinctness, you could not have one of the (cardinal) virtues without having them all. The conceptual objection claims that you cannot have real moral perfection without having all the powers and dispositions that ensure agreement with your morally perfect fellows, whether or not these powers and dispositions seemed, pretheoretically, to be moral ones.

To explain what is wrong with the conceptual objection, it will be helpful to consider an analogous argument from the history of philosophy. Along with a bevy of introductory philosophy students, the great political philosopher Thomas Hobbes probably fell prey to a tempting error. He noted that all motives of voluntary action are motives of the actor, or "self." Observing that ends of action must be regarded as choice-worthy or good from the actor's point of view, Hobbes slid over into the conclusion that all acts preceded by deliberation are self-interested, in the sense of aiming at what is good *for* the agent.[15]

Bishop Joseph Butler rightly denounced this reasoning on two grounds. First, it obscures important differences between such categories of motives as, for example, promoting a particular interest, promoting one's overall interests, promoting the interests of others, and doing one's duty. Second, it amounts to stretching the meaning of a well-understood term (such as "good for," or "selfish") so as to make an apparently substantive claim (such as "agents are motivated only by what is good for them" or "all acts are selfish") into a tautology.[16] When old habits of mind or conventions of meaning reassert themselves, however (as they apparently did with Hobbes), we may erroneously think and claim that we have established the original substantive thesis.

Hobbes's "argument" for psychological egoism is a clear example of intellectual theft, rather than honest toil. By lumping together importantly different categories of motives under the heading of "selfish" or "self-interested," Hobbes has fallen into the tempting trap of committing what may be called the *mixed-bag fallacy*. A trap of just this kind has firmly closed its jaws on the conceptual objector to our Complex Account of the need for government. This objector may, if she wishes, stretch the term "moral imperfection" to cover any features that prevent people from reaching practical agreement, but she threatens to bury interesting and useful distinctions among different sources of practical disagreement by employing such a mixed-bag category. Further, and more important, she thereby invites us to slide into the false conclusion that people who were morally perfect (in a more limited pretheoretic sense) would always agree on practical matters.

In the end, then, the conceptual objection essentially amounts to a verbal maneuver that, even if accepted, would not undermine the substantive claims of the Complex Account of our need for government. We can see this very clearly by employing a technical term, "archangels," to stand for those possessing moral perfection in the very strong sense favored by the conceptual objector. More precisely, archangels are people (or peoplelike creatures) possessing virtues of enough kinds and in sufficient degree that they would agree on all significant practical matters.[17] It would be correct to say, paraphrasing Madison, that we need government because we are not archangels.

Look, however, at how many and various the special properties of archangels would have to be. In addition to having full and correct beliefs regarding the content of moral principles and being perfectly conscientious, archangels would have to know and use all facts, be perfect reasoners, have flawless (and mutually converging) judgment in applying general principles to specific situations, and perhaps—to solve coordination problems—even be capable of reading one another's minds. Supporters of the Simple Account can take no solace in the conclusion that archangels, so characterized, could do without government, for—given the complex and various perfections archangels must have—this observation simply confirms the Complex Account, which attributes the need for government to a number of distinct imperfections in ourselves and our interactions.

The Voluntary-Settlement Objection

The second main general objection to the Complex Account of our need for government is based on the idea that morally perfect citizens, while they might disagree on significant practical matters, would simply settle their disagreements cooperatively, voluntarily, and peacefully. According to this view, *reasonableness*—in the sense of willingness to settle voluntarily practical disagreements by discussion and compromise—is itself a moral virtue that angels would possess in sufficient degree to obviate any need for imposed and enforced settlements.

On one interpretation, this voluntary-settlement objection becomes merely a version of the flawed conceptual objection: it claims that the

degree of reasonableness required to obviate the need for government
is implied by the very concept of moral perfection. This claim is
subject to the criticisms offered in the last section.

There is, however, a more plausible version of the present objection
which says that the requisite degree of reasonableness is attributed to
angels by the *correct substantive moral theory*. This version of the
objection is worth taking very seriously, for it does seem that such
moral theories as liberal pluralism, communitarian rights theory, and
rule utilitarianism would regard reasonableness as an important moral
virtue. For the sake of concreteness, I will here frame my reply to the
objection in the context of liberal pluralism—the view that there are
various valid conceptions of the good life and good society and that
advocates of different conceptions generally should be tolerant of each
other's moral beliefs and practices.

This reply consists in a general observation, followed by an independent game-theoretic argument spelled out in more detail. The general
observation is this: for the need for government to be obviated,
pluralist angels would not need to be just reasonable and tolerant,
they would have to give these second-order "interpersonal-relations"
virtues lexical priority over the substantive aims favored by their own
conceptions of the good. Otherwise, disputes would sometimes arise
among pluralist angels that they could not settle voluntarily by compromise or agreeing to disagree. These would be disputes involving
substantive values that rank higher for both parties than reasonableness.[18] It is easy to imagine, for example, disputes about abortion or
euthanasia being of this kind.

This point is reinforced by noting the following. Suppose we had a
unanimous agreement among liberal pluralist angels that tolerance was
the most important value of all. There would remain considerable
room for substantive disagreement about what tolerance does and does
not imply. Must we allow people to harm themselves, offend others,
create risks of harm to others, or even harm others if the harm is small
or only psychological? Are we offending against the value of tolerance
if we discourage acts of these kinds by intrusive sermonizing and
threats of withdrawal of future good relations or only if we employ
physical force or the threat thereof? On these practical matters even
the most angelic supporters of tolerance are bound to disagree and will
need an authoritative procedure for settling their differences.

There is a further objection to voluntary peaceful settlement as a
reliable alternative to government among the morally perfect. Suppose
we did have a population of angels, all of whom gave lexical priority to

settling disputes.[19] These angels (whether of the same or different types) may have first-order disputes for reasons we have seen, but whenever such disputes arise they will be settled easily by compromise, since both parties value agreement so highly. Let us therefore call these angels "compromising angels" (or "compromisers") and acknowledge that a society consisting only of compromising angels at a given time would be peaceable and just, without government, at that time.

The kicker is that this paradise of compromise is, without government, potentially unstable over time. To show this, I adapt, modify, and extend an argument of the evolutionary biologist Richard Dawkins.[20] The argument looks at the dynamics of the composition of angelic populations containing subgroups that have various behavioral dispositions (or follow certain strategies). It relies on two assumptions—the correlates of mutation and selection in Darwinian theory. First, there will be a small amount of change in the relative frequencies of various subgroups over short periods caused by randomness or external factors. In particular, an initially homogeneous population of compromisers will naturally develop a small minority of persons with different behavioral dispositions. Second, dispositions or strategies that are successful in a given time period are represented more frequently in the population in the next period, with the changes proportional to the relative degrees of success. Less pretentiously, this second assumption says that if (and to the extent that) a disposition or strategy works, more people tend to adopt it. That is, either people tend to *convert* from less successful to more successful strategies, or *new members* of the population are more likely to adopt the strategies that have been more successful (or both).[21]

I will now present a three-part analysis designed to show that an anarchic society initially consisting only of compromising angels is unstable in the sense that the introduction of a small population of angels following other strategies would eventually lead to a population largely consisting of angels who are not compromisers. Either the strategy of compromise is driven to extinction, or it is replaced by more sophisticated strategies that cannot guarantee peace and justice without government.

The first part of the argument introduces the polar opposite of the compromising angel: the "uncompromising angel" (or "uncompromiser"), who will not settle a first-order dispute except on his own terms. When two uncompromising angels fall into practical disagreement, neither will budge, and the dispute remains unsettled. This is the downside of being an uncompromising angel. The upside is that when a dispute arises between an uncompromising and a compromising angel, the latter—giving lexical priority to reaching agreement—will give in, while the former holds firm and captures the entire cooperative surplus available.

What will happen if a population of compromising angels is invaded by a small minority of uncompromising angels? The latter will get their way in each dispute that arises with a member of the other group and thus will have more success in attaining their first-order (moral) aims;[22] hence, over time, their representation in the population will increase. No matter what the new relative percentages of the two groups in the population are during a given time period, uncompromising angels will—on average—be more successful in that population mix than will compromising angels. As a result, the percentage of compromising angels will continue to decline period by period until that strategy is driven into extinction; nor can the compromisers make a comeback: since they do less well even when there are few of them, any chance increase in the percentage of compromisers will simply be followed by a new decline. The final result is a population consisting solely of uncompromising angels, whose practical disputes are never settled and who are therefore in the closest approximation to Hobbes's war of all against all that angels could be in. How sad that this decline, from the benign anarchy of compromise to the painful condition of festering disputes, is inevitable.

Perhaps, though, it is not. Perhaps, seeing the problems here, some angels will adopt *conditional* strategies that allow them to react differently to those they have found to be compromisers in past disputes and those they have found to be uncompromisers. In particular, the second stage of our argument explores what happens if we introduce the disposition to compromise except with those who have been uncompromising with one in the past. I will call a party having this disposition an "avenging angel" (or "avenger"), for if her initial willingness to settle is exploited by an uncompromising angel in their first dispute, she avenges herself by acting in an uncompromising manner toward that particular angel in future disputes.

The introduction of the avenging strategy lessens the relative advantages of being uncompromising by offering fewer opportunities to exploit others without reducing the benefits available to compromisers. (Compromisers interact with avengers just as they do with one another.) Is it sufficient, however, to shift the dynamics of interaction in favor of either or both of the compromising strategies? The answer must be equivocal.

When they are a small percentage of the population, avengers do not do well relative to uncompromisers. Most of their interactions will be first-time disputes with uncompromisers in which they are exploited. Further, the uncompromisers do better than the avengers in interacting with whatever compromisers there are. (They capture, on average, *all* rather than *one-half* the cooperative surplus available in a dispute with a compromiser.) If there are enough avengers around to begin with, however, so that a sufficient number survive after the compromisers have been eliminated in virtue of their sorry performance relative to the uncompromisers, the avengers may gain an advantage by withholding settlements from uncompromisers who have exploited them in the past while benefiting from settling disputes with one another.

Indeed, Dawkins's computer simulations indicate that while the compromiser strategy is destined for extinction, the outcome will be *either* a stable population consisting entirely of avenging angels or of uncompromising angels.[23] Which outcome results will depend on the initial distribution of strategies in the population and on other parameters such as the number of interactions in a time period, the relative value of compromise compared to getting your way and leaving a dispute unsettled, and how success in one period translates into increased numbers in the next period. This is not a happy result for the voluntary-settlement objector, for it shows that giving lexical priority to settling disputes voluntarily (being a compromiser) is an unsuccessful strategy, while combining this with angelic vengeance may or may not succeed in preventing an intolerable social outcome.

Perhaps Dawkins's analysis, which I have roughly followed so far, does not take us far enough. Will not angels view the uncompromising behavior of some of their fellows in an equally bad light, whether or not it has been practiced against them personally? Let us therefore imagine a new strategy, that of the "guardian angel" ("guardian"), who guards the moral aims of her fellow angels as zealously as she guards her own. In particular, she is a general avenger who compromises with all and only those who have compromised in all their previous disputes, whether with her or with others. Guardians in this sense always compromise with other guardians, compromisers, and avengers. When someone, however, has proven himself an uncompromising angel by once exploiting any member of these three groups, he can expect no compromise from any guardian in the future.[24]

Intuitively, it seems that the presence of guardians would doom the uncompromisers' strategy, for now uncompromisers lose a whole class of future opportunities for exploitation on committing their first act of exploitation and, hence, will fare less well. In other words, they will have less chance to move from victim to victim without running into other angels disposed to retaliate. They will be less successful than the other three types, or at least less successful than the guardians, and their strategy will dwindle into extinction.

There are two problems, however, with this final defense of the voluntary-settlement objection. First, there is a formal argument in the literature that, under conditions of free and perfect information, full rationality, and certain other restrictions, guardian-type strategies are not successful except when parallel avenger-type strategies are.[25] Second, under more realistic conditions, the guardian strategy has serious disadvantages compared to the avenger strategy. There are large information costs involved in being a guardian—you must be able to collect, interpret, store, and retrieve information about the past disputes of anyone you have a dispute with. This is far more difficult than the avenger's task of remembering whom his own past disputes were with and what the outcomes were. Further, while there are natural incentives to be an avenging angel—who wants to be exploited twice by the same person?—the incentives for being a guardian are unclear. Why should you punish someone for holding out for the fulfillment of her moral aims in a past dispute in which she was, in your view, just as likely to be in the right as her opponent?

Various theorists have suggested in other contexts that this kind of incentive problem can be solved by supposing that there are meta-norms that require punishment not only of violators of first-order norms, but also of those second-order violators who refuse to join in punishing first-order violators.[26] In our context, this would involve considering the strategy of metaguardian angels who are uncompromising not only with uncompromisers, but also with those who have given in to uncompromisers. I do not find this solution promising. Why should the same problem not arise at the next level when we ask about incentives for enforcing the metanorms, and so on, ad infinitum? Further, the information costs of individuals employing the metaguardian strategy are even more staggering than those of individuals employing the guardian strategy, for each must now keep track of how those she disputes with have acted in their own past disputes *and* in response to past disputes not involving them.

In the end, then, the guardian argument cannot save the voluntary-settlement objection. Indeed, I believe that a stronger conclusion is warranted. That argument, when properly understood, lends support to the view that even angels would need government to settle disputes, for government itself may be seen as a guardian angel, or, more accurately, as fulfilling the role of guardians in providing a mechanism that channels a society of angels into a desirable configuration. Because of centralization, it can reduce the information costs of keeping track of citizens' relevant past behavior; moreover, because of specialization of tasks—in which the responsibilities of (and expectations associated with) their roles provide officials with incentives to settle disputes among citizens on reasonable terms—government can be motivated to create and enforce settlements among disputing angels that, on the whole, resemble those the parties would reach if they were all reasonable compromisers.

The Futility Objection

Having sailed past the Scylla of the voluntary-settlement objection, we risk falling into the Charybdisian clutches of David Gauthier's futility objection.[27] According to this objection, government would be futile and useless among morally perfect people, because if a morally perfect person were unpersuaded by her opponent's arguments and offers of compromise on a particular issue, she would not acquiesce even in the face of government coercion. In other words, on issues where disputes among the morally perfect cannot be settled voluntarily among the parties (presumably because of strong principled differences), they cannot be settled even with the help of government. When government over angels is needed, it will necessarily be ineffective.

For the beginnings of an answer to this objection, we may turn to Hobbes, who notes that resistance to government requires, among other things, hope of success on the part of the resisters: "for it were madness to attempt without hope, when to fail, is to die the death of a traitor."[28] Now, it is unlikely that governors of a society of angels would put to death as traitors principled resisters to their policies. Nevertheless, by our definition of a government, these governors possess sufficient power to force compliance (e.g., by imprisonment, force, or threats) if need be. This means that, even if resistance to government decisions (outside of normal political channels) is not likely to be deadly for resisters, it will be known to be generally in vain.[29] For the futility objection to work, then, it must be the case that angels will generally resist unfavorable (from their point of view) government-imposed settlements of their disputes with other angels, even when they realize that such resistance will not succeed.

To suppose this, however, is to adopt a view of angels' attitudes toward peaceful dispute settlement that is the extreme opposite of that which was supposed in the voluntary-settlement objection. According to that objection, angels give lexical priority to the second-order value of peaceful dispute settlement over any first-order values to which they might be committed. By contrast, the futility objection views angels as giving no weight to peaceful dispute settlement with other angels when there is a conflict with significant first-order values. Neither of these extreme views seems at all plausible. It is certainly a reasonable moral position to attach some, but not infinite, weight in moral decision making to the importance of peaceful dispute settlement with other moral people; hence, many morally perfect people would see themselves as having considerable (but not necessarily always conclusive) moral reasons for acquiescing in the decisions of governmental bodies whose function is to settle such disputes.

In the previous section, however, I argued that angels' commitment to peaceful dispute settlement would not necessarily lead them to peaceful agreement with one another. How does having a coercive government make a difference? First, the government serves as a final public authority for enforcing settlements, ensuring that if one acquiesces in a compromise arrangement, one can reasonably expect others to follow its terms so that the elements of the compromise you approve of, as well as those you do not, will materialize. Second, government serves—and can be seen by angelic citizens to serve—some of the guardian-angel functions described in the last section. Third, our angels are, aside from their moral perfection, human beings like the rest of us, with their own personal and prudential concerns. Such beings are presumably capable of being influenced by threats of fines, imprisonment, and public disapproval, though to a lesser degree than we more sinful folk. This not only adds a motivational factor pointing directly toward acquiescence, it also adds assurance that other angels will abide by government rulings, thus stabilizing settlements that give opposing sides part of what they want.

We may summarize this by saying that the combination of the government's coercive power and its legitimizing influence (in virtue of its unique capacity to authoritatively settle disputes among citizens) will give most angelic citizens powerful reasons to acquiesce in its decisions, even when they disagree with those decisions on first-order moral grounds. This does not mean that angels will never resist their governments or that angels could never settle disputes among themselves, but it does mean that government would have a positive role in settling disputes peacefully, even among angels, facilitating settlement of many disputes that might otherwise lead to deadly social conflict.

To complement the theoretical discussion of this section, let me use a concrete example to illustrate the shortcomings of the futility objection. Consider abortion, an issue over which we might imagine morally perfect citizens disagreeing. One such citizen views abortion as the murder of an innocent human being and, hence, immoral, but the laws, enacted under reasonable democratic procedures and enforced by government power, allow abortion under many circumstances, and there seems little prospect of that changing. According to the futility objection, if this abortion opponent is morally perfect, the fact that abortion is legal should make absolutely no difference to him, even if it means that any acts of abortion protest he performs will be ineffective in stopping or limiting the practice overall. If he thinks intentional killers of the innocent should be stopped—even by killing them—he will kill as many abortionists as he can (since morally perfect people are perfectly conscientious and never fail to act on their moral principles).

It is clearly wrong, however, to think that a morally perfect person— even one having the beliefs described above—would necessarily act like this (as the futility objection supposes). Many such persons would be deterred from such extreme illegal action by the personal consequences of taking such action, the fact that other moral people disagree with him on the substantive issue, and the fact that abortionists are carrying out legal activities that are regarded by themselves and most of the members of the society as legitimate. Even angels—like these abortion opponents—can be influenced by government to comply with its rulings.

Conclusions

If the arguments of the last three sections are correct, the Complex Account of our need for government survives the three main objections that might be offered against it.[30] It is superior to the Simple Account, which wrongly identifies a single factor—our moral shortcomings—as the rationale for societies' needing authoritative dispute-settling mechanisms. That said, I hasten to emphasize two limitations on what my analysis, even if correct, shows. First, government has costs as well as benefits: economic costs of operations, danger of misuse of power, rent seeking by officials, and so on. A full justification of government among angels would have to go on to show that their need for government outweighs the costs if the government is properly designed. This task would be utterly trivial if Madison were right in suggesting that the normal problems of government would be nonexistent in a government of angels; but I doubt that he is.[31] Nonetheless, having morally perfect governors would substantially reduce the costs or risks of having government, thus making it plausible that the need to solve disputes authoritatively would outweigh the disadvantages of being governed—even for angels.

The second limitation should be obvious. Showing that moral failings are not the *only* source of the need for government does not mean they are not a source at all, or even that they are not the main—or most important—single source; indeed, they might be. In any case, the existence of this additional reason for needing government among nonangels (i.e., real people) suggests that we imperfect sorts need government even more than angels would.[32]

In closing, I will briefly mention how the project described in this essay develops a theme already hinted at in my earlier work.[33] There, I suggested that interpersonal conflicts in Hobbes's state of nature and the Cold War nuclear arms race (which represented the height of interstate conflict in the modern international state of nature) are not—as is often thought—simply a result of the immorality of the parties involved. Rather, they are at least partly the result of independent parties pursuing morally legitimate aims in a situation whose structure leads them into conflict. My present project, while limiting its focus to domestic political interactions, generalizes this idea about nonmoral sources of conflict to include sources besides interaction structures. In principle at least, being aware of the multiple sources of conflict should enable us to construct social strategies for minimizing and ameliorating conflict that are more productive than exhortations to the various parties to be more virtuous. It may therefore be useful to remember that government is a cross we must bear for more than our sins.

Notes

1. This essay originally appeared in *Social Philosophy and Policy*, vol. 12, no. 1 (Winter 1995): 1–18. It is reprinted with the permission of the estate of

Gregory S. Kavka and Cambridge University Press. An earlier version was presented at a symposium of the Pacific Division meetings of the American Philosophical Association in March 1990, in which Christopher Morris, David Gauthier, and Debra Satz were the author's fellow participants. The author thanks them and members of the audience on that occasion, as well as the other contributors to the *Social Philosophy and Policy* issue, for helpful discussion.

2. Alexander Hamilton, John Jay, and James Madison, *The Federalist* (New York: Modern Library, 1937), 337. This edition identifies number 51 as written by Madison or Hamilton.

3. For a recent sympathetic treatment of the marxist view that makes use of ideas from Kant and Rousseau, see Andrew Levine, *The End of the State* (London: Verso, 1987), 164–73.

4. A sophisticated philosophical work in the libertarian tradition is Robert Nozick, *Anarchy, State, and Utopia* (New York: Basic Books, 1974).

5. Gregory S. Kavka, *Governing Angels: Human Imperfections and the Need for Government*, in progress.

6. This characterization modifies, in a Weberian direction, the account of government offered in Gregory S. Kavka, *Hobbesian Moral and Political Theory* (Princeton: Princeton University Press, 1986), 157–60. It rules out classifying street gangs or the mafia as governments under normal circumstances, since these groups do not usually have the power to enforce their decisions (including on nonmembers in their territories) in defiance of public authorities and rarely claim the legitimacy of their doing so. When public authority has broken down or cannot penetrate a geographical area effectively run by a gang or group of rebels claiming legitimate authority in that area, this account properly allows the gang or rebel organization to count as the government of that area. Being a government, in my sense, clearly does not imply moral or political legitimacy, only the claim to it.

7. Reasonable completeness does not mean that the system has a precise answer to every possible practical question that might arise. It refers instead to the system that leaves no main area of moral concern unaddressed and that provides guidance appropriate to the tasks and capabilities of moral agents.

8. I plan to pursue these matters in Kavka, *Governing Angels*.

9. Cf. the discussion of the "burdens of judgment" in John Rawls, *Political Liberalism* (New York: Columbia University Press, 1993), 54–58.

10. Nozick, *Anarchy, State, and Utopia*, chap. 7. I ignore complexities in Nozick's position that are not germane to the present point.

11. For explanation and further discussion of such problems, with special emphasis on the Prisoners' Dilemma, see below, pp. 121–35, 138–61, and 172–88—Ed.

12. Such angels may have disagreements about the scope of moral principles, the theoretical meaning of moral terms, or the application of principles to specific cases.

13. Beliefs conforming to the agent's current evidence count as motivated

beliefs if the agent's motivations introduced a relevant bias in the gathering of evidence.

14. Shelley E. Taylor, *Positive Illusions* (New York: Basic Books, 1990).

15. Thomas Hobbes, *Leviathan* (1651; Harmondsworth: Penguin Books, 1968), 120, 192. For discussion, see Kavka, *Hobbesian Moral and Political Theory*, sections 2 and 3.

16. Joseph Butler, *Sermons,* Preface and Sermon XI, in A. I. Melden, ed., *Ethical Theories* (Englewood Cliffs, N.J.: Prentice-Hall, 1967), 238–39, 259–60.

17. For a somewhat similar use of the term, see R. M. Hare, *Moral Thinking* (Oxford: Oxford University Press, 1981), 44.

18. Cf. Jean Hampton, "Should Political Philosophy Be Done without Metaphysics?" *Ethics*, vol. 99, no. 4 (July 1989): 800–804.

19. Such angels are like the comic-strip character Caspar Milquetoast, whose "main goal is to avoid a quarrel. All else takes second place." See David Lewis, "Mill and Milquetoast," *Australasian Journal of Philosophy*, vol. 67, no. 2 (June 1989): 162.

20. Richard Dawkins, *The Selfish Gene* (Oxford: Oxford University Press, 1976), 198–201. In the argument given below, the "compromisers," "uncompromisers," and "avengers" correspond to Dawkins's "suckers," "cheats," and "grudgers," respectively.

21. New members may emulate successful present members, or success may lead to control of the resources needed to educate or indoctrinate new members in one's own mold. Note that these are cultural or learning phenomena. The analogy to biology is not intended to imply genetic transmission of relevant dispositions. Further, given cognitive complexity and moral pluralism, there is no single model of angelic behavior; hence, new members may adopt the dispositions of the more "successful" present angels without thereby acting immorally.

22. My analysis assumes that the number of first-order disputes one has, and who they are with, is independent of one's strategy.

23. Dawkins, *The Selfish Gene*, 200. Apparently, it is possible that, over the very long run, the population may flip back and forth between the two equilibrium states of being dominated by uncompromisers and by avengers.

24. Guardians may usefully be thought of as being like conscientious inhabitants of Locke's state of nature, who exercise the right to punish (by ostracism) transgressions of the laws of nature whether or not they themselves were victims of those transgressions.

25. Jonathan Bendoir and Dilip Mookherjee, "Norms, Third Party Sanctions, and Cooperation," *Journal of Law, Economics, and Organization*, vol. 6, no. 1 (Spring 1990): 33–63. The authors acknowledge (p. 43) that the formal assumptions needed to yield this result are quite restrictive.

26. Robert Axelrod, "An Evolutionary Approach to Norms," *American Political Science Review*, vol. 80, no. 4 (December 1986): 1095–1111.

27. David Gauthier, "Authority without Coercion: Reflections on Kavka and Morris," paper presented at the American Philosophical Association meetings, Pacific Division, March 1990.

28. Hobbes, *Elements of Law*, part 2, chap. 8, section 1; reprinted in Richard Peters, ed., *Body, Man, and Citizen* (New York: Collier Books, 1962), 369. For a useful discussion on this point, see S. A. Lloyd, *Ideals as Interests in Hobbes's Leviathan* (Cambridge: Cambridge University Press, 1992), 209–10.

29. It may not *always* be known to be futile, because potential resisters may not know that the government has sufficient force to defeat their challenge, that is, that the government is a "government" in our technical sense.

30. A fourth main objection is that angels would voluntarily set up a system of binding arbitration to settle disputes and promise to abide by the resulting decisions. In general terms, my reply is that to the extent adherence to settlements is voluntary, this objection is subject to the same sorts of problems as the voluntary-settlement objection: angels who rank other substantive values above agreement (and promise keeping) either will not promise to abide by the resulting decisions or will act in violation of those decisions when values that they regard as more important are threatened by adherence to them. On the other hand, if the decisions reached by arbitration are coercively enforced, then there is what amounts to a government.

31. Madison, in *The Federalist*, number 51, writes: "If angels were to govern men, neither external nor internal controls on government would be needed." I plan to argue against this claim, and discuss the problems of a government of angels, in *Governing Angels*.

32. Of course, the costs of government are, as noted above, likely to be higher among nonangels, so it is not immediately obvious in which situation there is a stronger net justification for government.

33. Kavka, *Hobbesian Moral and Political Theory*, and Kavka, *Moral Paradoxes of Nuclear Deterrence* (Cambridge: Cambridge University Press, 1987).

4

Market-Anarchy, Liberty, and Pluralism

Jan Clifford Lester

Introduction

I want to defend the view that market-anarchy is the best environment for liberty and pluralism.[1] To this end, I look at the nature of, and relationships among, various key concepts and what they denote. These things include pluralism, liberty, contract, the state, law, anarchy, the market, democracy, and nationalism.

By "pluralism" I mean merely different possible ways of life. I take its advocates to be seeking tolerance of different ways of life rather than seeing plurality as an end in itself (possibly to be promoted at the expense of liberty), but the very idea of liberty is highly problematic. I have written about it at much greater length elsewhere.[2] Here, I begin by stating my basic theory of liberty and explaining how it applies to the concept of contract. These are then applied to the other areas. The longest section examines the prejudice against market-anarchy as the route to liberty and pluralism, as typified by some writings of John Rawls.

Voluntaristic Interpersonal Liberty

Liberty, in its most general sense, signifies the absence of some sort of constraint on something. The topic here is interpersonal liberty: the absence of constraints on people by other people; or, more precisely, people interacting voluntarily without constraining, interfering with,

63

or imposing on each other—except to prevent or redress such constraining, interfering, or imposing. As "imposing" seems the most general of these terms, we will stick with that. Positively imposing on another is, therefore, contrasted here with merely withholding assistance—and preventing or redressing impositions. This sense of liberty is supposed to be the opposite of tyranny and totalitarianism: it is individual sovereignty. It is about voluntary association rather than selfish individualism (as its detractors sometimes misrepresent it). This is the liberty of libertarianism, classical liberalism, and common sense. As far as I can tell, no one has hitherto provided an adequate account of liberty in this sense. This failure is particularly striking and ironic among those calling themselves libertarians. We want a clear, or at least clearer, way of expressing this idea that is capable of dealing with various problems.

One important contrast with this sense of liberty is liberty as a mere zero-sum game whereby any loss in my interpersonal power must be exactly balanced by an increase in the power of others: if I lose the interpersonal power to exercise free speech then this must mean that others gain the power to keep me quiet. This position is even reached by the libertarian philosopher Hillel Steiner.[3] Such liberty cannot be protected or promoted *for* all; it can only be fought over *by* all. Unfortunately, people sometimes seek liberty in a way that entails this sense, and as a result people's real liberty and welfare tend to suffer. Classical liberals, such as Herbert Spencer, sometimes write of *equal* liberty and thereby seem committed to this zero-sum view, but equality, like democracy, is one of the various inconsistent accretions to classical liberal thought.[4] There are, of course, many other uses of "liberty" that it would make much more sense to replace with "ability," "opportunity," "want-satisfaction," "moral action," "self-realization," or any number of other things, but it would be a distraction to illustrate and criticize such examples here.

There are many different ways that people might impose on each other. We want to cover as many relevant types of imposition as possible. Subjective cost, as opposed to benefit, seems to catch this broad meaning. The ideas of cost and benefit here obviously relate to the person's spontaneous desires: those not manipulated by force or fraud. This rules out, among other things, conceptions of positive liberty that really involve paternalism. We can now define interpersonal liberty as "people not having a (subjective) cost imposed on them, that is, involuntarily, by other people," or, for short, "liberty is the absence of imposed cost."[5]

There are a few things we can note immediately about this formula. Such liberty admits of degrees: we can say that someone has liberty to the extent that cost is not imposed on him, and the libertarian policy will be to minimize any imposed cost. The idea of not imposing a cost is obviously something like J. S. Mill's problematic principle of not causing others harm.[6] Elsewhere I argue that imposed cost proves a clearer idea.[7] The contrast between imposing a cost and merely withholding a benefit is also supposed to capture and clarify the intuitive contrast behind the act-omission distinction,[8] for that contrast ultimately cannot be maintained, as there is no consistent and significant difference between mere action and inaction.[9]

We are interested only in what others really impose. An imposed cost is always on a person as a continuing agent. An imposed cost is never deducible from a mere momentary picture of a situation. The previous interactions among the agents have to be known. This might look like what Robert Nozick calls a historical principle rather than a patterned principle,[10] but it is not a moral principle: it is a conceptual point. Similarly, shooting someone dead could be an accident, euthanasia, execution, self-defense, and so on, depending on the historical circumstances and intentions. None of these descriptions is necessarily moral in intention. Someone could accept this conception of liberty while thinking that liberty is a bad thing. He could not do this if the theory were inherently moral. There is something that interpersonal liberty is, and whether it is morally desirable is a separate issue.

A crucial application of this theory is to the issue of contracts, to which we now turn.

Gift Contracts and Exchange Contracts[11]

Assuming that liberty is to be observed (for whatever reason or by whatever means), only explicit gifts of future property claims give others the claim to that property at some future time. Such gifts usually need to be recorded, possibly in formal circumstances and in front of reputable witnesses. It seems that this is understood because of the importance, and practical difficulty otherwise, of proving future-claim property transfers, and this popular understanding, or convention, means that casual statements of property transfer do not count.

If, however, we explicitly state and record that we give away our future claim to X, then the act of gift is thereby done. This is not merely promising at time T0 that we will give someone the claim to X

at time T1: we actually give him the property claim to X at T1 now
(at T0). Unless the other person imposes costs on us that require
compensation, we must surrender X at T1—for it will then no longer
be ours. The other person always has a libertarian claim to what we
explicitly give him a future claim to or contract to give him (if he keeps
his side of the contract and if we have acquired our property by
libertarian means). We cannot libertarianly insist that he instead accept
compensation merely for any inconvenience. The thing in question is
not our libertarian property. It counts for nothing that we might
happen physically to possess it.

Murray Newton Rothbard considers that contractual specific performance and contractual slavery cannot be libertarianly possible
because he thinks that this requires the person to "alienate his *will*"
and that this is logically impossible.[12] There is confusion over "alienate" here. It is true that we cannot alienate our wills in the sense of
making them cease to be *our attributes*, but that does not entail that
we cannot alienate those attributes that are us in the sense of making
them cease to be *our property*. Rothbard is conflating what is necessarily my attribute with what is necessarily owned by me. If his argument
were valid, then no nonhuman animal could be owned either, for
such animals also have wills that cannot be alienated in Rothbard's
conflated sense.

The contractual inheritance rule of entail is also quite libertarian,
contra Rothbard,[13] provided that we specify to whom or how the
property is to be dispersed in the event of the inheritor's breaking the
conditions of accepting his inheritance. Not to allow entail interferes
with the liberty—or, less oddly, libertarian interests—of the dead
person. Such libertarian interests can be understood in the way that
preference utilitarianism can allow want-satisfaction interests to extend beyond one's temporal as well as spatial limits. This might sound
more acceptable with other examples, such as dead persons' property
claims to be buried in the way they contracted for when alive (all such
claims obviously to be made on their behalves, rather as the claims of
merely unconscious living persons must be).

Therefore, forcing someone to stick to an honest contract or to pay
compensation that we agree to is not imposing a cost on him at all. It
might look like the imposition of a cost, but so might (if you do
not understand the circumstances) the recovery of any debt from a
complaining debtor or goods from a thief.

We are now in a position to consider the other areas.

The State, Law, and Anarchy

The state is an organization that coercively imposes[14] monopoly[15] control on persons and property. The state is thus inherently illiberal. It might be a practical necessity that the state's coercive imposition ultimately rests on the majority's opinion that this is acceptable (as famously argued in David Hume[16] and Etienne de la Boetie),[17] but that does not make the coercive imposition somehow libertarian, and it is an empirical point. The more powerful the state in terms of monopolizing superior arms and so on, the less authority it requires. We can conceive of a very powerful state that does simply whatever it wishes and in which a popular uprising would be a practical impossibility; we would still call it a state (and some states must approach this extreme, perhaps in preindustrial countries where the rulers buy foreign weaponry).

States do not have the explicit consent of, or explicit contracts with, their subjects. John Locke's view is that we tacitly consent to the state by not leaving its territory. He might as well have said that we tacitly consent to accept gangsters, murderers, or rapists by choosing to remain in an area they are known to occupy. As Hume argued in reply to Locke, there are ties of culture and habit that make it too expensive to leave. Even on the assumption that anarchy would be chaotic, and worse than the state, that still cannot turn a blunt denial of state legitimacy into tacit consent or contract. There has to be agreement in some form on both sides. This is clearly absent with the anarchist and at best hypothetical with the statist: if faced with a genuine contract that included taking away their individual sovereignty, how many people would really sign?[18] The state, it seems, rests on general opinion or culture or prejudice, rather than real consent or contract. Only the latter are consistent with liberty.

A state must rule (impose its control) to be a state, but there need be no written law. Laws are enforced social rules. They can exist without the state's encoding them or doing the enforcing. In fact, there are powerful arguments that state legislation is an antisocial interference with the spontaneously occurring systems of law that protect persons, property, and contract.[19] A monopoly protection agency (in the unlikely event that one should prove economic) would be paid to protect persons and property and hence would not be coercively imposed nor rule nor be a state. Libertarianism is logically compatible with contractual control, but that would not create a state as all noncontractors, including new generations, could ignore the controlling organization.[20] To finance its rule, it is logically possible that a state need not rely on taxation (money extorted by the state) or on inflating its coercive monopoly of currency: it could have sufficient voluntary donations. It is also logically possible that a state could tolerate a plurality of ways of life. Empirically, however, states are both massive consumers of tax money and Procrustean in their rule.

"Anarchy" means "no rule" (by literal etymology rather than pejorative connotation) in the sense of no imposed control of persons or property by the state. In a society where people interact without imposing costs on each other, no one can be ruled. Anarchy is thus linked to interpersonal liberty in an analytic way: to the extent that we have liberty, we approach anarchy; to the extent that we lack liberty, we approach totalitarianism. Law is thus quite compatible with anarchy, provided that it does no more than protect individual liberty. Enforced rules (laws) do not rule (impose control on) individuals if they are libertarian rules: they merely stop them from imposing costs on other people and their property. The mistaken idea that anarchy is incompatible with law, rather than with state rule, often causes people to dismiss anarchy too quickly.[21] This error is not merely common, it is almost universal.

The Market, Democracy, and Nationalism

The market is inherently anarchic (Karl Marx and Friedrich Engels attacked it for being so), though anarchy is possible without the market, if only in very small, primitive societies. Market-anarchy is contingently highly pluralist. "The market" has become a term of abuse for some people, but the expression is only another way of referring to voluntary exchange. The only liberal alternative to voluntary exchange is charity. The antimarketeer is not advocating charity. The illiberal alternatives include, in the property sphere: fraud, theft, robbery, extortion, and vandalism; in the personal sphere: deceit, assault, rape, slavery, and murder. To the extent that one objects to the market, one must effectively be advocating one of these.

The advocate of market-anarchy is not a utopian in the sense that he believes it to be an ideal end in itself. To be sure, the degree of market-created income certainly indicates the degree of public service as a good rule of thumb, and all state-funded work that the market or charity would not support is prima facie destructive of liberty and welfare—but income is not the only indicator of worth. If everyone were guided by immediate profit maximization, then there would be entertainment, technology, and prudence but there would hardly be art, science, and philosophy, and the best of these latter may eventually give more service over the generations (consider J. S. Bach, Sir Isaac Newton, and Plato). The world would surely be a poorer place without these pursuits, however, the labors of individuals and the wealth they produce in the market are more efficient when voluntarily given to the promotion of these things as they are perceived to be valuable. Market-anarchy is the best framework in which to cultivate them.

"Democracy" means rule by the people, and that requires some form of voting.[22] I know of no one foolish enough to advocate full-blooded democracy. Rather, people want it tempered by some liberal constitution. From a libertarian viewpoint, though, "liberal democracy" is an oxymoron (at least insofar as "liberal" means having respect for individuals' voluntaristic liberty): the more liberty individuals have, the less they can be ruled by the people (or anyone else). In practice, a liberal democracy is a substitute for all-out civil war. The vote-winning side imposes its rules on the others by force and the threat of force. Taxation and noncontractual regulation are themselves forms of aggressive imposition rather than peaceful persuasion.[23]

I generally agree with Murray Rothbard's and David Friedman's market-anarchist economic arguments; I have no economic arguments to add to those here. For instance, I endorse Rothbard's[24] and Roy Childs's[25] criticisms of Nozick's[26] argument for the minimal state and David Friedman's[27] reply to Tyler Cowen.[28] I shall not rehearse those arguments but merely urge people to read them (though I should say that even in his 1994 rejoinder[29] Cowen seriously underrates the significance of ideology: in a fully libertarian society, employees of so-called protection agencies[30] would regard as insane any instructions to extort money or protect criminals); nor will I fully tackle David Miller's rejection of free-market anarchy at the end of his book on anarchism,[31] as I do not think he seriously considers the market-anarchy explanations of public goods and law and order to be found in Rothbard and Friedman. I will, however, add a few words on nationalism.

Nationalism, as Miller uses the word, is the ideology that a society or culture needs its own state. Miller cites nationalism as a powerful ideology of identity that is opposed to anarchy. In this ideological sense, I am bound to agree with the opposition (though I see nationalism mainly as a propaganda tool to give the state legitimacy). That does not stop me from supposing that such nationalism will eventually be replaced by two things: a depoliticized affection for one's perceived geographical home and culture and a moral affirmation of liberty, which politics is correctly seen as destroying. As an anarchist, I therefore have no ideological nationality.[32] This can be contrasted with the more familiar idea of some ideological nationalists (Scottish and Welsh, for instance) who have not attained a separate state. When I call myself English, then, I mean only by geography and culture. On forms requesting my so-called nationality, I am tempted to replace this state-propaganda term with "subjection," for I cannot deny that I am a de facto subject of the declining British state (and a de jure subject of the infant European state).

What I wish to focus on in more depth now is the merely presuppositional dismissal of, or prejudice against, the market-anarchistic route to liberty and pluralism. I tackle some writings of only one erudite political philosopher, John Rawls. I chose him because his presuppositions are typical and his writings influential.

The Prejudice against Anarchy

Anarchical, not Metaphysical

In some writings by Rawls that are intended to clarify his position in *A Theory of Justice*,[33] we can see his presuppositions against anarchism brought out clearly. First, we look at "Justice as Fairness: Political not Metaphysical."[34] In this article Rawls is looking for a moral system of basic social rules, "the public conception of justice," that supports constitutional democracy. To be the more clear and robust, these rules are to be "independent of controversial philosophical and religious doctrines."[35]

Even if we grant that Rawls can achieve this goal, it is clear that he has sidestepped the clash with some political possibilities by simply refusing to consider anything outside some form of constitutional democracy. If there are no proper arguments against alternatives and he is trying only to preach a clearer understanding of constitutional democracy to the converted, then why should I criticize his writings? Because Rawls muddies the water, albeit unintentionally, on the natures of such things as liberalism, liberty, democracy, society, and justice in ways that are quite typical and that help to sustain popular views against anarchy.

Rawls writes of

> a conflict within the tradition of democratic thought itself, between the tradition associated with Locke, which gives greater weight to what Constant called the "liberties of the moderns," freedom of thought and conscience, certain basic rights of the person and of property, and the rule of law, and the tradition associated with Rousseau which gives greater weight to what Constant called the "liberties of the ancients," the equal political liberties and the values of public life. . . . Justice as fairness tries to adjudicate between these traditions. . . . [36]

The "liberties of the moderns," as listed, do seem to refer to people being free from interferences by others (with the possible exception of the rule of law, which might amount merely to state interference without any exceptions). The "liberties of the ancients," by contrast, seem to be the right to have a hand in interfering with the liberty of others, for politics always entails ruling (imposing control on) people. It is highly confusing to place liberty within the tradition with which it must be at odds; so "justice as fairness" must be more about striking a balance between individual liberty and democracy rather than about adjudicating competing claims within democracy, as Rawls states.

Though perhaps intending only to distinguish one society from another, Rawls drops into holistic views of society and justice without argument. He tells us that a society is "a more or less complete and self-sufficient scheme of cooperation" and that a sense of justice is "the capacity to understand, to apply, and to act from the public conception of justice which characterises the fair terms of social cooperation."[37]

A society is not a scheme in the sense that it is a systematic arrangement or single plan. One of the most important ideas that F. A. Hayek stressed is that what might look like the product of a systematic plan is often really a "spontaneous order" that has arisen polycentrically, or anarchically.[38] To the extent that we try to impose a systematic plan on such things, the result can be chaos. A society is more like the outcome of individual interactions in some geographical area. To view this outcome of individual interactions as a scheme might tempt one, as Rawls is tempted, to feel that one can be justified in imposing a better scheme despite the real schemes, or plans, of the millions of individuals that this must override.[39]

The same holism is assumed in defining a sense of justice as something that must be derived from the public conception. There is, however, no agent who is the public, nor are there sets of reasons that everyone accepts; there are only individuals with their own views on the matter. Perhaps Rawls is referring to the majority, but it is not clear why the majority's view must be regarded as ipso facto the correct view of justice.

"Fair terms of social cooperation" is also an expression that seems designed to lump together what are really quite distinct acts of cooperation.

We are told that one of the clearest differences between political conceptions of justice is between those that "allow for a plurality of opposing and even incommensurable conceptions of the good and those that hold that there is but one conception of the good."[40] Plato, Aristotle, Augustine, Aquinas, and classical utilitarianism are said to be in the singular category. Liberalism is in the plural category. This is supposed to be because in liberalism the conception of justice is "independent from and prior to the conception of goodness in the sense that its principles limit the conceptions of the good which are permissible."[41]

Can a theory of justice (basic moral social rules) ever be entirely independent of a theory of the good? These basic rules must themselves be thought good, or they would not be advocated. The real difference is that they can be limited (if deontological) while (teleological) classical utilitarianism and so on are fairly comprehensive. In fact, all systems of such rules (systems of justice) set good limits on the conceptions of the good but also allow some leeway for individual choice. With liberalism you must observe liberty in some sense, and otherwise you can do what you like. Now, constitutional democracy might allow for more diversity (if the constitution sufficiently limits the democracy) than most religions, but this is a contingent difference and a matter of degree: within most religions many kinds of lifestyle are possible as long as they do not flout the religion; within a constitutional democracy many kinds of lifestyle are possible as long as they do not flout constitutional democracy itself—but that is just what I want to do, the reason being that I believe that market-anarchy would be more liberal.

Rawls seems to feel it axiomatic that there would be maximum toleration of different lifestyles under some form of constitutional democracy. He is overlooking the anarchist argument that the state is a cause of strife because it creates the conditions for predation by a host of vested interests, that constitutional democracy is a way of setting people against one another in a negative-sum game. Intolerance of liberty and the destruction of wealth are the effects of this system. Pluralism could be better achieved by, as far as possible, respecting everyone's liberty to do what he wishes as long as he does not impose on others. This anarchist possibility is not merely left entirely unconsidered but is positively obscured by Rawls's accounts of the relevant concepts.

Anarchistic Consensus

In his article "The Idea of an Overlapping Consensus"[42] Rawls combines a tacit dismissal of anarchy, among other possibilities, with claiming for democracy several of the moral and social ideas that are fundamental to defending anarchy.

Rawls holds that within a constitutional democracy a "political conception of justice" that rests on self- or group interests would be a mere modus vivendi and hence unstable. Stability comes with a democratic system where there is "the support of an overlapping consensus."[43] A liberal anarchist can agree that a conception of basic social rules will not be as stable if it is based on pure self- or group interests. There is nothing about this idea that is more peculiar to democracy than to any other basic rules of social interaction, whether another kind of archy or even anarchy. Both extreme authoritarian regimes and extreme voluntaristic societies will tend to persist only insofar as the general populace feels approval of them and loyalty toward them.

While authoritarianism obviously limits the pluralism that Rawls feels is desirable, it is not clear how democracy could defend this pluralism better than anarchy. Rawls writes of having clear aims and limits to a constitution,[44] as though this is some guarantee of their being respected. In the United States the constitution has been eroded from the time of its inception. The very democratic mechanism has enabled interest groups to subvert liberties that would have been more stable left to unregulated, anarchic support.

The liberalisms of Immanuel Kant and Mill, and "many liberalisms" besides, are rejected because their doctrines are "not generally, or perhaps even widely, shared in a democratic society."[45] They are held to be too comprehensive to be practical for Rawls's purpose. What is needed is "implicitly shared fundamental ideas and principles."[46] He recognizes that it might not be possible to avoid comprehensive doctrines entirely but sees the crucial question as "what is the least that must be asserted; and if it must be asserted what is its least controversial form?''[47] The "fact of pluralism," we are told, makes an answer necessary if we are to reach a consensus.

Here Rawls is not merely rejecting "many liberalisms" that do not fit his purposes; he is rejecting full liberalism because he sees it as conflicting with other ideals, including that of democracy. From the anarchistic point of view, Rawls is really wanting to limit pluralism here with his own comprehensive view of how society should be organized. Pluralism does indeed make it desirable that we reach a consensus on liberal social rules, but the anarchistic answer to Rawls's question of the least that must be asserted, and in its least controversial form, must be "Live and let live," that is, "You let me live without interference and I shall not interfere with you." This would seem to be far more pluralistic than Rawls's implicit answer, which to the anarchist looks rather like "Rule and let rule," that is, "Let us share in the rule of everyone"—a Rousseauian travesty of individual liberty.

Of course, most people do currently see democracy as desirable and so, strictly speaking, "Live and let live" is controversial, but this is because people do not see that democracy is the enemy of liberal tolerance and wealth creation. Were Rawls to see this, he would surely agree that we should not pander to the prevailing conception of justice but, instead, argue for the anarchistic liberalism that is a better option.

Rawls deals with the criticism that an overlapping consensus is itself a mere modus vivendi. He thinks that with an overlapping consensus "the political conception of justice, is itself a moral conception."[48] Only where people are prepared to continue to support the system despite changes in the balance of power is there stability caused by an overlapping consensus rather than a mere modus vivendi; but, mutatis mutandis, this would apply equally to an anarchistic society: only where people are prepared to continue to give support to market-anarchy despite changes in their fortunes is there stability because of an overlapping consensus rather than a mere modus vivendi. Surely it is possible for people morally to affirm voluntary association at least as sincerely as state coercion, and the very existence of a democratic system constantly tempts and makes possible political actions at the expense of others, which must partly undermine any consensus.

The "method of avoidance"[49] is Rawls's expression for attempting to come up with a view that is maximally acceptable to all citizens from "religious, philosophical or moral" points of view. He thinks of "basic rights and liberties as taking certain questions off the political agenda"[50] because, "faced with the fact of pluralism, a liberal view removes from the political agenda the most divisive issues."[51] Rawls is analytically bound to be doing the exact opposite of what he asserts here. Politics is about what states do. To use the state to enforce certain so-called "basic rights and liberties," come what may, is not to take them "off the political agenda," but precisely to politicize them permanently. Rawls is really trying to rule other social systems out of (the state) court. One of the systems is anarchy with its greater tolerance of pluralism—the very thing he maintains that he wants to preserve.

We are told that eventually citizens may not be able fully to explain their agreement with each other because "they view the political conception as itself normally sufficient and may not expect, or think they need, greater political understanding than that."[52] They may come to affirm the system for its own sake. Again, this is just what a libertarian anarchist would expect to happen. Initially, people would be persuaded to accept anarchy on the egoistic basis that it is safer and more productive to live and let live. Eventually, people are likely to become more tolerant of freely chosen ways of life and simply feel that it is obviously immoral to interfere with them. Such tolerance is a vain hope in any political system, for politics necessarily entails the initiation of impositions by a monopoly agency, and this naturally provokes privilege, oppression, persecution, and retaliation—instead of the mutually beneficial cooperation that market-anarchy ensures.

Conclusion

Rawls is altogether representative of so-called liberals (in the modern sense). The problem is that none of them take liberty seriously and so cannot see that anarchy and the market are libertarian. They are more interested in inherently political rights; but rights that are inconsistent with liberty have malign unintended consequences. Such rights set up perverse incentives and moral hazards to such a degree that they undermine the very things they are supposed to be promoting. The things that the state guarantees or regulates are impoverished or destroyed to the extent that they are guaranteed or regulated. This applies to pluralism, health care, housing, pensions, education, roads, . . . you name it.

Such remains, however, the extent of antimarket prejudice in academia (where academics predominantly live off other people's taxes) that all such state failures are perceived to be the result of insufficient state regulation and provision. A few percent more of state spending here or a few more anticommercial regulations there and, we are told, all will be well. The spending is raised, the regulations imposed, and things are worse. That supposedly shows that we need even more.

Despite the intellectual resurgence of the market in recent years (initiated largely outside academia, in various private institutes[53]), there has not yet been a net reversal of state growth. State growth has been slowing down, however, and we may yet see genuine progress toward market-anarchy and the greater liberty and pluralism it allows. The role of the libertarian philosopher must be to dispel the presuppositions and conceptual confusions that impede a clear vision of this process. I hope that this, admittedly sketchy, essay has been a modest contribution to that end.

Notes

1. Market-anarchy would also stop the wars, economic slumps, taxation, and general welfare destruction that politics causes, but we are not looking at those here.

2. *Liberty, Utility, and Anarchy: A Philosophico-Economic Reconciliation* (forthcoming), from which this essay is adapted.

3. Hillel Steiner, "How Free: Computing Personal Liberty," in Phillips Griffiths, ed., *Of Liberty* (Cambridge: Cambridge University Press, 1983).

4. See the section titled "The Market, Democracy, and Nationalism."

5. Since coming up with this simple but comprehensive formulation of interpersonal liberty in 1989, I found that David Gauthier uses the idea of not imposing costs, though less consistently, in an attempt to derive morality contractually (David Gauthier, *Morals by Agreement* [New York: Oxford University Press, 1986]). He would also, unwittingly, be deriving the objective libertarian solution to problems but for certain key errors. In a state of nature he supposes that imposed costs do not require rectification unless social interaction takes place (pp. 207–12). He takes perfect competition to be a realistic criterion of market efficiency that the state can correct for without imposing costs (e.g., p. 97). He uses fantasy-world possibilities to decide what counts as imposing costs in this one (e.g., p. 263). Moreover, as Axelrod shows, iterated Prisoner's Dilemmas mean that Gauthier's elaborate theory of constrained maximization is quite unnecessary (Robert Axelrod, *The Evolution of Cooperation* [New York: Basic Books, 1984].

6. John Stuart Mill, *On Liberty* (1859; reprint Indianapolis, Ind.: Hackett, 1978).

7. See note 2.

8. The search for this contrast, with respect to the problem of abortion, put me on the path to libertarianism in 1979.

9. As argued, for instance, in Harry G. Frankfurt, "An Alleged Asymmetry between Actions and Omissions," *Ethics*, vol. 104, no. 3 (1994): 620–23.

10. Robert Nozick, *Anarchy, State, and Utopia* (Oxford: Basil Blackwell, 1974), 153–60.

11. In this brief section I have profited from reading Murray Newton Rothbard, *The Ethics of Liberty* (Atlantic Highlands, N.J.: Humanities Press, 1982), chap. 19, which I recommend despite its rights approach and the criticisms in what follows.

12. Rothbard, *The Ethics of Liberty*, 135.

13. See Rothbard, *The Ethics of Liberty*, 144.

14. That is, it uses force without having consent or contract, or without being in mere defense of persons and their property.

15. Competing states in one region are would-be states rather than real ones.

16. David Hume, "Of the First Principles of Government," essay 4 in *Essays: Literary, Moral, and Political* (1741–42; reprint London: Ward, Lock, and Tyler, 1877).

17. Etienne de la Boetie, *The Politics of Obedience: Discourse on Voluntary Servitude* (1577; New York: Free Life Editions, 1975).

18. In any case, a fully contractual organization would be quite libertarian and not a state at all.

19. See Bruce L. Benson, *The Enterprise of Law* (San Francisco: Pacific Research Institute for Public Policy, 1990); Lon L. Fuller, *The Morality of Law* (1964; New Haven and London: Yale University Press, 1969); Friedrich August Hayek, *Law, Legislation and Liberty*, three volumes (separate volumes in 1973, 1976, 1979; collection London: Routledge, 1982); and Bruno Leoni, *Freedom and the Law* (1961; expanded third edition Indianapolis: Liberty Press, 1991).

20. I would guess that such contractual control would be highly unlikely even for a few, small, eccentric communities.

21. For instance, James Buchanan has this assumption throughout his *The Limits of Liberty: Between Anarchy and Leviathan* (Chicago: The University of Chicago Press, 1975) and "A Contractarian Perspective on Anarchy" (in J. R. Pennock and J. W. Chapman, eds., *Anarchism: Nomos XIX* [New York: New York University Press, 1978] 29–42), despite having relevant works by Murray Rothbard and David Friedman in his bibliographies and notes. Lomasky also has this error (Loren E. Lomasky, *Persons, Rights, and the Moral Community* [Oxford: Oxford University Press, 1987], 109–10).

22. Can the market itself be seen as a sophisticated and fair form of democracy (with money as a store of voting power, which is voted to one by others)? That cannot literally be true as there is no rule in the market, only voluntary cooperation. The consumer is sovereign over only himself and his purchases.

23. For a fuller account of this thesis with respect to Karl Popper's defense of liberal democracy, see Jan Clifford Lester, "Popper's Epistemology versus

Popper's Politics," *Journal of Social and Evolutionary Systems*, vol. 18, no. 1 (1995).

24. Murray Rothbard, "Robert Nozick and the Immaculate Conception of the State," *Journal of Libertarian Studies*, vol. 1, no. 1 (1977).

25. Roy A. Childs, Jr., "The Invisible Hand Strikes Back," *Journal of Libertarian Studies*, vol. 1, no. 1 (1977).

26. Nozick, *Anarchy, State, and Utopia*.

27. David D. Friedman, "Law as a Private Good: A Response to Tyler Cowen on the Economics of Anarchy," *Economics and Philosophy*, vol. 10, no. 2 (1994): 319–27.

28. Tyler Cowen, "Law as a Public Good: The Economics of Anarchy," *Economics and Philosophy* 8 (1992): 249–69.

29. Tyler Cowen, "Rejoinder to David Friedman on the Economics of Anarchy," *Economics and Philosophy*, vol. 10, no. 2 (1994): 329–32.

30. I do not see why police, lawyers, and courts would not usually be separate, as they are now.

31. David Miller, *Anarchism* (London: Dent, 1984).

32. To think that everyone must have some such nationality is rather like thinking that everyone must have some religion—as would also have been normal at one time.

33. John Rawls, *A Theory of Justice* (Oxford: Oxford University Press, 1972).

34. John Rawls, "Justice as Fairness: Political not Metaphysical," *Philosophy & Public Affairs*, vol. 14, no. 3 (1985).

35. Ibid., 223.

36. Ibid., 227.

37. Ibid., 233.

38. On "spontaneous order," see, for instance, the index to Hayek, *Law, Legislation and Liberty*.

39. This mistaken, holistic view of society is epitomized by the young boy who, seeing a large gentleman walk by, asked his mother, "What's that man for?"

40. Rawls, "Justice as Fairness: Political not Metaphysical," 248.

41. Ibid., 249.

42. Rawls, "The Idea of an Overlapping Consensus," *Oxford Journal of Legal Studies*, vol. 7, no. 1 (1987).

43. Ibid., 1.

44. Ibid.

45. Ibid., 6.

46. Ibid.

47. Ibid., 8.

48. Ibid., 11.

49. Ibid., 12.

50. Ibid., 14.

51. Ibid., 17.

52. Ibid., 16.

53. Such as, in the United Kingdom, the Institute of Economic Affairs and the Adam Smith Institute, and in the United States, Atlas Economic Research Foundation, CATO Institute, The Independent Institute, Institute for Humane Studies, Liberty Fund, The Locke Institute, Pacific Research Institute for Public Policy, Policy Economy Research Center, and Reason Foundation.

5

Justifying the State[1]

David Schmidtz

Introduction

To escape the state of nature, people would submit to an absolute sovereign; therefore, absolute sovereignty is justified. So argued Thomas Hobbes. A minimal state, and only a minimal state, could arise by an invisible-hand process; therefore, the minimal state is justified. So argued Robert Nozick. In political philosophy, "therefores" often seem to come from nowhere.

My versions of these arguments are caricatures, of course, but many of us are also left wondering by the real thing. Do Hobbes's contractarian story and Nozick's invisible-hand story have anything to do with justifying the state? What would a story have to be like to engage such a task? These questions matter. Rational choice theories such as that of Hobbes (and after him, Rawls) and natural rights theories such as that of Nozick (and before him, Locke) are the wellsprings of current Anglo-American political philosophy, supplying not only our subject matter but our methods as well.[2] If they do not make sense, then generally speaking, neither do we.

There are two kinds of justification in political theory. Distinguishing between them can help us avoid being distracted by problems that are mere artifacts of contractarian methodology, only appearing to be relevant to justifying states per se. This helps us explain what is irreparably wrong with hypothetical consent arguments, why we find them appealing nevertheless, and what kind of argument can actually make use of that appealing hypothetical element. The distinction will also clarify the limited sense in which invisible-hand processes can be relevant to a state's justification.

Teleological and Emergent Justification

This is how Alan Nelson sees the current scene in political philosophy:

> In political philosophy, there is a general strategy for justifying states that has become dominant. The first step in implementing the strategy is to begin with some principles about morality and persons. . . . The second step is to show how a state would develop or could develop in sufficient accord with the principles of individual morality. The third step is to show that a state that does develop or would develop or could develop in this manner functions, in part, to promote morally desirable individual action. In Anglo-American philosophy this strategy has become so dominant that alternatives may seem hard to come by.[3]

The approach Nelson describes is widely practiced, so much so that he cannot be far wrong to call it dominant (and I shall follow him in doing so). Gregory Kavka, for example, correctly ascribes the dominant approach to Hobbes, and the contractarian tradition has yet to depart from it.[4] This is too bad, for the dominant approach muddles two quite separate methods of justification.

I call the two methods teleological and emergent justification. To justify an institution is, in general, to show that it is what it should be or does what it should do. The teleological approach seeks to justify institutions in terms of what they accomplish. The emergent approach takes justification to be an emergent property of the process by which institutions arise.

Teleological justification posits goals and compares practically attainable forms of government in terms of how they do or will serve those goals. Emergent justification posits constraints—specifically, constraints on the process by which the state comes to be. Emergent justification turns on a state's pedigree. Most and perhaps all of the historically important attempts at justification can be usefully classified as either emergent or teleological, although the distinction does not, of course, exhaust logical space in the way a less interesting distinction between teleological and nonteleological justification would. (An argument that the state commands our loyalty because it was teleologically justified in the past is neither emergent nor teleological, but neither is it an argument that many would care to defend.) In any event, I think there is much to be learned about a given argument by seeing how well it fits the emergent or teleological molds.

Consider some examples. One could argue that instituting a Leviathan is teleologically justified if a Hobbesian war would otherwise be inevitable. In contrast, one could argue that a Leviathan will be emergently justified if it emerges from the state of nature by consent. (For the moment, think of the appeal as being to actual or tacit consent. I discuss hypothetical consent arguments below.) This emergent approach has both invisible-hand and contractarian versions. In the former, the Leviathan's emergence is an unintended result of people individually binding themselves to the lord. In the latter, people bind themselves by collective agreement.

One also could justify particular policies or institutions in either of these two ways. For example, one could try to justify teleologically the passing of a certain statute by showing what the statute will accomplish, or one could try to justify emergently the same statute by showing that it was duly passed by the appropriate legislative bodies. To have emergent justificatory significance, the legislative process must not violate rights. (More generally, the process must respect whatever moral borders there are around persons, limiting what may permissibly be done to them.) This leaves open the question of whether the process's significance consists in the property of not violating rights or in some other property, but in either case, if the process violates rights, this will undermine such emergent justificatory significance as it would otherwise have had.

To show that a state actually emerged by consent would be a very strong form of emergent justification but, by the same token, showing that it did not satisfy this strong standard would be correspondingly weak as a basis for condemnation. In contrast, to show that a state emerged without violating rights would be a relatively weak emergent justification but, by the same token, showing that a state's emergence did not satisfy even this minimal standard would be the basis for a relatively strong condemnation. Any attempt at emergent justification ordinarily could be rebutted by showing that the process of emergence violated rights. Emergence by consent is very special in this respect, however, for consent is its own proof against rebuttal. Insofar as a state arises by consent, the only rights its emergence could violate are those that cannot be alienated by consent; hence, most, if not all, of the rights claims that might have rebutted its emergent justification will have been dealt with at a stroke.

Neither teleological nor emergent models are ethically self-contained. The teleological approach presupposes the legitimacy of certain goals. The emergent approach presupposes certain constraints applying to processes by which states arise. Both approaches presume some sort of position on the nature of moral borders around persons, in the one case because the state can be judged according to whether its emergence leaves such borders intact, in the other case because the state can be judged according to how well it serves the goal of protecting them. (Among the positions that a utilitarian version of the teleological approach may take, of course, is the position that the idea of moral borders around persons is "nonsense on stilts.")

Needless to say, chains of justification must come to an end, and no chain has enough links in it to satisfy everyone, but we can, in principle at least, specify how the two approaches to justifying the state link up to ethics in general. Although neither approach is ethically self-contained, it would be a mistake to infer that the teleological approach presupposes a consequentialist moral theory while the emergent approach presupposes a deontological moral theory. Consequentialists naturally endorse the teleological approach to justifying the state, but a consequentialist might insist that both kinds of justification are essential, out of a belief that if we do not insist that institutions be emergently justified, the institutions we ultimately end up with will not be teleologically justified either. An institution whose emergence tramples moral borders will probably trample moral borders as long as it exists, or so a consequentialist who cares about moral borders might reasonably fear. The emergent approach thus can appeal to consequentialists and deontologists alike.[5]

The teleological approach can be of similarly broad appeal. Of course, some deontologists may conclude that a strong enough emergent justification is sufficient in itself to underwrite the institution's claim to support. On the other hand, everyone cares about how governments perform, including Kantians. When a deontologist asks if the maxim "Support institution X" is universalizable, he will not be asking about the consequences of his contemplated support; yet, his maxim's meaning will still depend on the nature of institution X. Also, it would not be inconsistent with deontology to notice that institutions can and sometimes must be partly defined in terms of their functional properties. A deontologist may hold that the state's function, and indeed its duty, is to protect moral borders around persons and then to leave citizens to do as they please within those borders. Where a consequentialist would hold that the state's purpose is to promote the good, a deontologist may hold that the state's purpose is to promote the right.

Deontologists typically would not hold that the purpose of persons is to promote the right, for persons are ends in themselves, but states are not ends in themselves, or at least a deontologist need not view them as such. A deontologist may consistently judge that a state that protects moral borders satisfies such conditions as are necessary for it to command their support. At the same time, most deontologists would not consider possession of this functional property sufficient, for they would denounce a group that initially ran roughshod over moral borders so as to create and solidify the political power base that subsequently enabled the group (now calling itself a government) to protect moral borders more effectively. Thus, like some of their consequentialist colleagues, deontologists may judge that an institution must be justified not only teleologically but emergently as well.

Hypothetical Consent

How important is it to distinguish between teleological and emergent justification? Consider Hobbesian contractarianism. As Jean Hampton interprets the Hobbesian project, we must show on the one hand that creating a Leviathan is necessary to save people from Hobbesian war.[6] On the other hand, the assumptions we make in showing that a Leviathan is necessary must leave open the possibility that people will be able to create a Leviathan by consent. She offers an account of conflict as arising from human passions but rejects it "because it makes the sovereign's institution either unnecessary or impossible."[7] An alternative account of conflict as having its source in rational refusal to abide by unenforced contracts is "just as problematic for Hobbes's argument" because "it makes conflict so deep-seated that it is impossible to see how people can escape it. In particular, if people are unable to keep contracts in the state of nature, it would seem to be impossible for them to keep a contract to institute a sovereign."[8] In sum, the problem is that "Hobbes's account of conflict seems to generate sufficient strife to make the institution of the sovereign necessary, but too much strife to make that institution possible." Hampton has some interesting thoughts on how Hobbes might escape this dilemma.[9] The upshot of her argument, however, is that if the dilemma proves insoluble, then even granting Hobbes's premises, his

argument cannot justify absolute monarchy. Leviathan can emerge by
agreement only under conditions that make Leviathan unnecessary.

We leave aside details of Hampton's argument, for the point to make
here is that this dilemma is not so much a dilemma for Hobbes as for
the dominant approach as such. Once we abandon the dominant
approach and acknowledge the distinction between emergent and
teleological justification, the dilemma amounts to the following: On the
one hand, if people are able to make and keep contracts, a Leviathan
may be emergently justifiable, but it will not be teleologically justifiable
because it will not be necessary. On the other hand, if people are
unable to cooperate, a Leviathan will be teleologically justified, but it
will not be emergently justifiable because people by hypothesis lack
the wherewithal to create a Leviathan by agreement.

Cast in these terms, there is no longer a dilemma. Instead of
saying the necessary conditions for justification render justification
impossible, we now say only that the necessary conditions for teleological justification render emergent justification impossible. This forces
us to make a choice, but it is not a dilemma. Hobbes can happily
agree that emergent justification is impossible, for the purpose of his
contractarian exercise is to explain why the covenant is in people's
rational self-interest, not why rational bargainers would agree to it. If
the problem with the state of nature is bad enough to supply a
rationale for Leviathan, it does not matter to Leviathan's teleological
justification whether the problem is also bad enough to preclude
Leviathan's emergence by rational agreement.

What does matter is that, even if people are not rational enough to
create Leviathan by agreement, they surely are rational enough to
obey Leviathan once Leviathan is in place. Thus, the essential
Hobbesian claim is that with an absolute sovereign we have relative
peace, and without an absolute sovereign we have war. If correct, this
claim suffices to teleologically justify absolute sovereignty, regardless
of how or even whether absolute sovereignty emerges. Leviathan's
emergence by consent may be out of the question, but it is also beside
the point.

Let me elaborate, for the issue has significance for hypothetical
consent arguments in general. As an example of a hypothetical consent
argument, the Hobbesian argument looks like this:

(1) If Leviathan is the only alternative to Hobbesian war, then rational
    bargainers would consent to Leviathan.
(2) Leviathan is the only alternative to Hobbesian war. Therefore,
(3) rational bargainers would consent to Leviathan.

Once we reject the dominant approach, which this argument exemplifies, and treat emergent and teleological approaches as separate methods of justification, two things happen. First, we see that hypothetical consent arguments have no bearing on emergent justification. The Leviathan's emergent justification will be found in the Leviathan's actual history, or it will not be found at all. Second, we see that if the hypothetical consent story is an attempted teleological justification, then the point of the story is to compare the Leviathan to its alternatives, rather than to give an account of its history, which means that the real work being done here is the teleological work of (2). Once we have (2), nothing is added by going on to get (3).

Of course, consent can be a sign that Leviathan is preferable to Hobbesian war. More generally, consent can be a sign that a government is teleologically justified. (That is, what warrants hypothesizing consent in the first place is that people would have good reasons to consent.) A government can be teleologically justified, however, even if collective action problems would prevent the sign of its justification from materializing. Admittedly, the likelihood of strategically minded individuals holding out for special concessions from the rest of the collective threatens to falsify (1), for even bargainers who see an urgent need to create Leviathan may still have rational reasons to impede its creation by holding out for special favors. Had hypothetical consent offered the possibility of emergent justification, one might be concerned to find ways of getting around this problem. Such concerns, however, are utterly irrelevant to the state's teleological justification, for the falsehood of (1) is only an obstacle to moving from (2) to (3). Since, once we have (2), there is nothing to gain by moving to (3), it makes no difference to the state's teleological justification whether (1) is true or false. So the hypothetical consent argument is as irrelevant to teleological justification as it is to emergent justification. The truth value of premise (2) is relevant to Leviathan's teleological justification, but the argument as a whole is not.

Moreover, although consent may be, among other things, a sign that a government is teleologically justified, consider what happens if we try to use hypothetical consent as a sign of teleological justification. Let us formalize the idea that hypothetical consent is a sign of Leviathan's teleological justification as the opposite of (1), namely: if rational bargainers would consent to Leviathan, then Leviathan must be the only alternative to Hobbesian war. We can then employ this premise in the following argument:

(4) If rational bargainers would consent to Leviathan, then Leviathan must be the only alternative to Hobbesian war.
(5) Rational bargainers would consent to Leviathan. Therefore,
(6) Leviathan must be the only alternative to Hobbesian war.

The difficulty in using hypothetical consent as a sign of teleological justification now becomes clear. When we actually observe consent, we can take our observations as data. If (5) was based on observation, it would be unobjectionable, but we do not observe hypothetical consent—we assert it. To warrant this assertion, we must argue for it. How, then, can we argue for (5)? We cannot appeal to (6) as a basis for (5), because we are supposed to be deriving (6) from (5), but any reason we give for hypothesizing consent in (5) would have to be something like the teleological justification implied by (6). In other words, we need something like (6) before we would have reason to hypothesize the rational consent in (5) as a sign of the truth of (6). Hence, hypothetical consent cannot do any real work.

Let me stress: the complaint here is not that (5) is false but rather that we would need to know that (6), or something very much like (6), was true before we would be warranted in asserting (5). Therefore, even if the argument is perfectly sound, it is still a bad argument. It is a bad argument because we cannot verify its soundness—that is, we cannot verify that premise (5) is true—unless we have prior knowledge that its conclusion is true.

More generally, if we actually observe people consenting, then that in itself is reason to suppose that they would consent under those circumstances. Absent actual observations, we cannot simply assume that people would consent to something; we have to give reasons why they would or should consent. (So if I say the state is justified with respect to you because you would have consented to it under the appropriate conditions, you might quite reasonably respond by asking, "What makes you think I would have consented?" My answer would have to be that a rational person such as yourself would have good reasons to consent.) If we discover a good reason why people should consent to the state—call it "reason X"—we will then be free to contrive hypothetical stories about rational agents reacting to reason X by consenting to the state, but the real story will already have been told by reason X itself. (The hypothetical story adds nothing whatsoever. It certainly does not add consent, since the story is only hypothetical.) In other words, hypothetical consent cannot constitute justification; to suppose hypothetical consent is to presuppose justification. Hypothetical consent proceeds from teleological justification rather than to it.

Distinguishing between teleological and emergent justification has helped us see that there are two quite different arguments in Hobbes, that they do not stand or fall together, and that ultimately the teleological strand of the Hobbesian argument is the only strand with justificatory potential. More generally, the distinction suggests that hypothetical consent arguments are also combinations of two separable strands of argument. The emergent strand has no justificatory potential, however, for a state can be emergently justified only in terms of the process by which it actually arose. The teleological strand has justificatory potential, but the realization of this potential is presupposed by, rather than supplied by, the argument that rational agents would consent under the hypothesized circumstances.[10]

Actual Consent

Does this mean that the emergent approach never has justificatory potential? No. Unlike hypothetical consent, actual consent has justificatory force over and beyond the teleological force of the reasons people have for consenting. Freely given consent is intrinsically a kind of authorization; by consenting, one gives others a right to expect from oneself that which one has consented to do, to give, or whatever.[11]

Actual consent also is neither particularly rare nor difficult to secure within a range of typical human endeavors. To give an example not directly relevant to the creation of governments, we observe consent on a small scale whenever we observe an ordinary exchange of goods between two people. What do we ordinarily think of as justifying such exchanges? There are two answers. We may argue that the exchange's results further the participants' goals (better than their alternatives). For epistemic reasons if nothing else, however, we usually are more inclined to focus on whether the process of negotiation and exchange is unforced, not fraudulent, and so on. In other words, when the process accords with these and any other constraints applying to it, it fully realizes the justificatory force latent in actual consent. The first approach is teleological, looking to the exchange's outcome. The second is emergent, looking for compliance with constraints on the process by which the outcome arises.

Two questions arise concerning the emergent approach. First, what sort of large-scale process would provide the same kind of justification that emerges with the small-scale process? Second, does this process ever actually occur on a sufficiently large scale to justify a state emergently? Consider contractarianism as a theory about how emergent justification might work. In a contractarian bargaining process, members of a large group seek a collective agreement. Consent to the agreement is taken as a sign that the agreement is mutually advantageous. It is by no means a guarantee, however. (At least, it does not guarantee ex post advantage, which is presumably what bargainers really care about.) People enter the agreement without the benefit of hindsight, and actual consent does not presuppose rationality in the idealized way that hypothetical consent does; but actual consent carries emergent force regardless, so long as, for example, failures of foresight are not attributable to fraud.

Of course, translating the prospect of mutual advantage into actual consent is a problem. It may be good strategy for a given person to drive a hard bargain, withholding assent to a mutually beneficial collective agreement for strategic reasons and thereby putting the entire group in limbo unless it accepts the holdout's demands. If it does accept the holdout's demands, it may find that the supply of holdouts is inexhaustible. (Ideally, rational bargainers might see this very fact as a reason not to hold out, but since we are discussing the possibility of actual consent, we do not get to assume that people conform to our notion of what is ideal.) We might hope for collective bargaining to produce actual consent to the state. Realistically, however, we must admit that individual self-interest stands in the way. The obstacles to collective bargaining that we might wish away when we construct hypothetical bargaining environments are, in the real world, serious obstacles indeed.[12]

There is an alternative. Contractarian accounts of the state's emergence are distinguishable, at least in a rough sense, from invisible-hand accounts. In contractarian models, intentional collective action leads to an intended and mutually agreeable result. In invisible-hand models, bargaining occurs among shifting and relatively small subsets of the collective. The larger scheme of stable society evolves through a series of relatively small-scale exchanges and is an unintended result of such exchanges. There are various agreements between individuals, but there is nothing resembling an agreement to create the emerging social order. The social order emerges spontaneously.

Invisible-hand processes thus preserve the contractarian process's tendency to produce mutually advantageous outcomes, while reducing the scope for, and localizing the consequences of, strategic behavior.

Why? Because there is no wider agreement to be thwarted by strategic holdouts. If a person drives too hard a bargain, his would-be trading partners go elsewhere. An invisible-hand emergent justification need not require everyone (or any arbitrarily selected percentage) to consent to the details or even the general character of the emerging social order. There is no collective action problem because there is no collective action.

Consequently, the invisible hand is much more likely than collective bargaining to generate a government by consent. It gives an affirmative answer to our question about whether the kind of consent we observe on a small scale also drives large-scale processes, but this advantage over collective bargaining has a price, for it raises another question. Consent drives both large-scale and small-scale processes, but does large-scale justification emerge from the large-scale consensual process in the same way that small-scale justification emerges from small-scale consensual process?

Unfortunately, when the large-scale process in question is an invisible-hand process, the answer has to be no. The problem is that people consent to individual transactions rather than to the order that spontaneously emerges from them. In other words, that an outcome arose by consent does not entail that people consented to it. (Analogously, people are willingly doing what produces the greenhouse effect, but that does not mean they are consenting to its production.) It seems that the importance of the kind of invisible-hand process described by Nozick, even if it were actually to occur, is analogous to the importance consent has in a two-person exchange when the parties consent without really knowing what they are getting into. It does mean something, but not necessarily a great deal.

We have been considering the invisible hand insofar as it pertains to justification by actual consent. Actual emergence by invisible-hand process weaves into the resulting distribution of power and wealth the kind of rights claims that actual consent can create but hypothetical consent cannot. In contrast, what we get from hypothetical consent is (as with contractarianism) a story about how emergent justification could occur—or perhaps we get a covert but still real teleological justification appended to an unnecessary story about people consenting to it because it is teleologically justified. For a state, however, to be justified on the ground that people consent to it, people have to consent to it.

Thus, Ronald Dworkin's comment on Rawlsian contractarianism[13] also applies, with a vengeance, to Nozick's invisible-hand story;

whatever role actual invisible-hand processes play in emergent justification, invisible-hand stories are merely stories. They are not even pale forms of the actual process. In fact, the problem is worse for hypothetical invisible-hand processes than for hypothetical social contracts. At least a hypothetical social contract presents the emerging state as something to which ideally rational agents would consent. A hypothetical invisible hand, however, does not do even this. What emerges by invisible hand is not what ideally rational agents hypothetically consent to. Rather, the thrust of an invisible-hand story like Nozick's is that the state could conceivably emerge as the unintended result of a series of actions, each having consent. Such a story does not depict the state as having even hypothetical consent.

Teleology and Hypothesis

The previous remarks notwithstanding, hypothetical invisible-hand processes can have considerable justificatory force, but not in emergent justification. I suggested that a hypothetical consent story could serve as a sign of teleological justification. Actually, there is a more important role for hypothetical invisible-hand stories in teleological justification. We care, or at least we should care, about invisible-hand processes because most of what goes on in society is influenced by them. Our society's economy, its political system, even its ecology, have characteristics that are products of human action but not human design. We must take the invisible hand's pervasiveness into account before we can begin to say what form of government is teleologically justified. That is not to say, however, that the invisible-hand process per se has moral weight. Rather, it is to say that outcomes have moral weight and that invisible-hand processes play a pervasive role in shaping outcomes.

The teleological approach, rather than using invisible-hand models to show how a state emerged (which would be irrelevant to teleological justification), instead uses them to help predict what would follow from a state's instantiation. If individually rational activity will not undermine what otherwise is a collectively rational institution (i.e., will not push it in the direction of either anarchy or tyranny), such stability speaks in the institution's favor, compared to less stable alternatives. In contrast, if only extensive coercion can prevent an institution's collapse or only an eternally vigilant citizenry can stop it from sliding toward tyranny, such instability is a potentially fatal flaw.

When we compare alternatives, we have to consider not only what the alternatives are but also what those alternatives tend to become.[14]

Invisible-hand models developed en route to teleological justification may be purely hypothetical, but that is not a problem. The importance to teleological justification of hypothetical models is clear. We care about what will happen if we create a given kind of state. Creating a hypothetical model of it gives us the best information we can get short of actually going ahead and trying it. (Of course, if the historical record shows that people actually have gone ahead and tried it, so much the better, information-wise.) So an invisible-hand story can be hypothetical and yet serve as part of a teleological justification, as long as the story is realistic. (In particular, since its purpose is to help us predict an outcome rather than to supply the outcome with a pedigree, the depicted process need not be fair.) Its purpose is to show how alternative forms of government would actually turn out as responses to real problems.

Conclusions

I began by distinguishing between emergent and teleological justification. By helping us to see where one kind of justification ends and another kind begins, this distinction helps us avoid the dominant approach's tendency to generate puzzles that have no bearing on substantive problems in justifying the state. We can, for example, analyze hypothetical consent arguments as (possibly sound) teleological justifications joined to superfluous models of consensual processes that have emergent justificatory force only when they actually occur. I also discussed the role that purely hypothetical invisible-hand stories might play in teleological justification as thought experiments that can help us predict what would follow from a state's instantiation.

I read Hobbes as having an argument that Leviathan is teleologically justified. The way I read Nozick, the backward focus of his argument makes it irrelevant to teleological justification. Moreover, the hypothetical nature of the argument makes it irrelevant to emergent justification. His approach can suggest contrasts in terms of the possibility of emergent justification, but not in terms of emergent justification as such. Showing that only a minimal state can possibly be emergently justified would show something, but it would not emergently justify the minimal state.

We can judge states in terms of how they arose, we can judge them in terms of how well they actually function, or we can judge them in terms of how well they would function if instantiated. In all three cases, the nature of the justification in question is obvious. The first is emergent. The second is teleological. The third is both teleological and appropriately hypothetical. In contrast, Rawls and Nozick have asked us to judge states (or the principles that inform their institutions) in terms of whether they would emerge from a suitably described starting point. Explaining what such an exercise has to do with justifying states is a tall order.[15]

Notes

1. This essay is a revised version of an article that originally appeared in *Ethics* 101 (October 1990): 89–102. It is reprinted with the permission of the author and The University of Chicago Press.

2. See Thomas Hobbes, *Leviathan* (New York: Macmillan, 1962); John Rawls, *A Theory of Justice* (Cambridge, Mass.: Belknap, 1971); John Locke, *Two Treatises of Government*, ed. Peter Laslett (New York: Cambridge University Press, 1963); and Robert Nozick, *Anarchy, State, and Utopia* (New York: Basic, 1974).

3. See Alan Nelson, "Explanation and Justification in Political Philosophy," *Ethics* 97 (1986): 154–76, 155.

4. Kavka provides the following reconstruction of the Hobbesian argument. Note the parallel between it and (juxtaposing the second and third steps) Nelson's justificatory schema. (*a*) Anticipation (i.e., engaging in preemptive first strikes) is a more reasonable strategy in the state of nature than is lying low, but the collective result of this individually rational strategy is war and misery. (*b*) The problems encountered in an appropriate kind of civil society are less severe than the problems of insecurity and anticipation in the state of nature. (*c*) Therefore, rational parties in a state of nature would form a civil society of an appropriate kind in order to escape that natural state (see Gregory Kavka, *Hobbesian Moral and Political Theory* [Princeton, N.J.: Princeton University Press, 1986], paraphrase of pp. 108–9). Contractarianism is, roughly, the theory that states are justified either by obtaining the consent of their citizens or by being the kind of state that rational agents would consent to.

5. A principle that specifies how institutions legitimately may arise is a principle of emergent justification. If asked why we are using that particular principle rather than some alternative, we may give various reasons. Perhaps the principle is one we all agreed to use or perhaps using that principle has the best results, but regardless of what we deem to be its rationale, it is still a principle of emergent justification, that is, a principle that specifies how

institutions legitimately may arise. For example, being ratified by a constitutionally bound legislative body is one way in which an institution can be emergently justified. Although we look to the legislative body as a vehicle for emergent justification, however, we remain free to judge the legislative body itself in terms of how it functions, as well as in terms of how it emerged.

Moreover, some criteria of emergent justification do not emerge by human action at all; hence, the nonevent of their emergence can be neither defended nor criticized. We could, for example, claim that we have certain moral rights by nature and that, to be emergently justified, a state must emerge without violating them. One could not emergently justify a particular set of natural rights claims, however, for their emergence is not an issue. Therefore, unless there is a third kind of justification, the only way to justify natural rights claims is to justify them teleologically. Chapter 3 of David Schmidtz, *The Limits of Government: An Essay on the Public Goods Argument* (Boulder: Westview, 1991), argues that the state can be emergently as well as teleologically justified in assuming the exclusive right to punish, even if individuals have a natural right to punish and even if they do not voluntarily give up that right.

6. Jean Hampton, *Hobbes and the Social Contract Tradition* (Cambridge: Cambridge University Press, 1986).

7. Ibid., 63–68, 73–74.

8. Ibid., 74, 79.

9. Ibid., 136 ff.

10. John Simmons rejects hypothetical consent as a basis of political obligation. Simmons believes that people can acquire political obligations only by their own voluntary actions. Simmons, however, distinguishes between what we are obligated to do and what we ought to do. It can for example sometimes be true, according to this distinction, that we ought to help a little old lady across the street even though we are not obligated to do so. In this respect, governments are like little old ladies. Even if actual consent is the only sound basis of political obligation, we sometimes ought to obey a government because of that government's virtues even though we have no obligation to do so. See A. John Simmons, *Moral Principles and Political Obligations* (Princeton: Princeton University Press, 1979). Although this need not be considered a problem, I see Simmons's move from "obligation" to "ought" as circumventing the commitment to voluntary action as the basis of political obligation that grounded his rejection of hypothetical consent models to begin with. Given Simmons's claim that legitimizing the state requires a deliberate act but justifying it does not (p. 199), the mark of a successful justification is that the justification reveals the virtues of certain governments, and the fact that they have such a justification weighs in favor of obeying them regardless of whether we have consented to them. This move is a move to what I call a teleological approach.

11. At times, Hobbes himself seems to appeal to the justificatory force of actual consent. For example, Hobbes says (in his conclusion) that a person

becomes subject to a conqueror by promising, through express words or other sufficient (possibly tacit but nonetheless actual) sign, to do as the conqueror commands. He also says that commonwealth by acquisition and commonwealth by institution (chap. 17) differ only insofar as people consent out of fear of the conquering sovereign in the former and out of fear of each other in the latter (chap. 20). We could read this as a purely descriptive account of the ways in which sovereigns actually emerge, or we could read it as a discussion of how sovereigns come to be emergently justified.

12. Of course, collective bargaining would be less problematic if it could be ratified by less than unanimous consent. Indeed, Kavka supposes that

> unanimity is not required. So long as the arguments for a given provision are compelling enough to command *nearly* unanimous (e.g., 95 percent) consent among the parties as characterized, the possible or probable existence of a stubborn minority of extremist refusers is no bar to the adoption of the provision. (p. 219)

Perhaps, but if a procedure ignores dissenters, this is a bar to emergent justification, notwithstanding the fact that the barrier might be surmountable. I think Kavka's claim is best thought of as an insight about teleological justification, namely, that we do not need unanimity in order to have the kind of consensus that counts as evidence that a provision will function well. Actually obtaining 95 percent approval of a certain provision generally indicates that the provision is teleologically justified, and a relatively tiny dissenting minority is not as such a contraindication. (It could become a contraindication, however, once we look at the specific issue; if the issue is whether the minority should pay higher taxes than the majority, dismissing the minority voters as eccentrics would be, at best, a mistake.)

13. See Ronald Dworkin, "The Original Position," in Norman Daniels, ed., *Reading Rawls* (New York: Basic, 1976), 17.

14. Edna Ullmann-Margalit says that "even if the invisible-hand explanation turns out not to be the correct account of how the thing *emerged,* it may still not be devoid of validity with regard to the question of how (and why) it is *maintained"* ("Invisible-Hand Explanations," *Synthese* 39 [1978]: 263–91, 275). This point about the invisible hand's explanatory role is analogous to my point about its justificatory role; whether the invisible-hand processes that accompany an institution will incline that institution to evolve in a desirable way is generally relevant to whether the institution is teleologically justified.

15. Gregory Kavka has suggested to me that the Rawlsian thought experiment has a heuristic value. It helps us discover, appreciate, and express the elements of a state's justification. This seems right, although the message of the section on hypothetical consent is that the thought experiment's value can be no more than heuristic and that the real justification it helps us appreciate and express, if it helps us at all, will be a teleological justification. If I were to try to connect Rawls's project to justification, I would not argue that rational

agents or even their noumenal selves would endorse Rawls's two principles. Instead, I would adopt Rawls's definition of a well-ordered society as an explicit standard of teleological justification and then argue that, by adopting institutions that satisfied Rawls's two principles, a society would be well ordered, that is, would advance the good of its members according to a public conception of justice (p. 5). Something like this is what it would take to underwrite the presumption of teleological justification on which the hypothesized endorsement by rational agents (or by their noumenal selves) depends.

6

Anarchism and Skepticism[1]

Jonathan Wolff

The Methodology of Justification

Can we justify the state? That this question fades in and out of focus is not an original thought.[2] One natural response to the question is incomprehension. We can hardly doubt that there is a question of what type of state we should have, but it is far harder to see that there may be reason to think that we should not have a state at all. What, after all, is the alternative? Many people thinking about this for the first time fall into a form of simple pragmatism or consequentialism: it is just obvious that we need the state—we could not manage without one.

Even if we accept—which perhaps we should not—that we do need the state, it is not difficult to push the issue a step further. The problem of political obligation can be motivated by considering the existence of political power: the claimed right of one person to set rules that others must follow or else be punished. The state concentrates political power into the hands of the few, who together are given a monopoly right to exercise coercion. How can it be, though, that these people—typically no wiser, more intelligent, or virtuous than the norm—can have such a right to intervene in the lives of others? This is the anarchist challenge: what can be the moral basis of an individual's or group's right to rule? The problem of political obligation requires an answer. What moral reasons are there for departing from a state of nature where no inequalities of political power exist? Why not anarchy?

What sort of question is this? Or rather, where is it supposed to lead? Suppose that no one can devise a defense of inequalities of political power that satisfies everyone. There is no obvious reason to think that the anarchist position is inconsistent, so we can presume that many anarchists will not be budged by whatever arguments their opponents manage to produce. Does this mean we should reject the state? Or should we continue to accept it, but worry? Or is some other response appropriate? In particular, should we assume that any failure to rebut the anarchist challenge constitutes an argument for (some form of) anarchism?

Some philosophers have certainly argued in this way. Two of the most prominent in the literature are M. B. E. Smith[3] and A. John Simmons.[4] Similar positions are adopted by Joseph Raz[5] and Leslie Green.[6] The failure to justify the state generates a view that has been called critical philosophical anarchism:[7] critical because it is based on criticisms of arguments for the justification of the state and philosophical because, I suppose, such people have not engaged in active political movements for the abolition of the state.

In a way, we seem to have reached an impasse. There appear to be powerful philosophical reasons for objecting to the existence of the state, but there are equally powerful, perhaps less philosophical, reasons for accepting the state. Should we try to settle the debate by accepting the greater authority of philosophy? Or of common sense?

My argument in this paper is that the critical philosophical anarchist position has been given too much weight in this debate. Those who have undertaken the task of defending the state have, in general, accepted that it is up to them to prove that the state is justified, whereas critical philosophical anarchists have often been content simply to point out the flaws in those arguments. They presume that the state is morally problematic (and are right to presume this) and set the challenge to see how it can be justified. Perhaps anarchism, however, is morally problematic, too. Argument is thus needed to show that it is justified, if it is.

To shed light on this issue, it will help to consider another philosophical debate, which at first might seem rather far removed but in fact bears certain similarities: skepticism about knowledge. Consider how this is set out in Descartes's *Meditations*. The topic of the First Meditation is whether we can know anything for certain. The common-sense belief that we can often achieve certainty is confronted by several waves of doubt: the arguments from mistake, from dreaming, and from the evil demon. Thus, a philosophical challenge is mounted, and the problem of knowledge is motivated. The possibility that I might be dreaming or being deceived by an evil demon is enough to cast doubt on every one of my claims to knowledge. To restore myself to knowledge, these skeptical doubts need an answer.

Some philosophers argue that no answer can be given, at least within the terms in which Descartes has set the challenge. Philosophical skeptics deny that we are justified in many or any of our claims to knowledge, yet others find this conclusion literally unbelievable. Commonsense claims about knowledge might be wrong in some details, but it is not credible that we know virtually nothing. Again, philosophy and pragmatic good sense seem to come into conflict. Again, we have an impasse.

Many will argue that in both cases we should—initially at least—prefer the skeptical position. The skeptical position makes a negative claim: there are no convincing ways of defending political power or justifying claims to knowledge. The burden of proof surely falls on those who wish to make the positive claim that the state is justified or that we do have knowledge. On this view, then, the skeptical and anarchist positions are granted a privileged position in the debate. If we cannot conclusively defeat Descartes's dreaming or demon arguments, then we have to accept that our beliefs are never (fully) justified, and we thus become epistemological skeptics. If we cannot convincingly explain why there should be inequalities of political power, then we have to accept that the state is not (fully) justified, and we thus become philosophical anarchists.

Of course, there are important disanalogies in the examples. For example, there are few, if any, serious skeptics about knowledge. There are many serious philosophical anarchists,[8] and so it would be unfair to stigmatize philosophical anarchism by associating it too closely with a view that virtually no one adopts. Furthermore, the two arguments use different methodological strategies: epistemological skepticism proceeds by suggesting a possible alternative explanation for our normal perceptual experiences; philosophical anarchism proceeds by pointing out an apparent moral defect in the state. There is thus no exact structural similarity between the two cases. Nevertheless, there is one important feature they have in common that I wish to emphasize: both the skeptic and the philosophical anarchist assume that the burden of proof is on the opponent. Are they right to make this assumption?

This is clearly a matter of some significance. It may be impossible, for example, for defenders of the state or of normal claims of knowledge to meet the standards of proof that the anarchist and skeptic presuppose, but this does not rule out the possibility that they might be able to meet some lower standard. Therefore, before we can attempt to justify the state, we need to know what is going to count as a justification.

We can bring this point out by pursuing the analogy with skepticism one further step, by considering an attempt to deal with skepticism that involves a refusal to grant it the privileged position in the argument it claims for itself. I want to look at W. V. O. Quine's response to the dreaming hypothesis—that for all I know this is a dream, and so I have no knowledge at all.

For Quine, the fact that it is possible that this is a dream is not sufficient to cast doubt on our claims to knowledge.

> Experience might, tomorrow, take a turn that would justify the skeptic's doubts about external objects. Our success in predicting observations might fall off sharply, and concomitantly with this we might begin to be somewhat successful in basing predictions upon dreams or reveries. At that point we might reasonably doubt our theory of nature, even in its broadest outlines.[9]

Quine sets up what he takes to be a neutral test for comparing our normal knowledge claims against the dreaming hypothesis: the prediction of our future sensory stimulations. The test for any theory, argues Quine, is how well it predicts our observations, so a fair contest between common belief and skepticism is to see which one best predicts our future sensory stimulations. Now it is possible that the dreaming hypothesis could win. Perhaps we will find that more of our predictions come true if we assume that this is all a dream: perhaps this will happen in the future. It is much more likely, though, that most predictions on that basis will fail and common belief will do a much better job. On a level playing field, then, common sense defeats skepticism.

I am not concerned here to evaluate the success of Quine's rebuttal of skepticism—many will feel that his playing field tilts too far in favor of common sense—but I am much more interested in the general strategy. Rather than granting the skeptic a privileged position in the debate, Quine has sought out a neutral standpoint from which the claims of skepticism and common sense can be treated as equal competitors. Can we do a similar thing for the debate about political obligation: find a neutral standpoint from which to assess the competing claims of the anarchist and the statist? I want to consider whether Rawls's contractualism offers such a standpoint.

The Hypothetical Contract

One immediate objection to the idea that Rawls's contractualism could provide the neutral ground on which the problem of political obligation can be fought out is that Rawls's own view of political obligation is not contractualist. In contrast, Rawls argues that there is a "natural duty" to support those just institutions that apply to us.[10]

It will bring Rawls's view into sharper focus if we respond to this objection. Certainly we should accept that Rawls presents his view in the terms stated: there is a natural duty to obey those just institutions that apply to us. If our state is (tolerably) just, then each of us has an obligation or—Rawls would prefer to say—a duty to obey that state. So far, though, this is a superficial theory. What are natural duties for Rawls, and how do we know what they are? Are they, for example, given by the law of nature, revealed by reason? Rawls's answer is that the natural duties are those duties that would be accepted by people in his original position; hence, Rawls's theory of political obligation turns out to be contractualist in exactly the same way as his theory of distributive justice: at bottom Rawls is a hypothetical contract theorist of political obligation.[11]

Can contractualism provide a neutral standpoint? Perhaps this is doubtful. Indeed, it would seem to be playing back into the hands of the anarchist, for a contract requires unanimity, and so a single dissenter is enough to wreck the chances of creating the social contract. To put this another way, political obligation is universalistic, in the sense that all those who reside within a state's borders are supposed to be obliged, yet contract theory is voluntaristic: one has obligations only if one has voluntarily brought them on oneself. It does not take much imagination to see the problems of trying to defend universal obligation on voluntary foundations; this is the problem that has plagued contract theory.

If we thus insist that the only possible foundation for political obligation is an explicit contract, assented to by all members of society, then we will be unlikely to avoid anarchism. Of course, many people will accept that it is better to contract into the state: this provides a way both of settling disputes peacefully and making decisions concerning the population as a whole. We can reasonably predict, however, that some will refuse to assent out of principle (in the belief that the state is intrinsically immoral) or self-interest (out of fear of being outvoted on a regular basis) or just to make trouble. If contractualism is a neutral standpoint, then it seems anarchism is the likely winner.

Of course, to reject contractualism for that reason would be to beg the question against the anarchist, but there are other reasons to object to this form of contractualism. First, we must not forget that Rawls's contractualism does not appeal to an explicit contract, but to a hypothetical contract: a contract people would make under certain circumstances. For this reason Rawls's theory is not, strictly speaking, voluntaristic. This helps in one way. We can specify the circumstances so that everyone makes the same choice. Therefore, we avoid the problem that some individuals might refuse to consent; but this solution has its apparent costs. No doubt there are ways in which we can specify the hypothetical circumstances of the contractors so that they will all choose to join the state, but perhaps we could specify them a different way, so that they make a different choice. For example, if we imagine people placed in Hobbes's state of nature, it seems fairly obvious that such people would contract into the state. If, however, we depict it as some anarchists have done—a situation of peace, harmony, and freedom from want—the state might appeal to no one.

That is our first difficulty: how should we specify the hypothetical circumstances of the choosers? This leads to a second and more fundamental problem. As Ronald Dworkin has argued, a hypothetical contract is not a contract, so it is wrong to assume that a hypothetical contract carries with it the justificatory force of an actual contract; neither is a hypothetical contract a "pale shadow" of a contract.[12] How, then, can we understand how an argument from a hypothetical contract is meant to work? The basic form of a hypothetical contract argument is that individuals in a certain hypothetical situation—the state of nature, or the original position—would make a contract with particular terms. Our problem is what this is meant to show. Why should we not simply respond: so what?

There are many ways in which hypothetical contract theory has been understood.[13] For present purposes, however, the central divide is between what we could call a hypothetical rational contract and a hypothetical reasonable contract. To understand the difference, consider an ordinary commercial contract, which is an example of an actual, rational contract. In the simplest case two parties come to an agreement for mutual benefit. Each seeks to gain and realizes that the contract is instrumental to this: to do better for myself, I must enter a contract with burdens as well as benefits. If terms cannot be agreed, no contract is made. The parties are then in a bargaining game. If they are to advance their interests, they must come to some agreement, but it is also possible that they will reach no agreement. In that case no contract is struck, and we remain in the precontract situation. We can thus represent the parties as bargaining away from a break point. In the normal case a number of possible contracts would represent a profit for both parties: each tries to do the best she can from among these possibilities, knowing that the other is also trying to maximize profit. In the end, most likely, a mutually profitable compromise is reached.

The break point is the default position in case of disagreement; similar observations apply in the more complex case of a multiperson contract. Each person has a veto. Therefore, for an agreement to be made, all parties must agree. While it is true that any subgroup can make a contract independently, what it cannot do is bind a dissenting minority to the majority decision. Those who do not sign the contract are not bound by it.

According to the theory of the hypothetical rational contract then, to show that people in the state of nature would make such a contract is to show that the state is in everyone's interests, in the sense that no one has a good reason for exercising his or her veto. On many views this can be only the first step in an argument to show that we have political obligations, and further steps are necessary to complete the argument, but we already have enough detail to see exactly why the rational hypothetical contract seems to favor anarchism. Suppose there are people who do not believe that the state is in their interests. They might even be right. If so, then the hypothetical contract fails at the first hurdle: we cannot show even that the state is in the interests of all. We seem left, therefore, with philosophical anarchism.

The theory of the reasonable hypothetical contract—Rawls's theory—is quite different. It rejects the idea that we are bargaining away from a break point. The social contract is not like a commercial contract in which we are choosing whether or not to make an agreement with others. Rawls has several reasons for saying this, but the most important is the form of motivation he attributes to the contractors.[14] He does not assume that they are narrowly self-interested, out for everything that they can get, nor does he simply widen the notion of "interest," assuming that people sometimes have an interest in the fortune of others. Rather, he assumes that individuals are reasonable in that they are prepared to moderate their claims out of a concern for others and are willing to propose and honor "fair terms of cooperation."[15] That is, rather than seeing the contract as merely instrumental to the pursuit of their interests, reasonable contractors value cooperation with others in itself (although, of course, not at all costs).

One important formulation—partially endorsed by Rawls—of the motivation behind reasonable contractors has been provided by T. M. Scanlon: moral agents are moved "by the desire to be able to justify [their actions] to others on grounds they could not reasonably reject (reasonably, that is, given the desire to find principles which others similarly motivated could not reasonably reject)."[16]

More generally, Scanlon writes: "An act is wrong if its performance under the circumstances would be disallowed by any system of rules for the general regulation of behaviour which no one could reasonably reject as a basis for informed, unforced general agreement." Scanlon's work is to provide a contractualist moral theory. Rawls's project is narrower in scope: to generate contractual foundations for political philosophy. Here we need not address the question of whether contractual foundations can be generated on this basis for the whole field of morality. The present issue is the purchase this approach gives us on the issue of the justification of the state.

Modifying and applying Scanlon's ideas to the special case of political obligation,[17] we can now see the basic contrast between the idea of the rational contract and the idea of the reasonable contract. The rational contract has the following features:

(1) It takes individuals to be pursuers of their own individual goals (perhaps self-interested, but also perhaps not).
(2) Agreement is seen as having only instrumental value: as a way in which disparate individuals can achieve their separate goals.
(3) It defines a break point in the case of nonagreement.
(4) If there is unanimous agreement, then the correct or just outcome is the result of that agreement.
(5) If there is no unanimous agreement, then the break point is the correct position. (Each person thus has a veto.)
(6) The range of possible agreements is defined by the set of Pareto improvements over the break point: that is, the set of possibilities that improves everyone's situation as compared to the break point.

Thus, as we saw, this model of agreement as bargaining away from a break point will avoid anarchism only by chance. To put this more clearly, the state will turn out to be justified only if it satisfies more of every individual's preferences than the status quo. If this is not so, then the feasible set will be empty. Furthermore, it will be guaranteed to be empty if we allow people to have a very strong preference for anarchy and there is at least one such anarchist. If we discount such preferences, then the feasible set may or may not be empty.

The reasonable contract, by contrast, has the following features:

(1) It takes individuals as pursuers of their individual goals but constrained by a desire to justify their behavior to others on grounds that could not reasonably be rejected.
(2) It supposes that agreement is seen, at least in part, as desirable in itself.
(3) No break point is defined.
(4) If there is unanimous agreement, then the correct or just outcome is the result of that agreement.
(5) If there is no unanimous agreement, then some other procedure will legitimately be used to determine the outcome (for example, majority rule).
(6) The range of possible agreements is defined by the set of arrangements that could not be reasonably rejected.

In practice, the main difference between these approaches comes from the fact that, on the second model, the parties place considerable weight on the idea of reaching agreement, provided that others are similarly accommodating. Thus, the fact that someone is worse off than he or she might be under some notional break point (say, generalized egoism) is not a conclusive reason for rejecting that arrangement. By contrast, on the model of the rational contract such an arrangement would not even figure in the feasible set of outcomes.

On the model of the reasonable contract, then, we consider individuals as committed to the idea of finding a common set of arrangements such that no one could reasonably reject those arrangements. It may be, of course, that there are many possible arrangements; in that case we must choose between them on some other ground. Note, though, that there must, in principle, be at least one arrangement that cannot be reasonably rejected, even in the case of tragic choices, for options can be reasonably rejected only in the light of alternatives. To make the point in a graphic way, suppose there are only two possible arrangements: one in which all the red-haired people die and one in which all but the red-haired people die. In some sense it might seem that we can reasonably reject both, but if these are the only two options, then this is utopian. Either we must find some particularly salient feature of choice (there are fewer red-haired people, or the red-haired are more valuable) or an acceptable procedure for the choice.

We cannot simply reject both options; hence, the feasible set is context dependent.

My suggestion is that we should treat the reasonable contract as a neutral standpoint from which we can assess the competing claims of different forms of anarchism and statism. I will also argue that, on this playing field, statism wins; but first we must examine some obvious objections: that there is no deep distinction to be made between rational agreement and reasonable agreement and that even if there is such a thing as reasonable cooperation, it favors the state only by begging the question and so is not neutral at all.

Why might someone refuse to accept the distinction between the rational agreement and the reasonable agreement? One reason for this claim is that acting reasonably is, we might think, a self-effacing form of acting rationally. That is, my long-term goal is to do as well for myself as possible, but after a little experience in life one comes to realize that one does better by being reasonable. Life is a series of episodes of cooperation, and few opportunities are granted to those known to be unreasonable. It is thus rational to appear to be reasonable, and the best way of appearing so is to be so.

A likely response is that this gets the phenomenology of being reasonable wrong. A reasonable person simply wants to justify his or her behavior to other reasonable people: there is no ulterior motive in mind. This is not, however, conclusive: it might be most rational not only to be reasonable but also to school oneself to act and believe as if it were of independent value to be reasonable.[18]

Anyone determined to reduce the reasonable to the rational will not be deterred. Nevertheless, an explanation is owed of why one should seek to reduce the one to the other. Rawls's view is that no one untainted by philosophy or rational decision theory would feel such a project necessary or desirable.[19] Why should we seek an integrated theory of action this way?[20] Even if we do seek it, so far it is only a claim that the reasonable can be reduced to the rational. We have yet to see how the reduction is to be carried out in detail.

This approach, then—born from a conviction that the reasonable must be reducible—is not compelling; yet there may be other problems in trying to set out the distinction. One of the characteristics of the reasonable contract is that a decision procedure is invoked in the case of nonagreement. This is also, however, often a feature of rational contracts: commercial contracts often involve clauses about who will arbitrate in case of disagreement, and so this feature apparently fails to distinguish the two ideals.

Note, though, that terms calling for arbitration in a commercial contract will be binding only if all parties to the contract agree to them (ignoring the possibility that the situation is covered by positive law). On the other hand, the reasonable contract claims authority even over those who refuse to accept any arbitration principle. Reasonable people may aim to achieve universal agreement, but they are satisfied with the agreement of the subclass of the reasonable. No one has an unrestricted veto, not even a veto over the choice of arbitration principle. It is true that individuals may reject or veto certain arrangements, but only on reasonable grounds. If a person tries to insist on such a veto on what is widely perceived to be an unreasonable basis, then he or she can be overruled. Why? Because that person is behaving unreasonably—there is little more to be said, except to explain why in detail.

Some will think that this makes the idea of the reasonable contract highly unreasonable: illiberal, or dangerous even. This seems an exaggeration, but it is worth being clear that the idea of the reasonable contract gives individual choice a somewhat lesser role than it is often accorded, at least by the rhetoric of liberal and libertarian thought, and it is verging on the dishonest to pretend otherwise. The fact that some people refuse to agree with a scheme that claims authority over them is not, on this theory, a sufficient reason to refuse the scheme such authority. The question is whether the people are refusing on reasonable grounds. That itself can be a matter of dispute and interpretation, but the basic point is that one individual's choices can be outweighed by the interests of others—certainly not in all the cases in which utilitarianism would yield such a result, but in some, at least, and perhaps some others, too.[21]

I am sure that this is not enough to allay all fears about the apparent illiberality of the reasonable contract, but perhaps nothing could. I now want to move on to a second objection to the idea that the reasonable contract can be used as a neutral framework to assess the competing claims of the anarchist and statist: that it begs the question in favor of the state.

The main reason for this objection is that the reasonable contract encourages us to seek a system of rules. Is this not already a prejudice in favor of the state? This objection, though, is surely mistaken. Why should the agreed rules not be no rules, or socially enforced rules, rather than coercively enforced rules? There is nothing in the idea of rules alone that begs the question in favor of the state.

Furthermore, the idea of reasonable agreement embodies certain assumptions that the anarchist should find congenial. It is interesting to note that most traditional approaches to the defense of the state appeal in one form or other to self-interested motivation. Traditional contract theory starts by attempting to persuade individuals that they will be better off by joining the state. Fairness arguments point out that, for almost all individuals, the benefits of the state outweigh the burdens, but the argument from the reasonable contract no longer treats the issue of self-interest as alone decisive.

Of course, individual self-interest could hardly be ignored, but whether or not the state is justified turns on the question not of what every given individual can gain from the state, but what sort of arrangements can be justified to all reasonable people. In some cases, then, it might be reasonable to require some people to make some level of sacrifice. Given the profoundly moral basis to most forms of anarchism, this outward-looking reorientation away from self-interest should be welcomed. I therefore claim that we have found our neutral standpoint. It is not obvious whether, from this standpoint, we could reasonably reject either the state or anarchy. Let us call the anarchist who accepts this standpoint the "reasonable anarchist." The question is whether the reasonable anarchist can remain an anarchist.

The Justification of the State

An argument from Rawls suggests that reasonable anarchism cannot be sustained, and so the state emerges victorious. Rawls's argument—in fact virtually all the arguments I shall discuss in the remainder of this paper—is broadly familiar. Putting such arguments into the contractualist framework, however, will help us see their force and what they achieve. Rawls's central claim is that distributive justice requires a "basic structure" of justice, a system of major social institutions, including the political constitution and central economic organization.[22] A second premise (assumed but not argued for by Rawls) is that a basic structure requires enforcement by the law and, hence, the existence of the state. The third and final premise is that reasonable people should be concerned about distributive justice. From these it follows that it is unreasonable to reject the state: thus the reasonable contractualist cannot be an anarchist.[23]

Let us consider these premises one by one and the inference to the conclusion. We will then be ready to reflect on the nature and significance of the argument.

Why does distributive justice require a basic structure? Rawls addresses this question in what is, in effect, his reply to libertarian theories of justice, such as that of Robert Nozick. Nozick has, so it first appears, a purely procedural account of distributive justice: if goods are justly acquired and justly transferred, the outcome is ensured to be just. Rawls rejects this for several reasons, but the most important point is that, according to Rawls, the free market, left entirely to itself, will tend to erode justice—as if, he says, the invisible hand leads us in the wrong direction: to the formulation of oligopolies and inequalities of opportunities.[24] Even among people of goodwill there is no way of avoiding this through individual behavior: there is no set of rules restricting individual behavior that would prevent injustices from arising. We cannot coordinate our actions in that way: at the very least any such set of rules would be too complex for us to follow; so, Rawls contends, we must accept "a division of labour between two types of social rules":[25] those rules governing our day-to-day economic behavior, such as rules against theft, fraud, and so on; and those that help create a background of basic justice, such as inheritance tax. If we are serious about distributive justice, then we need to generate institutions of background justice: a just basic structure.

Nozick might accuse Rawls of having the wrong theory of distributive justice. Nozick is fully aware that free-market transactions will not reliably generate any pattern of holdings, but on Nozick's view, so much the worse for patterns.

It would take us too far afield to try to settle this issue here, yet it is worth noting—something often missed—that Nozick's own theory of distributive justice was chosen, in part at least, independent of its merits as a theory of justice, because it does not require institutions of basic justice to support it. This is because Nozick appreciates that, once this much is conceded, it is a short step to the justification of the state. In introducing his view, Nozick remarks:

> Against the claim that [an extensive state] is justified in order to achieve or produce distributive justice among its citizens, I develop a theory of justice (the entitlement theory) which does not require any more extensive state [than the minimal state].[26]

We are thus given the distinct impression that the entitlement theory is devised to avoid an argument for the extensive state, whatever its own individual merits as a theory of justice (which, of course, Nozick thinks are considerable[27]). It is arguable, though, that even Nozick's minimal theory of justice requires at least a minimal state—it is not compatible with anarchy. Institutions appear to be necessary, if not to regulate the rectification of transactional injustice (theft and fraud) then to ensure that society adheres to the Lockean proviso that no one should be made worse off than they would have been in the state of nature. Rawls's arguments continue to apply: no plausible set of rules governing individual transactions could plausibly ensure that this proviso is met.

Nozick, of course, does not avail himself of this argument for the minimal state, because he takes his task to be the refutation of the anarchist, rather than to argue for the preferability of the state from a neutral standpoint. So far, however, I have tried to render plausible only the first step in the neutral argument for the state: that distributive justice requires institutions of basic justice. Bearing in mind the argument just made—that even Nozick's theory appears to require such institutions—we see that this particular argument is not premised on Rawls's theory of justice; rather, it applies provided that one does not adopt a purely transactional theory. Despite Nozick's rhetoric, it is now widely accepted that his own theory cannot be described that way for the reasons I have given.

While the above considerations seem to me strong, I must concede that they do not actually prove that distributive justice requires a basic structure. One possible line of reply is to say that Rawls and his followers simply have lacked imagination. Rawls has given no general argument for the impossibility of achieving distributive justice without a basic structure: all he has done is spread some doubt. A more plausible response is to say that the anarchist ought to adopt Nozick's view of property but apply it in a more rigorous way: perhaps without the Lockean proviso.[28] If, on this basis, one can maintain a purely transactional theory of distributive justice, then justice can, in principle, be secured without a basic structure. (For my part, I reject such an account of distributive justice on traditional egalitarian grounds, but I cannot attempt to argue this here.) I will continue to assume, however, that Rawls is right: distributive justice requires a basic structure.

Premise two in the argument, which we shall examine shortly, was that a basic structure of justice requires law and hence the state, and the third premise was that reasonable people have good reason to be concerned about distributive justice. (A further background assumption is that they have no better reason to be concerned with something else that conflicts with the demands of distributive justice. We will return to this.)

Why should reasonable people be concerned about distributive justice? Perhaps this does not need much argument. A reasonable person is prepared to moderate his or her claims in the light of claims of others. It is hard to see how such a person could be indifferent to claims about distributive justice. A reasonable person, to adopt Scanlon's approach, wishes to regulate his or her behavior according to rules that no one could reasonably reject. You could reasonably reject rules that treated you unjustly: as a reasonable person, such rules should be unacceptable to me, too. Indeed, Rawls goes so far as to define a reasonable person as someone who is prepared to propose and honor fair terms of cooperation. I will thus take it as established that reasonable people should be concerned with distributive justice (but this is not, without much further argument, to say that they should be committed to any particular conception of justice).

The remaining—and hence key—question is whether achieving a basic structure of justice requires the coercive intrusions of law and the state and, if it does, whether the state has an unacceptable opportunity cost. Here we run up against familiar twin anarchist challenges to the state: first, a just basic structure can be achieved without coercive intervention; and second, permitting agents of the state such coercive power will do more harm than good. In one version agents of the state will inevitably use that power for their own ends to the detriment of the people as a whole, so even if distributive justice is harder to achieve without the state, the disadvantages of the state are such that we will do better without it.

One peculiarity of this debate is that, superficially at least, both the anarchist and the statist can be made to appear to hold an inconsistent position. The statist believes that people are insufficiently good to live without the state but that the agents of the state can achieve a level of benevolence unattainable by other human beings: when given power and opportunity, they will not use it for their own ends. The anarchist, by contrast, mistrusts individuals sufficiently to suppose that they will misuse power but trusts them to behave when they are not subject to coercive restraint.

Of course, this dilemma is oversimplistic in many respects. The statist will argue that we require the state, not because we are all insufficiently good, but because we are insufficiently organized. Broadly, most of us are reasonable people, but we cannot coordinate our actions as we wish without the state. Furthermore, unreasonable people do exist and will seek power, and so the ideal state needs to contain structural safeguards so that no one can abuse his or her power. The anarchist response is more complex: there is something especially corrupting about power, which can undermine our otherwise reasonable motivation. This corruption is so serious that it outweighs whatever benefits coercive organization brings with it.

To take this a little further, consider again our naive starting point. I suggested that a first reaction to attempts to question the existence of the state is a form of pragmatism or consequentialism: it is obvious that we need the state. A likely anarchist rebuttal is that it may be obvious that we need something, but it is not so obvious that we need a state. To think so is to confuse organization with coercion. It is true that society needs certain structures of cooperation, even of enforcement, but there is no reason to believe that such structures need to be backed by coercion. To believe so would be to accept a demeaning vision of ourselves and our fellow beings. Voluntary organization is all the organization we need; hence, reasonable con-tractors can reject the state as intrusive and unnecessary.

But is it? I have assumed that the great majority of people are reasonable in the sense outlined. Let us distinguish two cases. Either everyone is reasonable or some part of the population is unreasonable, or, we might say, antisocial, in varying degrees. If we continue to assume that Rawls is correct to claim that achieving distributive justice requires a basic structure, would a society entirely composed of reasonable people need coercive structures to underwrite its basic structure? Rawls apparently believes that even under such circum-stances no one could reasonably reject the state. Perhaps he is wrong: this is a question about what can be achieved on a purely voluntary basis between people of goodwill. The situation is quite different in the second case, though, if we assume that at least some people are unreasonable. Coercion to secure a just basic structure seems essential in the face of people—perhaps quite a number of them—who are prepared to engage in antisocial behavior.

Some anarchists think that this argument begs the question. A common anarchist response is that antisocial behavior is an effect of living under a (necessarily corrupt) state, and so the state is a cause of the very behavior that its existence is supposed to remedy. There are two things wrong with this argument. First, even if it is true that the state is the cause of our corruption, the fact is that we are now corrupted. As Rousseau well understood, removing the state would not be a way of removing our corruption: in fact, it would be a way of allowing it a free rein. There is no way to return us to innocence.

Second, and more important, there is something self-defeating in the argument that the state is both corrupt itself and the cause of antisocial behavior. If the state is both undesirable, yet also the cause of antisocial behavior, how could it have come into existence? Not by the deliberate action of the antisocial, for, by hypothesis, the state is the cause of antisocial behavior. Of course, it is possible that reasonable people could have created a state, which in turn, as an unintended consequence, exerted a pernicious effect on them, but it is hard to believe that the state is the sole cause of antisocial behavior.

More plausible explanations of the existence of the state are that either it was a response by the reasonable to contain the unreasonable or it was, at least at first, devised by the unreasonable to further their own ends.[29] In other words, if the state exists, then that is argument enough that we need some form of state! In the terms of the idea of the reasonable contract, even if—contra Rawls—the state is not necessary among reasonable people, the fact of the existence of unreasonable people makes it so.

These considerations constitute a powerful defense of the state from within the terms of the reasonable contract, but I am conscious that there is more to be said on both sides. The argument is not over yet, but what I do hope to have made convincing is that these arguments about power and organization are the terrain over which the justification of the state is to be fought and that the method of reasonable contractualism provides a framework and forum in which such debates can be conducted.

To argue for anarchy, it is not enough to point out the peculiarity of the state and the difficulties with many of the arguments in favor of it. Rather, in contractualist terms, it has to be shown that reasonable people seeking agreement on the nature of the social world would prefer anarchy to the state. Some anarchists try to do just this. We can admire their courage, but we do not have to agree with them. The defense of the state, we may say, needs only to meet the burden of proof assumed in the civil, not the criminal, courts: not beyond reasonable doubt, but by the balance of probabilities.

Notes

1. Versions of this paper have been presented at Kings College, London, the University of Wales, Lampeter, and the University of Kent, and I am

grateful for the many useful comments I received on those occasions. I would also like to thank Vittorio Bufacchi, Andreas Follesdal, George Klosko, Jan Narveson, and Jack Sanders for their extremely helpful written comments on earlier drafts.

2. Bernard Williams, "The Minimal State," in J. Paul, ed., *Reading Nozick* (Oxford: Blackwell, 1982), 27–36.

3. M. B. E. Smith, "Is There a Prima Facie Duty to Obey the Law?" *Yale Law Journal* 82 (1973): 950–76.

4. A. John Simmons, *Moral Principles and Political Obligations* (Princeton, N.J.: Princeton University Press, 1979).

5. Joseph Raz, "The Obligation to Obey the Law," in his *The Authority of Law* (Oxford: Oxford University Press, 1979).

6. Leslie Green, *The Authority of the State* (Oxford: Oxford University Press, 1988).

7. I take the term from Chaim Gans, *Philosophical Anarchism and Political Disobedience* (Cambridge: Cambridge University Press, 1992).

8. Myles Burnyeat wrote an influential paper entitled, "Can the Skeptic Live His Skepticism?" in Myles Burnyeat, ed., *The Skeptical Tradition* (Berkeley: University of California Press, 1983). One might equally well ask, "Can the anarchist live her anarchism?" For an amusing illustration of the problems from writings within the anarchist tradition, see Wordsworth Donisthorpe, "The Woes of an Anarchist," included in Benjamin Tucker, *Instead of a Book* (New York: B. Tucker, 1893).

9. W. V. O. Quine, "Reply to Stroud," *Midwest Studies in Philosophy* 6 (1986): 475. This aspect of Quine's view was first brought to my attention by Burton Dreben.

10. John Rawls, *A Theory of Justice* (Oxford: Oxford University Press, 1972), 115.

11. Although Rawls is quite explicit about it, this aspect of his view of political obligation seems to have been lost in subsequent debate. This, I think, is partly a consequence of A. John Simmons's influential discussion in chap. 6 of *Moral Principles and Political Obligations*, in which he deliberately detaches Rawls's view from its contractual foundations, claiming that "[Rawls's] arguments on these points stand on their own feet, independent of his unique 'hypothetical contract' justifications" (p. 144). This claim would be more convincing if Simmons had been able to tell us what these supposed independent arguments for the view are, but he does not. Rather, he provides a number of counterexamples to the doctrine that we have a duty to comply with those just institutions that apply to us, without considering whether Rawls's hypothetical contract arguments provide resources for a reply.

12. Ronald Dworkin, "The Original Position," in N. Daniels, ed., *Reading Rawls* (Oxford: Blackwell, 1975), 16–53.

13. For some discussion, see my "Hobbes and the Motivations of Social Contract Theory," *International Journal of Philosophical Studies* 2 (1994): 271–86.

14. My interpretation of Rawls is based on *Political Liberalism* (New York: Columbia University Press, 1993) and in particular on Lecture 7, "The Basic Structure as Subject."

15. See Rawls, *Political Liberalism*, pp. 48–65, for a fuller discussion of the concept of "the reasonable."

16. T. Scanlon, "Contractualism and Utilitarianism," in Amartya Sen and Bernard Williams, eds., *Utilitarianism and Beyond* (Cambridge: Cambridge University Press, 1982), 116.

17. Rawls and Scanlon use the method to devise, or at least to assess, principles: Rawls, principles of justice; Scanlon, moral principles. My project is rather different and perhaps more ambitious. Can we use the method to assess possible sets of institutions (including coercive institutions)?

18. For instructive discussion of such possibilities, see Derek Parfit, *Reasons and Persons* (Oxford: Oxford University Press, 1984), part 1.

19. Rawls, *Political Liberalism*, 52.

20. One reason is that, unless an agent can be represented as maximizing some goal—albeit a theoretical construct—that agent will be behaving irrationally by the formal standards of rational decision theory and so is vulnerable to exploitation by others: an irrational person can be turned into a "money pump." Even if it is correct, however, that rational behavior requires the apparent maximization of something, this does not show that reasonable action is reduced to rational action, for rational agents, in the sense under discussion, are defined in a substantive sense: as those who seek to maximize particular actual goals—their own interests and, perhaps, certain interests of certain others. The theory of rational action underlying the idea of the rational contract thus attributes substantive goals to rational agents. The point that all formally rational agents can be represented as maximizing something is a way of reducing both the reasonable and the substantively rational to the formally rational; not a way of reducing the reasonable to the substantively rational.

21. The value of choice, after all, requires defense. Cf T. M. Scanlon, "The Significance of Choice," in S. McMurry, ed., *The Tanner Lectures on Human Values*, vol. 7 (Salt Lake City: University of Utah Press, 1988), 151–216.

22. Rawls, *Political Liberalism*, 265–69.

23. Note that an argument from distributive justice cannot justify all the functions of the state and, hence, not all our political obligations (e.g., the liability to pay taxes to fund defense). See George Klosko, "Political Obligation and the Natural Duties of Justice," *Philosophy and Public Affairs* 23 (1994): 251–70. Thus, the suggestion here is only part of a complete view. For another part, see my "Political Obligation, Fairness, and Independence," *Ratio*, New Series 8 (1995): 87–99, and for a sketch of the whole, my "Pluralistic Accounts of Political Obligation," in *Philosophica*, forthcoming.

24. Rawls, *Political Liberalism*, 267.

25. Ibid., 268.

26. Robert Nozick, *Anarchy, State, and Utopia* (Oxford: Blackwell, 1974), xi.

27. See in particular Nozick, *Anarchy, State, and Utopia*, chap. 7. For my own assessment of the merits of Nozick's view, see my *Robert Nozick: Property, Justice, and the Minimal State* (Oxford: Polity; and Stanford, Calif.: Stanford University Press, 1991), especially chap. 4.

28. For arguments that we should reject the Lockean proviso, see John T. Sanders, "Justice and the Initial Acquisition of Property," *Harvard Journal of Law and Public Policy* (1987).

29. Some such story seems to be given by Rousseau in his *Discourse on the Origin of Inequality* (Middlesex: Penguin, 1984). For a brief discussion, see my "Hobbes and the Motivations of Social Contract Theory," 281.

7

Games, Anarchy, and the Nonnecessity of the State

Howard H. Harriott

Introduction

Anarchism as a political doctrine is thought by many philosophers to be indefensible. This is due in part to a misunderstanding of what anarchism might entail. It is often assumed that anarchism implies the absence of order, and consequently it is sometimes seen as the very rejection of political life.

The essential claim of most anarchists is that human social organization and cooperation are realistically possible without the coercive and centralized apparatus of the state. Arguments purporting to defend anarchism by this route have been thought to be highly implausible on the grounds that they must make unrealistic assumptions about human voluntariness and the ability of persons to act collectively without coercion. Some critics have thought that unless the anarchist assumes a harmony of interests among individuals (a highly unlikely situation), the idea of voluntary cooperation without coercion is impossible.

The claims of anarchism could be greatly advanced if the above negative perception of the anarchist's thesis could be disarmed. As I hope to show in this paper, a theoretical and empirical defense of anarchism is indeed possible, and we have strong grounds for supposing that human beings in the absence of the state would be able to achieve cooperation without coercion or Leviathan-like control.

One type of argument of interest, supporting the view of the necessity of the state, emerges from a very plausible argument frequently advanced for the state, often going under the title of "the economic argument for the state," or "the public good argument for the state." The intuition guiding this argument for the state seems on the face of it reasonable. Put in its most logical form, it asserts the following:

(1) The state has an important and essential function, namely, the provision of public goods, such as schools, lighthouses, public order itself—items that individuals would perceive as highly desirable and essential for collective well-being.

(2) Individuals are basically egoistically motivated and thus will not voluntarily contribute to the creation of such goods because of their tendency to free ride wherever it appears rational to do so.

(3) The result of such tendencies is that public goods are underproduced or will not be produced at all, to everyone's detriment, since they undermine cooperation.

The state is thus pragmatically necessary, in order to provide for individuals that which they acknowledge as valuable but will not contribute to voluntarily.

The essential thrust of this argument is that the motive of self-interest in individuals is so weak that they lack the necessary wherewithal to act collectively without coercion and thus that it is unreasonable to assume that agents so characterized can move beyond the myopic decision-making strategy of narrow self-interest.

Undermining this argument, as I hope to do here, requires the clarification of some notions that appear in the many versions of the argument. The first among these is the notion of "public good." Public goods are frequently understood as contrasted with private goods. Public goods, unlike private goods, satisfy two conditions: those of nonexclusiveness and nonrivalry. Nonexclusiveness of a good implies that once it is produced, no one can be excluded from enjoying it. Nonrivalry entails that the utility enjoyed by any individual does not detract from the utility levels that others might enjoy. There are some who challenge the hard and fast nature of this dichotomy, but the basic argument is not undermined by the possibilities. Next, the provenance of the argument outlined above is clearly that of economics, with its attendant notion of the rational agent as one whose motivational concerns lie in maximizing his or her utilities.

Testing the Strength of Voluntariness

The challenge for anarchists who argue that humans are fully capable of providing many of the goods that the state is allegedly needed for is to prove that human beings, unencumbered by government paternalism and coercive activities, are indeed able to do so. Anarchists who look closely at the actual performance of government in the production of important public goods—such as environmental protection, for example—balk at the claim that government has succeeded in this and other domains. To prove the case, though, that people can function without government, one must defend the view that voluntariness and cooperation are much more likely to arise spontaneously than conventional arguments would suggest. A successful argument against the state ought to give us good reasons to believe the limits of human cooperation to be much less narrow than that supposed by economic theory.

There are a number of arguments that have been offered from anthropological evidence that are very convincing and that show that there is nothing inevitable about the state. This evidence conflicts with the thesis that, without the state, humans have been incapable of social organization adequate to provide for social needs. Many statists might well concede that all these anthropological claims concerning acephalous societies are true but argue that they have little evidential bearing on humans today who have experienced the large nation-state and, as well, the "market experience." Such statists then conclude that short of some miraculous and unbelievable harmony-of-interests situation among human beings, we cannot assume that the economic perception that human beings will tend to free ride is a faulty assumption.

Before we can show the claim of the statist about the limits of cooperativeness among human beings to be unfounded, we need to set up our argument carefully. I advert to a game-theoretic formulation of the public-goods problem and in particular to the Prisoners' Dilemma formulation. Understanding this formulation of the public-goods problem is essential for the points I wish to make about the possibility of voluntariness. I selected the Prisoners' Dilemma game because of its relative simplicity and centrality in modeling the very problem of free riding that we need to show as surmountable without a Leviathan-like solution. It needs to be stated, though, that despite the pervasiveness of Prisoners' Dilemma scenarios in political and ethical life, not all public-goods problems are best formulated as Prisoners' Dilemmas.[1]

The Prisoners' Dilemma Formulation of the Public-Goods Problem

The scenario that is amenable to a game-theoretic formulation is as follows: Consider a world of two individuals, A and B, who are both desirous that some good should be realized. Each player has one of two strategies: either contribute to the production of this joint good or let the other produce it alone in the hope that the other might take the initiative and produce the good without help. Suppose that it costs 12 units to produce the good in question no matter how many choose to do it and that if the good is produced, it yields 5 units to each person. We assume that the benefit that accrues to each person is a function of the cost, the yield, and the number of contributors. In this case, suppose that the net benefit to each player is given by the following formula:

$5 \times$ (number of contributors) − individual cost of producing the good

Thus, if both A and B choose to contribute, then each gets a net benefit of 4 units. If neither A nor B decides to contribute, then there is zero net benefit for both, since neither contributes to the cost. If A produces the good alone, his net benefit is −7 units, while B obtains a net benefit of 5 units. B thus obtains a free ride. A symmetrical situation results if B contributes and A does not.

One way of representing this situation is through the notion of a two-person game. Implicit in the notion of a game is the assumption that the action choices of any player are influenced by the choices of the other player. This distinguishes the situation from decision contexts where one is acting purely against nature (as in individual decision making). In very simple terms, we can represent the problem in a game formulation incorporating strategies (action choices of each player); with row for player A and column for player B, the cells represent the payoffs to each player when the combination of strategy choices is made by the players. We thus have the following so-called agent-normal form of the game:

	B produces	B does not produce
A produces	4, 4	−7, 5
A does not produce	5, −1	0, 0

Figure 1

Such a game has a Prisoners' Dilemma structure (named for the situation described by A. W. Tucker[2]) and illustrates the following phenomenon: Both players as rational agents would like the collective good to be realized (rather than not at all), but each would prefer that the other should incur the costs. Suppose each player promises to contribute. In the absence of any binding agreement, each has an incentive to renege on his promise to contribute since each may hope the other will pay the lion's share. The fact that the good is a public good and deemed desirable means that each person is aware that the other can benefit from the labor without penalty once the good is produced. Such a situation constitutes a wide variety of social situations in which agents have mixed motives about each other and in which each cannot guarantee that the other can be trusted not to free ride. The interesting question that now arises is this: what can be predicted to follow when rational players face these kinds of strategic situations?

Given the situation described, figure 1 models the sort of situation that is typically advanced by those who argue for the necessity of the state. They argue game-theoretically that the outcome of a one-shot game of the sort described above is such that it is rational according to the economic theory of rationality to suppose that we should expect that both players will not produce. An undesirable situation is likely to obtain: a wanted public good will not be supplied; hence, statists argue, we need government to provide us with what we know we want but are too motivationally impoverished to provide without coercion.

The logic behind this conclusion depends on understanding what the basis of the solution to a game is, for the cogency of the statist's bleak solution depends on claims about what rational players are likely to do and not do when confronted with Prisoners' Dilemma-type situations. It is to this that we must now turn.

The game theorist John Harsanyi[3] has pointed out that the main problems facing the players of a game include the problem of finding a unique solution to the game, that is, the choice of a particular strategy pair with its associated payoffs, and the question of the stability of that payoff. Once the players find a strategy combination that suits them, they should not be tempted to deviate from it. Part of the metacriteria for a good theory of social behavior modeled by game theory is that we should obtain outcomes that are in some plausible sense rational and stable.

The standard conceptual device that has informed legions of game theorists concerning the rational solution of games—especially those of the noncooperative type—has been the so-called Nash equilibrium. It has been the intuition of many that a rational solution to such a game as the Prisoners' Dilemma must emerge from the set of strategies admitted by the Nash criteria.

The Nash solution criterion for the two-person game typified by our public-good game is as follows. Suppose that we have a two-person game (with two pure strategy options available for each player); then we say that a strategy pair, one for each player $<s_1, s_2>$, is a Nash equilibrium solution if, for each player, the strategy choice selected is a best reply to the strategy choice of the other. By "best reply" I mean that each player cannot increase his payoff by switching to some other available strategy given a particular strategy choice by the other player in the game.[4]

In standard (orthodox) Nash equilibrium game theory, the ideal situation is to find that a game scenario has a unique pair of best-reply strategies, one for each player, for this defines a stable and self-enforcing equilibrium solution to the game. If we can agree that rational self-interested agents can find in Prisoners' Dilemma situations a stable and self-enforcing solution to their public choice problems, we will have established a strong analytic plank for anarchist claims.

The logic of the Nash solution applied to our players A and B can now be evaluated. Given the story as we have told it, what is it rational to expect as an outcome? To find if a Nash solution exists, we have to see whether among the players' possible strategies there is at least one pair of strategies $s = <s_1, s_2>$ such that each is a best reply to the other. Each player has two (pure) strategies: produce/do not produce. Suppose player A decides to go for "produce"; then B's best reply is to go for "do not produce," but it is clear that if B independently and in absence of knowledge of A's choices goes for "do not produce," then A's best reply is not the strategy "produce" but rather the strategy "do not produce."

It is clear from the game scenario that the rational and Nash equilibrium solution of the game is that both players are rational in choosing the strategy of "not producing," which is clearly undesirable. The desirable outcome in the northwestern corner of the diagram in which both benefit and which would be better for both players collectively is not attainable. That solution—which yields both players a payoff of 4 units each—is the Pareto-optimal outcome, in the sense that if both players are able to select the cooperative strategy pair <produce, produce>, they would generate the socially best outcome. It is the failure of players rationally to reach this outcome that has provided the impetus to the free-ride argument and that has made an important argument for the state prima facie plausible. Statists say that the existence of Prisoners' Dilemmas serves to show the pragmatic necessity of the centralized state. They claim that, but for the state's activities to solve these public-good problems, the goods will not be provided.

Anarchist Rebuttals to the Statist Analysis of the Prisoners' Dilemma Game: The Analytic Arguments

Anarchist thinkers who take a public-good argument to be the strongest statist defense of the state can provide a strong counterattack to its prima facie plausibility without abandoning the basic insight of game-theoretic reasoning. Two sorts of anarchist responses tackle head-on the game-theoretic formulation of the argument for the state. Collectively, they provide in my view a firm rebuttal of game-theoretic versions of the public-good argument for the state. I refer to these as the analytic arguments from formal game theory modeling and the experimental arguments for the possibility of human cooperation in the absence of a centralized state. I take the view that the analytic arguments for the possibility of human cooperative solutions to the Prisoners' Dilemma provide important insights into the kind of realistic possibilities that are needed to realize cooperative institutions, but I do not consider these arguments, which show the possibility of rational agents choosing cooperative strategies, to be a decisive rebuttal to the statist. In fact, the analytic arguments are much weaker than some anarchists are willing to concede.

Let me turn first to the analytic arguments. Critics of the statist argument have seized on the observation that its refutation requires the establishment of two things: first, that there is the possibility of escaping the Prisoners' Dilemma without some sort of coercive solution of the Leviathan type and, second, that egoistically inclined agents can reason their way via some sort of "rational deliberational dynamics" into the cooperative solutions. The insight here is that what sustains rationality in securing cooperation is, inter alia, the notions of trust and reputation and that if we engage in repeated interactions of the Prisoners' Dilemma sort, rational agents may find the cooperative strategies in repeated games, for repeated interaction allows the transmission of information about players' past responses and hence provides the possibility of learning. Agents who engage in repeated Prisoners' Dilemma situations may discover conventions of cooperation and coordination not available in a world of one-shot games.

Prudential reasons for cooperation, in a manner suggested by David Hume, might also emerge.

Axelrod's "Tit-for-Tat" and the Emergence of Cooperation

Two types of nonequivalent theoretical arguments have emerged that seem to provide sound rebuttal to the statist's case. These may be seen as attempts to show the possibility of the emergence of cooperation in Prisoners' Dilemma settings without centralized coercion. Both are based on the insight that cooperation can emerge through repeated interaction. The problem they both show with the statist argument is that a too-restrictive modeling of the agent in the public-good situation might be the fault. One view, developed by Robert Axelrod,[5] considers what kind of strategies might succeed in a world of egoists who are free to choose from a wide range of strategy responses in repeated interactions. Axelrod shows that a type of conditional cooperation can emerge among players if they repeatedly interact in the sort of public-good game we have outlined. Roughly, of the possible strategies that players can adopt if they engage each other repeatedly, a tit-for-tat strategy used by both players can lead to the cooperative outcome. Analytically, the tit-for-tat strategy can be defined recursively for each player thus: Given an iterated Prisoners' Dilemma situation, a player plays his cooperative strategy on the first round and then in succeeding rounds imitates the strategy of the other player on succeeding rounds.

Under these conditions the cooperative solution will emerge. It is claimed that this strategy has advantages over other possibilities that could theoretically be initiated by a player in a repeated Prisoners' Dilemma interaction. For instance, an alternative strategy choice might be to cooperate on the first round and then defect indefinitely after the first defection (a very vengeful strategy) or to cooperate no matter what the other player does (a martyr strategy) or to play a randomized probabilistic strategy of cooperation and defection.

It is held by some that the rational adoption of the tit-for-tat strategy can emerge as a self-enforcing strategy choice by agents who may then discover the benefits of cooperation. It is held too that the insight of this case shows a number of ingredients that a strategy might require in an egoistical environment in order that cooperation, once established, may persist. Axelrod thinks that successful strategies must be clear (the strategy signal is easy to read), nice (the strategy is nonprovocative, in that defection from the cooperative strategy is never initiated), provocable (the strategy is not indifferent to defection by the other party), and forgiving (the strategy will foster cooperation conditional on reciprocal cooperative choices by the opponent). Tit-for-tat obviously does this better than any of the other three rival strategies I have postulated.

Taylor-Type Repeated Prisoners' Dilemma Games

It has been shown by Michael Taylor[6] that if we model the Prisoners' Dilemma game in the context of a possible infinite repetition of those games, then we can prove that the situation can lead to players' finding the cooperative strategy. Provably, rational players may discover the Nash equilibrium in these situations. The argument turns on treating the situation faced by players caught in our Prisoners' Dilemma situation as one in which they participate in a Prisoners' Dilemma supergame—essentially an infinite repetition of this game. With mathematical adjustments to the notions of strategy, payoff, and equilibrium and varying the technical conditions in various ways, game theoreticians have been able to prove the possibility of player convergence onto the cooperative solution in this enlarged supergame structure. Indeed, a class of theorems establishing this claim goes under the heading of the "folk theorem of noncooperative game theory."[7] Informally, and perhaps not transparently obvious, the folk theorem implies that any individually rational strategy in a repeated Prisoners' Dilemma game can be an equilibrium.

What is of theoretical interest in the above implication of the folk theorem is that it shows the possibility of cooperation as a realizable strategy. That is, in our case of A and B engaged in repeated play of the public-good game outlined in figure 1, A and B can find a strategy that permits cooperation in that larger game.

It is necessary to see the logic of this without undue technicality, as I hope the following brief explication suggests. For this we need to advert to some of the concepts that interpret the folk theorem. Consider the Prisoners' Dilemma supergame as an infinite repetition of the basic Prisoners' Dilemma game between A and B. Each play of the game, beginning with the first, is called a stage Prisoners' Dilemma game of the infinite supergame. The notion of a strategy in a one-shot game must now be extended to the notion of a strategy plan for playing this larger supergame. Just as in the discussion of the Axelrod game, we might think of possible strategy plans for A as follows: "always go for 'produce' in every repeated play," or "do not produce forever after the first use by the other player of his noncooperative strategy." As for the concept of payoff in this larger supergame, we assume that both players will discount future payoffs by some discount factor a. The payoff in the larger supergame is just the geometric average of the infinite stream of payoffs that each will obtain in the infinite repetitions. In the case of the players in our public-good game we can consider that A is in an infinite play with B, receives the payoffs $\{u_1, \ldots \ldots u_n \ldots \}$ in the sequence of plays of the game with a discount factor of say $a = 0.8$. His payoff in this larger supergame thus would be the convergent sum:

$$u_1 + (0.8) u_2 + (0.8)^2 u_3 + \ldots \ldots$$

In the simple example of our public-good game outlined in figure 1, but now played repeatedly, a selection of a strategy plan by A to cooperate on every round and a similar choice by B to play his cooperative plan to play "produce" on each round would yield a payoff for A of:

$$4 + 4(0.8) + 4(0.8)^2 + \ldots \ldots \ldots$$
$$= 4 [1 + (0.8) + (0.8)^2 + \ldots \ldots]$$

Since the sum within the square brackets is a geometric series, the payoff to A is $4/(1 - 0.8)$, which is 20 units.

Objections to the Analytic Arguments

There are important statist objections to the claims made for the game models presented briefly above concerning the matter of the possibility of cooperation. These objections provide a source of additional objections to the anarchist claim that must be met. Models, of course, either represent an underlying reality satisfactorily or they do not. They can be judged only in terms of their epistemic virtues. Do they fit well, explain, and provide insight?

Statists might want to challenge both the Axelrod and Taylor models on the strength of their realism and the probability that the conditions they describe are realistically possible. Consider first the model given by Axelrod, with its claim that the evolution toward cooperation in Prisoners' Dilemma situations can be effected by players discovering a tit-for-tat strategy. The model mimics a process of cooperation. The fitness of this strategy has even been demonstrated by simulation in computer experiments that pit it against other possible strategies, but a problematic aspect of the Axelrod strategy is that tit-for-tat does not seem to be a highly likely outcome when self-interested egoists go to work in an environment where misjudgment and misperceptions can take place, as might occur with players in environments where signals can be subject to noise.

Let me now turn to the case of cooperation via the supergame model. In this case the folk theorem appears at first to render the anarchist case unassailable, but the proof of cooperation that is offered by the theorem is too generous. It proves too much, since it does not predict one unique solution to the supergame that coincides with the cooperative solution. The folk theorem shows that it is rational to play a cooperative strategy in the supergame if we equate rationality in noncooperative games as coextensive with the choice of a Nash equilibrium point. In a supergame setting we also find that a Nash equilibrium yielding the payoff $<0,\ 0>$ also obtains if both players choose their defect strategy plan of never cooperating. Another way of stating the objection to anarchists who rely on a supergame type of argument is that, because of the abundance of Nash equilibrium points, we do not have enough of a rationale for supposing that the cooperative solution will be uniquely chosen.

Let me illustrate this point with respect to supergame strategies applied to our public-good game mentioned earlier. Suppose that the game is played repeatedly, the same payoff structure on each round. There are many possible strategy plans that might be invoked in the larger supergame. Consider three of the many possibilities, and assume that each of the two players can choose any of the three strategy plans described below.

(1) M: a martyr strategy in which one plays the cooperative strategy: "produce no matter what the other player does."
(2) T: tit-for-tat, characterized by the rule: "cooperate on the first round and do what the other player did on his previous move."
(3) D: "always defect no matter what the other player does."

With these three strategy plans for playing the supergame, we can work out a game matrix depicting the payoffs that will occur if A and B each select from the three strategies above. The following game matrix results when we apply the discount rate of $a = 0.8$ to the various strategy combinations that may be chosen by both players:

	B uses M	*B uses T*	*B uses D*
A uses M	20, 20	20, 20	$-35, 25$
A uses T	20, 20	20, 20	$-7, 5$
A uses D	25, -35	5, -7	0, 0

Figure 2

To see how these matrix entries arise, we need to compute only one case. Let us suppose that A chooses T (tit-for-tat) and B selects M (the martyr strategy); then in the repeated game A nets 20 units and B obtains 20. These payoffs arose in the following way: when A plays T under the assumption of B's commitment to cooperation, he obtains a total payout of

$$4 + 4(0.8) + 4(0.8)^2 + 4(0.8)^3 \ldots \ldots$$

which is a geometric progression whose sum is 4/0.2, that is, 20. Quite similar reasoning yields the sum of 20 for B.

What is of significance here is that in the supergame, the reasoning of the players need not yield the inferior outcome of $<0, 0>$, as was apparent in the one-shot Prisoners' Dilemma game.

Indeed, recent advances in game theory have neither substantially helped nor, in fact, hindered the anarchist's claims about cooperation. Some theorists have attempted to move their considerations in the direction of what is termed "equilibrium refinements." These theoretical moves consist of attempts to provide rationally defensible conditions that may serve to eliminate some of the many Nash equilibrium solutions that can arise in repeated game contexts. Those committed to equilibrium refinements presuppose that unique predictions for repeated games must emerge from the set of Nash equilibrium solutions. Indeed, the problem of understanding rational action in repeated game contexts is made even more complex by the fact that plausible solutions can be advanced for some of these games whose rationales do not lie in Nash equilibrium reasoning.[8] At any event, this explosion of complexity within the framework of repeated games has weakened the earlier confident theoretical claims that the analytical arguments alone appeared to offer. Game-theoretic formalizations of the anarchistic solutions are still clearly of great value, but the empirical testing of these claims has taken on a greater urgency.

The Experimental Approach and the Experimental Defense

For all the sophistication of the analytic arguments, critics of those arguments claim that the assumptions concerning rationality that are needed are too unrealistic to model anything in the real world. For some critics, the theoretical defenses of anarchism via supergames are far removed from real rationally inclined agents. For critics such as Michael Hechter,[9] the conditions assumed in the supergame presentation, for example, go beyond what is reasonable. In the supergame construction, for instance, we must assume that players have perfect information about past plays of the game and strategy choices of all other players. With players lacking these "super-rational" abilities, it would seem that some doubt can be cast on the result if anarchists purport to claim that such cooperative structures could be expected to emerge in the absence of centralized state control. What sort of response is possible here?

It is clear that without the possibilities of testing their claims empirically, the anarchist's case is only half-made. The statist's bald claim is that in almost all social contexts in which free riding is a possibility, free riding will be likely to occur. The anarchist faces the challenge that (1) we have evidence of the operations of states and their coercive control in the provision of public goods; (2) we have, apart from older acephalous societies,[10] no scientific proof that agents today faced with Prisoners' Dilemma situations can resist the lure of free riding without strong external sanctions—enough at least to engage in sustained collective action; and (3) we have a strong belief by many social scientists that free riding is a pervasive human phenomenon, so pervasive that it would undermine most cooperative structures.

I believe that this latter thesis is false and that considerable support exists in experimental evidence from recent work both in social psychology and in what is now termed "laboratory economics."[11] This latter domain of inquiry involves an attempt to model economic and other social processes by means of experiments typical of what is the norm in the natural sciences. By this means, a certain kind of skepticism about the arguments for anarchism concerning cooperation can, in my view, be met and possibly disarmed.

Let me consider briefly three sorts of cases that might undermine the intuitions of statists for whom the free-ride hypothesis is taken as an almost obvious truth. The first is that it is clear on reflection that the urge to free ride cannot be as strong as those statists suggest, for vast areas of human social life support cooperative structures without the coercive threat of centralized authority. Think here of voluntary associations that people readily form or join to support causes of special interest, for example, public television by subscription, local volunteer groups to help the aged, charitable donations by individuals, and an array of cooperative community tasks. Indeed, it is reasonable to conjecture that motivations to cooperate in social life may be sometimes destroyed by government interference in the production of those goods.

Consider now work of a more scientifically respectable nature in social psychology. Quite a number of studies in carefully controlled experiments yield results that are in conflict with the free-ride assumption. A large body of literature is compatible with the view that the operation of prosocial motivations in persons persists in many instances where a free-ride advantage can be obtained without the risk of detection. One experiment—among many in the current literature—is the following example, which I dub the "wallet experiment" of Hornstein and his associates:[12] In these trials, wallets containing a small sum of money were scattered around New York City on a daily basis, with minimal details about the owners enclosed (name, address, telephone numbers, etc.). Common sense might have supposed a low return rate, given the opportunistic possibilities available to those who found them. The results of these experiments were that in some situations unexpectedly high rates of return were recorded, far higher than would be assumed by the perception of human nature inherent in the free-ride assumption. Such very surprising results have been replicated in different experimental designs by social psychologists, results that confound free riding and self-interest predictions.

Let me now turn to a final example. Since anarchist arguments against the statists turn on the statists' use of the Prisoners' Dilemma game in formulating the public-good problem, we might render the statist case that much more implausible if we were able to show that the prediction of free riding could be cast in doubt in a realistic model of real players in empirical tests that mimic Prisoners' Dilemma versions of the public-good case. The anarchist case could be advanced if we were able to test the extent to which humans can sustain voluntariness and cooperation without coercion. Statist theories predict free riding where the anarchist theories of the sort we have advanced suggest the real possibility of stable cooperation. It is here that I believe experimental arguments can help if the anarchist case is to be freed of charges of a merely romantic and unrealistic utopian attachment to the possibility of cooperation.

Consider what the statist might be inclined to suggest as the best prediction in the following variation on the public-good game that I mentioned earlier, between A and B. Imagine that both are issued 100 tokens each for each of ten successive periods of play. The particular scenario they face is this: on each round of play, each may choose either to place all his or her tokens into a private account or to place his or her set of tokens into a joint investment account that yields a return proportionate to the sum total that is in the amount jointly invested. Each player makes his or her decision at each stage, ignorant of the current choice of the other player. Let us suppose that there is a return to each player proportionate to the sum of tokens placed in the joint account, say, 7 cents for each 10-token unit. Whether one contributes or not, one is entitled to the proportionate share of the returns in the joint account. In addition, each token left in the private account yields 1 cent.

It is obvious that if A chooses to play the cooperative strategy of putting all his tokens into the joint venture and B does the same, each will obtain as gain $(0.7) \times (100 + 100) = 140$ cents. If A plays the cooperative strategy and B goes for defection, then A nets 70 cents and B nets $100 + (0.7) \times 100 = 170$ cents. Given the symmetrical situation, the numbers are reversed if B cooperates and A defects. It should be clear that this particular model is in fact an instance of a Prisoners' Dilemma, with a payoff structure given below.

	B cooperates	*B does not cooperate*
A cooperates	140¢, 140¢	70¢, 170¢
A does not cooperate	170¢, 70¢	100¢, 100¢

Figure 3

The model clearly mimics the public-good problem and is amenable to empirical testing. The mechanism described above is one of a number of voluntary contribution mechanisms that have been devised to test the theoretical prediction of free riding. In fact, it is an instance of a widely used scheme originated by Mark Isaac, James Walker, and Susan Thomas.[13]

What outcome would one suppose to be likely, given that the above public-good game were played once only, or if it were replicated ten times? Statists who ordinarily accept the standard account of Nash equilibrium as the legitimate game solution predict that in the one-shot game, both parties will select their noncooperative strategies. Some even argue that in the tenfold repetition of the game where the finite duration is known to both A and B, a backward induction argument predicts a use of the noncooperative strategy by both players on all rounds.

What has been the result of study of empirical trials of these designs? Contrary to the view of the defenders of the free-ride hypothesis, the results do not, for the most part, support the claim that free riding is pervasive. Rational choices by real agents give support neither to free riding in the one-shot Prisoners' Dilemma game nor to finite iterations of those games.[14] Indeed, the Nash prediction of zero cooperation is disconfirmed in many such studies and under several variations of the conditions under which the games are played. For instance, the noncooperative Prisoners' Dilemma game may be played with absolutely no communication or with some allowable preplay communication where "cheap talk" may be permitted, that is, talk that might be useful to both players but that does not bind them into any preplay agreements.

Conclusion

Evidence such as that described above speaks against the statists' view that human cooperative propensities are slight and thus undermines their view that the anarchist defense of the possibility of cooperation resides solely in analytic arguments. Of course, given the very experimental nature of the more recent work, anarchists may have to confront another objection to any result we might obtain on such experiments, especially if they prove unfavorable to statists' overall hopes. In experimentation in the natural sciences as much as in the social sciences we confront the "Duhem-Quine" problem: are our results delivering genuine phenomena, or are we witnessing in some subtle way the consequences of our research design? I believe that there is no certain response to this possibility except to say that replication and variation sometimes reveal the existence of stable phenomena, and the real possibility of cooperation is one such. In summary, both the analytic and the empirical game-theoretic arguments—at least when deployed together—provide a strong case against statists and a challenge that has not yet been fully met.

Notes

1. For a discussion of various ways of understanding public-good problems that may not be Prisoners' Dilemmas, see, for example, Jack Hirschleifer and John Riley, *The Analytics of Uncertainty and Information* (Cambridge: Cambridge University Press, 1992). The formulation that is employed here I learned from William Riker and Peter Ordeshook, *An Introduction to Positive Political Theory* (New York: Englewood Cliffs, 1973).

2. A. W. Tucker is the late Princeton mathematician who invented the original story behind the Prisoners' Dilemma game that has spawned a vast literature in ethics and politics.

3. See John Harsanyi, *Rational Behavior and Bargaining Equilibrium in Games and Social Situations* (Cambridge: Cambridge University Press, 1988).

4. The notion of a Nash equilibrium can be defined in very precise mathematical terms. My characterization follows that of John Harsanyi in using the idea of best reply because of its intuitiveness in explaining the ideas of both uniqueness and stability. An equilibrium solution can be characterized as a pair of best-reply strategies, one for each player in the game. The Nash equilibrium concept is of central importance because Nash proved that every noncooperative game has at least one equilibrium point in terms of mixed or pure strategies.

5. Robert Axelrod, *The Emergence of Cooperation* (New York: Basic Books, 1984).

6. See Michael Taylor, *Anarchy and Cooperation* (London: John Wiley & Son, 1976), and his further work, *The Possibility of Cooperation* (Cambridge: Cambridge University Press, 1987).

7. For more careful statements of the folk theorems and of the important variants on repeated games, see, for example, Robert J. Aumann, "Repeated Games," in George R. Feiwel, ed., *Issues in Microeconomic Theory and Welfare* (Albany, N.Y.: SUNY Press, 1985), 209–42, as well as Sylvain Sorin, "Repeated Games with Complete Information," in Robert Aumann and Sergiu Hart, eds., *Handbook of Game Theory* (Amsterdam: North Holland, 1992), 71–107. The term "folk theorem" has stuck because the result of the folk theorem has been known to game theorists for quite a long time, though no one has claimed to be its discoverer.

8. The problems here would take us far afield from what needs to be established for present purposes, but for interesting critiques of the status of the Nash solution as the source of a rational solution to any noncooperative

game, see David Kreps, *Game Theory and Economic Modeling* (Oxford: Oxford University Press, 1991), and Ken Binmore, *Fun and Games* (Lexington, Mass.: D. C. Heath, 1992). For important ramifications for the study of rationality and collective action under different modeling situations, for example, where the players make a finite and known number of plays, see David Kreps, Paul Milgrom, John Roberts, and Robert Wilson, "Rational Cooperation in Repeated Prisoner's Dilemma," *Journal of Economic Theory* 27 (1982): 245–52.

9. See Michael Hechter, "Comment: On the Inadequacy of Game Theory for the Solution of Real World Collective Action Problems" in Karen Schweers Cook and Margaret Levi, eds., *The Limits of Rationality* (Chicago: University of Chicago Press, 1990), 240–49.

10. For an interesting discussion, see Michael Taylor, *Community, Anarchy, and Liberty* (Cambridge: Cambridge University Press, 1982).

11. The methodology of "laboratory economics," or experimental economics, gained its initial impetus from early pioneers such as Vernon L. Smith, who argued that many economic theorists paid too little attention to experimentation. He proceeded to construct experimental tests of economic theories. See Vernon L. Smith, *Papers in Experimental Economics* (Cambridge: Cambridge University Press, 1991).

12. Harvey Hornstein, Elisha Fisch, and Michael Holmes, "Influence of a Model's Feelings about His Behavior and His Relevance as a Comparison Other on Observers' Helping Behavior," *Journal of Personality and Social Psychology* 10 (1968): 220–26.

13. The testing of free riding in a variety of situations has been the subject of numerous experimental studies in the last twenty-five years. A classic study is Vernon Smith, "Incentive Compatible Experimental Processes for the Provision of Public Goods," in V. L. Smith, ed., *Research in Experimental Economics*, vol. 1 (Greenwich, Conn.: JAI Press, 1979). Many of the studies use the Isaac-Walker-Thomas mechanism or some variant of it. See Mark R. Isaac, James M. Walker, and Susan H. Thomas, "Divergent Evidence on Free Riding: An Experimental Examination of Possible Explanations," *Public Choice* 43 (1984): 113–49. For examples of alternative mechanisms, see, for example, Thomas R. Palfrey and Howard Rosenthal, "Testing for Effects of Cheap Talk in a Public Good Game with Private Information," *Games and Economic Behavior* 3 (1991): 183–220.

14. An analysis of many of the results of these experiments does not at all show that free riding never occurs; rather, that the extent to which it does occur in a variety of settings is far less than would be expected by the theoretically guided expectations of statists. Like all experimental results, these are open to interpretation and criticism.

8

Self-Contradictory Contractarianism

Anthony de Jasay

Can it be rational to will the state?—or to will it away? Why societies need states, and if they do, what kind of state meets their need, remains an evergreen quandary that each generation has been pondering anew, often with some passion. That this should have been the case is perhaps odd, considering that societies and states live much like Siamese twins, or so we perceive them. Our current usage of the two words "society" and "state" is revealing: a society would not be fully fledged, complete, and deserving of the name if it lacked a state of its own. It is probably a sound conjecture that if we nevertheless keep questioning the nature and necessity of the link and keep producing justifications for it, it is because of the discomfort we feel in the face of two of its attributes that seem to clash. One is that this link forces us, sometimes with great severity, to do what we would not freely choose to do and to forbear from what we would choose. It is doing so, not at some finely drawn moral margin, but over a major part of our feasible choices. In particular, it takes the lion's share of individually earned and owned resources and uses them in ways that the individual in question would not have chosen, for otherwise there would be no call for choosing them collectively. The other is that all this seems, in some more or less obscure manner, legitimate: the state's force weighs on us with our consent, and we could not reasonably want to have it otherwise.

The clash, which seems tantamount to masochism in the individual and to a dilemma of coexistence in the group, has been reconciled time and time again by successive versions of social contract theory; yet

137

the discomfort subsists, and explanations-cum-justifications of the state are renewed in ever more sophisticated and elegant forms, lately somewhat clarified by game and decision theory.

Three main reasons tend to be invoked for why the state of nature, in the sense of an attempt by large groups of people to interact to mutual advantage without recourse to a sovereign state, is not viable or is at least wastefully inefficient.

The first is that whenever individual benefits from a common enterprise are not directly proportional to the individual contributions,[1] the assumption of burdens and the distribution of the resulting benefits is potentially conflictual. It is possible for some to get a better deal if others get a worse one. In such situations, the cost and incentive structure of social cooperation has the makings of a Prisoners' Dilemma: it is good if all contribute and benefit, but it is better for each to benefit more and contribute less, and best of all for each to contribute nothing. Rational men dispose accordingly. They do not contribute, do not fulfill their promises to contribute, and default on agreements providing for reciprocal contributions. There will thus be no systematic cooperation among them without the systematic and putatively impartial use of force, or its threat, to enforce reciprocal promises. Any entity that has the will and the authority backed by overwhelming force to perform this function is a state. (Needless to say, the argument does not imply that a state is, nor that it can in theory or in practice possibly be, limited to this function.)

Under the same heading, it is also said that if agreements could not be enforced, then there also could be no agreement on how to divide the fruits of cooperation and division of labor. Income distribution is a function of factor ownership; unless property rights in (nonhuman) factors of production are first agreed, the distribution of the surplus because of cooperation is subject to a bargaining problem, which may not be soluble. Before cooperation, the division of labor, and "the market" become possible, therefore, the state must define property rights, that is, decide who owns what.[2]

The second reason calling for the state is that if, in spite of the first reason, cooperation is nevertheless possible, then so is free riding on the back of it, and both burdens and benefits will be "unfairly" distributed unless the state prevents this.

The third reason that is frequently cited, though no rigorous argument supports it, is that even assuming systematic and universal cooperation, successful bargaining about the resulting surplus, and no free riding in the ordinary sense, a distribution of net benefits could still emerge that may not be just or, since the justice of distributions is in the eye of the beholder and cannot be ascertained in the same way as matters of fact can be, would not be felt just by a substantial part of society. This would put sustained cooperation in jeopardy. To save it, the state must—and only it can—bring about the redistribution that engenders the required degree of social cohesion.

Only the first of these reasons is really decisive. The case for the necessity of the state, derived from rational choice theory alone, stands or falls with it. The others, and their numerous progeny that crop up in political agendas, are either derivatives of it or, if they have independent status (e.g., problems of fairness), are not intersubjectively valid. If the first reason for the state does not hold, it must generally at least be possible, though not assured, to realize mutual advantage and overcome social dilemmas (*n*-person games whose dominant equilibrium is Pareto-inferior, for example, the "war of all against all," or the "tragedy of the commons") by agreement. For the divergence between what is rational for any individual player and for all the players taken collectively springs from the irrationality of relying on mutually beneficial reciprocal promises if it is indeed the case that breaking the promise secures a better outcome ("payoff") for any party, whatever the other parties to an agreement may choose to do. Contracts, then, are never willingly honored. Now, if promises are kept and agreements do bind, any collectively rational outcome, that is, any interaction whose effect, including any negotiable externalities, is at least weakly Pareto-superior to its next-best alternative can ultimately always be brought about by a contract whose execution is assured, that is, one which it is individually rational to conclude.

The only interactions that could not be contracted for and required the intervention of the state would be ones whose effects on the parties were Pareto-noncomparable, good for some but bad for others. Here, the state would be needed, not because contracts do not bind, but because if they do bind, the prospective losers would refuse to enter them. Imposing the Pareto-noncomparable solution just the same by the threat of force is to be deemed good, to be carried out and commended, if the bad of the losers is deemed smaller than the good of the gainers from the interaction. This is, of course, not a question of fact, but a value judgment calling for, and intended to justify, controversial political action. It may have merit, but it is not intersubjectively defensible.

If contracts do bind, however, it is never very obvious why any change that is Pareto-superior should not become the equilibrium solution of a cooperative game, why the costliness ("transactions cost") of such solutions should be an obstacle as long as they still yield a net benefit that is divisible, and why coercive arrangements requiring the maintenance of a state are expected to be, all in all, less costly and more efficient than voluntary ones. Whichever way we turn the various supports that have been provided for the body of theories that explain why it is rational to have the state, only the problem of keeping promises is crucial and indispensable.

*   *   *

> Thus bridges are built; harbours open'd; ramparts rais'd; canals form'd; fleets equip'd; and armies disciplined; every where, by the care of government, which, tho' composed of men subject to all human infirmities, becomes, by one of the finest and most subtle inventions imaginable, a composition, that is, in some measure, exempted from all these infirmities.

In thus ending the famous passage of the Treatise where two neighbors agree to drain a meadow, Hume certainly does not seek to belittle the blessings of government,[3] nor does he directly rule out the idea that its invention, even if in historical fact it was not, *could* have been inspired by the good its subjects expected to reap from their subjection to it and the harm they trusted it to protect them against. His "Of the Original Contract"[4] is not really concerned with what could or could not have been agreed, but rather with what was not—a flank attack to which contractarianism, with its "as if" reasoning, is arguably not vulnerable. More central and more deadly to the theory of the state as an instrument that rational men would have chosen is his account of what comes first, the possibility of binding agreements or the state as their enforcer.

This is the parting of the ways between Hobbes and Hume. The latter is categorical in asserting that the great enabling conditions of civilization are prior to the state, rather than being interdependent with it, let alone being brought about by it: "the stability of possession, its translation by consent, and the performance of promises . . . are, therefore, antecedent to government."[5] Nothing in Hume suggests that political authority, however fine and subtle an invention it may be, is one that rational men would will and could not reject on pain of ceasing to be rational. On the contrary, he has no doubt that obedience to the government is the effect, and not the cause, of justice, where justice is defined as the due performance of promises;[6] yet, if agreements bind prior to the state, how can the imperative need for it arise?—as distinct from the question of how states in history actually arose, and why they are obeyed once they have arisen.

For Hume, the evidence shows state power to be exogenous to society, springing "from quarrels, not among men of the same society, but among those of different societies";[7] it originates "in usurpation or conquest,"[8] is obeyed by habit and domesticated by continuity. There is evidence to show neither that it is endogenous nor that it is an indispensable element of any viable society. If there were evidence, or if deductive proof were possible, social contract theory would long ago have become uncontroversial, a stagnant backwater.

In fact, we have no firm clue to what good the state is a necessary condition of. If, for rational men, keeping onerous promises is dominated by breaking them, it could follow that some kind of protostatal authority is needed for a benign social order, but the premise of promise breaking is neither a conceptual truth residing in the nature of promises nor entailed in expected utility maximization or any other, perhaps less demanding, form of rationality. It is contingent on the facts of the case, and inferences from it may grossly fail to hold in the most prevalent and important social settings. It is an empirical fact that the state does stand ready to enforce onerous promises of a certain ("legal") kind; hence, the question of "anarchic" compliance does not arise, and if hypothetically it did, it could not be answered. It cannot sensibly be argued that the reason why the state enforces certain promises is that otherwise they would be broken, for we can only speculate about what would happen if there were no state (or, as in certain societies where it has recently collapsed, there were just the memory of one, preserved in broken-down institutions, lost virtues, and perverted social habits). We do see a historical regularity—one state to one society most of the time—but it would be abject functionalism to believe that this proves anything about the necessity or efficiency of the link between them. It is on the strength of this historical conjunction that many inductive claims about the state as a defining feature of civilization have been advanced. They are worth what induction is worth. Failing a more compelling deductive ground, Hume's step of conceding legitimacy to the state on conventional grounds is conceding plenty.

Contractarian theory is vastly more ambitious, seeking as it does to find a ground for legitimacy that, if established, would be nearly unassailable, without having to concede anything to resigned acquiescence, unthinking convention, and force of habit. Its ground is that since a possible society endowed with a state can be shown, on commonly agreed criteria of rationality, to be preferable to all other possible ones that lack a state, it is as if the society-cum-state had been chosen by unanimous rational agreement. If this argument stands up, it is of course immaterial that it has not in fact been chosen, but by courtesy of exogenous events has helpfully arisen in time, without having to be chosen in the first place.

To sustain such an audacious argument is to go out on a long limb. Attempts to see whether it will break have not, I think, been well fitted to the purpose. Such attempts have tended to find that it will bear, variously, a liberal, a Lockean, or a minimal state. These findings presuppose the possibility of agreement and then find a plausible set of terms on which to agree. To presuppose the possibility, however, is to suppose the hardest logical test already withstood. Testing the limb one more time, without this tacit presupposition, is the main object of the present essay.

*   *   *

Curiously enough, at the base of contractarian theory we find no such presupposition. On the contrary, it is the very impossibility of agreement that creates the need for agreement—a paradox whose putative resolution along the road bears watching. The base is formed by Hobbes's two cardinal propositions. The first asserts that though it is better for all to have peace, it is better still for each to invade the property of the other, with the result that all will be at war—a recognizable Prisoners' Dilemma situation, where the individually rational choice leads to a collectively irrational outcome. The second proposition is that mutually contingent promises are irrelevant and might as well not be made: "covenants . . . are vain breath." Without the second proposition, the first would lose its effect, for Prisoners' Dilemmas could always be evaded by mutually agreeable binding agreements.

Since all are aware of the force of the second proposition, and since the outcome, peace, which it renders inaccessible, is at least weakly preferred by each (i.e., "collectively rational") to the accessible equilibrium outcome, war, it is individually rational for all to reach for what appears to be an obvious instrument obviously within reach that will render accessible the peace that is collectively rational.

This instrument, the sovereign state, may be specified in the Hobbesian or the Lockean manner; the former deals with the necessary and the possible, the latter with the desirable and the commendable. These differences need not concern us at our level of inquiry. Whichever specification is adopted, enough features remain in common for the instrument to qualify as a state—to put it briefly, the common consent to found one if it does not yet exist, and to accept it as legitimate if it does.

*   *   *

This argument is going too well and too fast for its own lasting good and could do with a mild challenge and a brief halt before proceeding. For it may be questioned whether, in the Hobbesian paradigm and its diverse formulations, it is really individual rationality that opposes the collective one and must be overridden or rather its lack or its submersion under the weakness of will and the strength of the passions. The latter, in particular, is a widely favored reading of Hobbes.[9] Like many of the other classics, Hobbes's theory contains inconsistent elements. His reasoning exposing the "Foole," in particular, thoroughly undercuts the whole case he makes for wanting and accepting a sovereign. Since the Foole is demonstrably irrational or at least a fool, and since it is demonstrably best for each, individually, to respect "covenants without the sword," rational men can freely covenant with one another to keep the peace or jointly to adopt any other cooperative strategy they see fit; they have no use for the Leviathan unless it is to protect them from irrational ones and fools; but wouldn't that be cracking nuts with a steam hammer? I shall leave this question to one side for now.

Other inconsistencies, though of lesser import, are more obscure. Jean Hampton painstakingly explores most of them.[10] One, the role Hobbes sometimes assigns to the passions, however, can bear some further observation. It seems to me a mistake to equate the Hobbesian "passions" of fractiousness, eminence, and glory seeking with irrationality and to oppose them to the other, presumably rational, Hobbesian project of preemptively invading another's property as the best strategy for self-preservation. Glory, eminence, and self-preservation are alike in that they all function as final, noninstrumental ends. (If they could be shown not to be final, we could always put in their place the even more final ends with respect to which they were supposedly functioning instrumentally and carry on from there.) Final ends are all "passions" in the sense of being noninstrumental. They are neither rational nor irrational. If reason had any grip on them, they would be seen not to be final; they would be unmasked as instrumental. Reason, "the slave of the passions," can only guide practice with reference to the ultimate objectives the practice is intended to attain. It operates in the form of a hypothetical imperative: *if* this is your "passion," *then* do such-and-such. It does not dictate action with reference to itself; it must ultimately refer to something that is a datum for, and beyond, reason. It thus dictates the course of action that best leads to the satisfaction of such "passions" as govern people's ordering of available alternatives. Reason does not dictate what "passions" it is rational to have.[11] Both glory seeking and self-preservation can be perfectly consistent with the choice of "warre,"—or not, as the empirical case may be. "Warre" would be irrational, not if it were motivated by glory seeking or some other passion, but if it failed to assuage the passion in question.

If rationality can, however, dictate either "warre" or peace or perhaps a mixed strategy between them, depending on which "passions" it is a slave of, the state becomes, not a universally rational instrument, but a rational instrument with respect only to certain passions and an irrational or a redundant one with respect to others. It would all depend on what passions people do in fact have; contractarianism would not be a consequence of rational choice in general, but of particular contingent facts that may or may not obtain.

What happens to the theory if all act rationally, but some are moved by radically different "passions" from others? Alternatively, what happens if some act rationally given their ruling passions, while others are inconsistent, have disorderly preferences and no ruling passions, and are unpredictable? Would it be rational for one subset of society to want a social contract and create a state, not to serve their own "passions" in isolation, but as a strategic response to the anticipated actions of others motivated by other passions or to the risks of wrongly anticipating the actions of those whose motivation is disorderly and unpredictable? The question has not, to my knowledge, been raised in the contractarian literature. The answer is not obvious and looks many layered; but there is a presumption that creating a state would compound the problem the fully rational subset faced in the state of nature, for suppose that given the sort of "passions" they have, their equilibrium strategy was peace, provided the complement also chose peace, but they did not know what passions, if any, governed the latter's choice. A state controlled by the fully rational subset could ensure that the others did not choose "warre," but a state falling under the control of the others may well allow them to choose "warre" or to introduce an altogether new, unforeseen strategy set where the best available strategy for the fully rational is to submit to gross exploitation by the others or simply to their sheer, pointless, and stupid inconsistencies.

Be that as it may, the contractarian case is not made of such heterogenous material. It deals with a society where everyone is similarly rational and where the preferences of some are not shaped by passions vastly different from those of others. Assuming such a society as part of the theory's initial conditions is both a measure of its ambition and a source of its paradoxical nature.

The archetype as well as the common fount of every dilemma that appears to oppose individual to collective rationality is a master dilemma: the dilemma of contract, whose unique equilibrium solution is nonexecution of the contract, or "no contract." Obvious enough in itself, it is both a Prisoners' Dilemma and an explanation of why all genuine, properly defined Prisoners' Dilemmas, which it is in every player's interest to transform into cooperative games, are condemned to remain what they are, namely, noncooperative games.

In the dilemma of contract, after an exchange of onerous promises, if the first party performs as promised, a rational second party will default on his promise, since he has already had the benefit of the first party's performance and no further benefit would accrue to him from his own performance. Since his promise was onerous, he would in fact lose by not breaking it; moreover, this is common knowledge, and the first party is aware that his performance would be unrequited; therefore, he will not perform in the first place. Since this is common knowledge, too, concluding a contract that both parties know they will both default on would be a pointless exercise.

This has troubling implications. In the commonsense view of the contract, one party's promise is given because the other's is given, and both expect the other to execute the contract. In fact, the will theory of the contract tells us that it is the declared intention of each party to perform as promised, relied on by the other party, that creates the binding contract. If the execution fails or is in dispute, a party to the contract may seek remedy by applying to some third party, who may be an adjudicator leaving enforcement of the judgment to the plaintiff, as in early Roman legal practice, or an adjudicator-cum-enforcer, a sort of mechanic who fixes what got broken, but it is not the latter who creates the contract; it is the parties who do.

Noncooperative game theory, however, shows that rational parties can have no intention to perform and would not do so even if in a pregame setting they had intended to, and any declaration to the contrary on their part is an irrelevance. Obviously, reliance by either party on the promise of the other is absent, but if there is an enforcing agent programmed to remedy default, it is the intentions that become irrelevant, and the declarations relevant, for if they have been made in suitable form, the enforcing agent will exact their execution or the reparation of the consequences of nonexecution. It is as if it was the existence of the agent, or rather the expectation that it will act as it is programmed, that transforms irrelevant gesticulations and pointless exchanges of words into binding contracts.

It is crucial to the understanding of the putative resolution of the dilemma of contract that while an enforcing agent can, under certain conditions, enable the parties to pass from n-person noncooperative to (conflictually) cooperative games by entering into binding commitments, the interaction between the agent and either party remains a two-person noncooperative game. Nothing proves the possibility of a binding contract between the parties and the enforcing agent; there is no meta-agent that could, and would, enforce this contract. If there were, the parties would need a binding metacontract with this meta-agent, to be enforced by a supermeta-agent, and so on forever. An enforcing agent as a tool of the principal parties would presuppose an infinite regress of enforcing agents, each superior to the last.

Either party chooses between two strategies, to perform or to default. Which looks to be the better choice depends, in this game, on the expected reaction of the enforcing agent. The enforcer can act against the defendant only if it is able, either alone or in combination with the plaintiff, to threaten the defendant with sufficient force to make the latter prefer compliance to defiance. In addition, the enforcer must also expect to do better for itself if it enforces than if it does not.

The usual, albeit tacit, assumption of the enforcing agent acting as a programmed automaton, making no strategic choices, has no foundation in rational choice. Making this assumption is to assume away the principal-agent problem. Principals might wish the agent to enforce their contracts (at any rate, plaintiffs would; that defendants would is less evident). But will it comply? The agent has a set of alternative strategies of its own, choosing to enforce only if and to the extent that it finds doing so payoff maximizing for itself. What it expects to be payoff maximizing for itself depends, in turn, on the power of the several principals and their expected payoffs from performing or defaulting, from complying with enforcement or resisting it, and their expected payoffs from making the enforcing agent perform its duties or letting it default. For good measure, it also depends on the mutual consistency or otherwise of the several expectations, which, of course, is generally the case in noncooperative games.

                                   *   *   *

Locked into the first-order, master dilemma that denies them the instrument of the contract and hence the escape into cooperative interactions, state-of-nature societies would, according to received theory, at every turn get caught on the horns of derivative, second-order dilemmas whose individually rational equilibrium solutions were collectively irrational, Pareto-inefficient. There must be, to be sure, countless such interactive situations. In each, however, there are four types of possible outcomes or payoffs for each player, and each player ranks them in the same descending preference order: "free riding," "reciprocal cooperation," "noncooperation," and "sucker." For well-known reasons that we need not rehearse, the dominant strategy of each player is not to cooperate, unless the dilemma of contract is first overcome, binding mutual agreements become possible, and the game is transformed. Some standard types of such dilemmas loom particularly large in the popular consciousness and in political theory.

The oldest is probably the dilemma of tort. Life and limb are vulnerable, and, as Hume charmingly put it, property has the inconvenience of "looseness and easy transition from one person to another."[12] If the players respect each other's bodily integrity and property, and each knows that the others do, all are well off. If one trespasses while the others respect, the trespasser is better off still, and the trespassed-on is worst off. If all take costly precautions against being trespassed on, however, all are worse off than they might be if they all respected, but this is still the best that each can do for himself, given that the others have the same preferences as he and the same strategies are available to them.

The public-goods dilemma is the standard dilemma that has attracted the most attention from economists and social theorists. Suppose a good is to be provided by a public for itself in a manner that (wholly or partly) dissociates the getting of it from the paying for it. This may be, perhaps, because it is too costly to reserve the good for the payers and to exclude access to it by nonpayers or because it is deemed preferable for policy reasons to demand no payment or only little payment. It may then be collectively rational but individually irrational to volunteer to pay. Since this is true of every member of the given public, a public composed of rational individuals only cannot voluntarily provide the good for itself. (This result, if it holds, holds regardless of the characteristics of the good, i.e., of whether it is a "public good" in the textbook sense, with particular properties as regards "excludability" and "nonrivalness." It depends solely on the assumption of full or partial independence of individual contribution from individual benefit.)

In the dilemma of teamwork, the members of the team choose

between working and shirking. If all work, all are well off, but as long as enough others work, each member is better off shirking than working. Each knows that if he nevertheless chooses to work, he will be exploited by the shirkers. The equilibrium solution is that all shirk, and there is no teamwork.[13]

If enough soldiers stand up behind a parapet and shoot at the approaching enemy, a few get shot, most do not, and they can defend the frontier. The national defense dilemma results from the fact that standing up and risking being wounded promises, for each soldier, inferior payoffs to ducking, whether the other soldiers choose to shoot or to duck. It is good if the enemy is repulsed, better still for each if he ducks while the others repulse it, worse if the enemy is not repulsed because too few stand up and shoot at it, but worst of all if one gets shot in vainly trying to repulse it. The dominant equilibrium, therefore, is that everybody ducks and the enemy is not repulsed.

The good Samaritan, at some cost to himself, stops and helps the victim he finds by the wayside. The bad Samaritan passes the victim by and saves the cost of helping him. He reckons that if another Samaritan who passes by is a good one, the victim will be helped and all will be well. If the other Samaritan is also a bad one, neither will help the victim, because being the sucker who stops and helps while the other speeds by to his destination is the worst possible payoff. Since each Samaritan knows this of the others, none will want to be the only one who stops, and there will be no good Samaritan acts, only a Samaritans' dilemma. Any Samaritan who falls victim to misfortune will be left by the wayside, though it would be better for all if they were helped in case of need and could rely on binding contracts of mutual aid.

The escape from every one of these dilemmas is tacitly or explicitly contractual. It leads through the escape from the dilemma of contract, which, in turn, leads through contract enforcement by an agent other than the parties themselves. The agent itself cannot be bound by contract to the parties as its principals if it is true that binding contracts require an agent for enforcement, since the supposition of an enforcing meta-agent to make the agent fulfill his contract would have to rely on the notorious infinite regress. A suggested, and I believe unsuccessful, solution to this impasse is treated below. If the impasse is a genuine one, the interaction of the contracting parties and the agent is a noncooperative game, where each player acts in what he thinks will prove to be in his best interest if every other player acts in *his* best interest.

Severely simplified, the game would follow something like the following schema: There are *n* players—*n*-1 citizens, who are the contract parties, and one state that the citizens have created in the pregame to enforce their contracts. For brevity, the former will be called Principals; the latter, the Agent. In extended form, players make strategy choices at each node of the game tree, and go on to the next node accordingly. At the first node, Principals choose between transferring power to the Agent (handing over their arms to it, giving it access to their other resources) or retaining power. The expected payoffs depend on how many other Principals choose to transfer. If enough do, and the Agent is made strong, "retain" is weakly superior, for the Principals who retained power reap the same benefits from enforcement at future nodes of the game as the ones who transferred but can better resist enforcement against themselves. On the other hand, if not enough Principals transfer and the Agent lacks power, "transfer" is weakly superior, for this strategy at best succeeds in empowering the Agent and, hence, provides for future enforcement. If it does not, because too little is transferred, the Principals can at worst recover from the weak Agent what little they transferred. Under these assumptions, the first node would yield a mixed strategy by which some Principals would transfer power and others would retain it (or where all would transfer some proportion of their power), making the Agent strong enough but leaving all or some Principals with some means of resistance.[14] (How retention of power is achieved need not be specified, but there seems to be a range of possible practices, from the concealment of arms to tax evasion—or at least "tax planning.")

The Agent itself cannot be bound by contract to the parties who are its principals if it is true that binding contracts require enforcement by an Agent not party to the contract. The Agent, if it were party to the contract, could not be relied on to enforce it against itself. As I argued earlier in this essay,[15] the supposition of a binding contract between contract parties and an enforcer entails the supposition of an infinite regress of enforcers (basically the same truth is expressed in the old rhetorical, and vain, question of *quis custodiet ipsos custodes*—who is to oversee the overseers?).

As is to be expected, the same paradox recurs at the level of every derivative social dilemma, whether it is of the tort, public goods, teamwork, defense or Samaritan type. One illustrative instance is Leslie Green's trenchant statement of the paradox in terms of public goods.[16] Instead of dealing with the enforcement of contracts as a precondition of cooperation and vice versa, he deals with authority as a precondition of the capacity to produce public goods and vice versa. Authority, commanding obedience that overrides self-interest, is a (higher order) public good. It must first be generated in anarchy. Anarchy either can or cannot generate public goods. If it can, what need is there for authority? If it cannot, how can authority ever be generated in the first place? Green goes on to argue, I believe plausibly, that what he calls first-order public goods are more likely, because they are less difficult, to be produced in anarchy than is the authority that is supposedly required to overcome the public-goods dilemma and ensure their production. There is, then, no contractual exit from the state of nature: if the state is to be created by contract, it cannot be created, since it is its own antecedent condition.

*   *   *

It is, alas, a mistake to dismiss the finding about the contract as a mistake. Jean Hampton judges it to be such and dismisses it by positing an "empowerment" convention that produces the same performances as would the social contract if it existed and could be enforced.[17] Under the convention, most people come to obey the ruler, making him their Agent. Some people (the Agent's agents) punish transgressors of the convention. If people benefit from the convention, it will not unravel. Since it is in the Agent's interest that it should not, he will wield his power in a manner beneficial to the people.[18] Once the people discover the agency relationship, "they will be able to play their proper role as principal."[19] This is a puzzling assertion: Hampton appears to resolve the principal-agent problem by assuming that it has been resolved—but it has not. For "playing their proper role as principal" is no doubt meant to convey that they fully control the agent, as if he had no objectives of his own or no discretion to pursue them; but if this is the case, what possible interest can he have in the survival of the convention that empowered him? If it is not the case, the principal-agent problem subsists. The agent, once empowered, must have some discretion in using his power, and the problem of enforcing the due performance of his side of the implicit bargain with the people is logically the same as it would be in the putative social contract. The people, by transferring their own power to him, have accepted the role of the "first performer," the ruler is left with the role of the second, and whether we call this game structure a contract or a convention does not change matters. If it is a convention, it is a conflictual one depending on enforcement in the same way as the contract.

Suppose, counterintuitively, that the best payoff of the ruler is some discretionary use of his power but that the second-best payoff, where he totally lacks discretion and acts as an automaton, an inanimate tool in the hands of his principal, is still positive. This is the interpretation most favorable to Hampton. The people as principal must both empower the ruler and ensure that he gets only his second-best payoff, which is no doubt the understanding at the base of the convention.

Enforcement of the ruler's performance in the game is supposedly provided for by a strategy option that the people somehow retain in a metagame or extra game,[20] that is, to depose him if he takes liberties that they did not mean to allow him. It is not clear how, in practice, such an option can be retained. Talk[21] of object-language and metalanguage á la Tarski or umpiring a baseball game and fixing the rules of baseball or laws and rules of recognition á la Hart help not at all in explaining the quite different problem of how power is both transferred to the ruler and retained by the people for the purpose of taking it back from the ruler if he abuses it.

It is, we are assured, a mistake to believe that this is a paradox, for "in modern democracies" the people are the "overseer of their rulers' performances"[22] and can depose them. Let it be noted, in passing, that Hampton's people act individually in letting themselves be "subjugated," but "interdependently"[23] when they depose their subjugator, which rather begs the question of collective action instead of answering it. It is a fallacy of composition to believe that if a group as a whole has some capacity, parts of the group must have parts of the capacity. Be that as it may, however, what the people depose, if they do depose, is a government, to be instantly replaced by another. They do not depose the state and have in normal times no power to do so, nor do they dismantle it partially, nor can they materially change the discretionary powers, opportunities, and rewards that control of the state confers. Whether a change of government will really and lastingly constrain and transform, in a beneficial manner, the way the ruler—any ruler as agent—seeks to enlarge and use the discretion that constitutes the whole point of his wishing to rule is admittedly an empirical question. Neither the history of democracy nor that of other forms of rule abound in encouraging answers, but they are in any case secondary to the more fundamental problem of the rationality of reciprocal promises (whether they are explicit contracts or merely tacit understandings) to perform certain onerous actions nonsimultaneously—a problem of irrational or at least inopportune choice that Hampton denies.

Her convention is depicted as a pure coordination game that all would rather play than not, which it quite clearly is not. This may be the cause of the obscurities in her argument. Some conventions, as is well known, are pure in the sense that both universal violation and universal adhesion are Nash equilibria; violation does not dominate. If enough people adhere, it is best for each and for all to adhere. No one can increase his payoff (reduce his burden) at the expense of other parties to the convention by violating it. Language, the use of money, and the rule of the road are the paradigmatic examples. Some authors, notably David Lewis, reserve the very name "convention" to such games.[24] Other, nonpure coordination games[25] leave room for conflicts of interest. As long as enough people adhere to them, it is better for each to violate than to adhere. Respect for property, "share and share alike," "women and children first," or waiting in a queue are such conflictual conventions, and they unravel unless enforced by some sanction (though, happily, for many essential conflictual conventions the mildest kind of sanctions suffice). Now, in Hampton's empowerment convention there is a sizeable conflict, for the payoff from "obey" is at least weakly dominated by the payoff from "transgress" if others obey and a fortiori if they do not.[26] Since this is so, the strategy her people are supposed to choose at the immediately preceding node of the game, namely, "transfer your power to the ruler," is, to use the technical term, not subgame-perfect, for "retain your power" would have given (better) access to the superior payoff yielded by "transgress." This convention, then, either cannot get off the ground or must unravel if it does. It is characteristically a social dilemma with the same structure as Prisoners' Dilemmas, where the collectively rational solution is individually irrational and cannot be attained. In this, it is no better than the social contract.

*   *   *

My argument must not proceed to its preordained terminus without first coming to terms with a particularly daring quasi-contractarian diversion whose success, paradoxically enough, would have rendered all contractarianism, and hence my critique of it, otiose. I am referring to David Gauthier's widely remarked attempt[27] to show that it is individually rational for people to act in a way demanded by collective rationality in social dilemmas. This way is the abandonment of "straightforward" in favor of "agreement-constrained" maximization, where the latter course yields the Pareto-superior, collectively rational solution for the set of constrained, but not for the straightforward, maximizers. If this is so, it is irrational to remain a straightforward maximizer and make do with the Pareto-inferior solution; hence, constrained maximization will be positively selected, crowding out straightforward maximization.

Since individual rationality suffices to bring about the collectively rational solution, there is no need for an instrument of agreed coercion to enforce it, nor for a further, higher instrument to enforce this instrument's enforcing function, and so on; nor would it make sense to impute to the subjects of a preexisting state a will to obey it as if in compliance with an "as-if" social contract. Consequently, the state could not be legitimized as the necessary condition of equating the individually with the collectively rational. If Gauthier had succeeded, he would have provided one proof of the possibility of ordered anarchy. This is not to suggest, however, that his lack of success—if that is indeed how his enterprise must, or will come, to be seen—is a sign that other possible proofs are not likely ever to be found.

The prevailing view taken by game theorists tended to be that "constrained" maximization is irremediably inconsistent with rational action in games whose strategy sets and payoff structures correspond to the Prisoners' Dilemma. The knockdown argument is the bold one that the statement "Noncooperation is the sole and dominant equilibrium" must be accepted as analytic, implicit in the description of all such games. A cooperative strategy equilibrium, corresponding to constrained maximization, cannot possibly be read into this game description, though it can perhaps be derived by suitably altering the description and transforming the Prisoners' Dilemma into some other game by changing the available strategies, the payoffs, or both. The least radical variation, employed by many social theorists to explain cooperation in conflict, is to introduce iteration: if the game is one in an expected consecutive series of Prisoners' Dilemmas—where at least some of the same players will play in some consecutive games and where players do not know which, if any, game is the last one of the series in which they will play—and some other not too difficult conditions are satisfied, the payoff structure is transformed and cooperation is the best of two or more possible equilibria. Gauthier, however, explicitly rejects (*Morals by Agreement*, 169) recourse to this transformation, for he wishes his thesis to be perfectly general and not contingent on such particular social facts as iteration and so on. He manifestly wants to drive the coach and horses of a cooperative solution through the Prisoners' Dilemma, not replace it with a different and less harsh game, albeit one closer to everyday reality.

Why he thinks he can do this is best understood by first recapitulating the received theory that explains why it cannot be done. A rational player's promise that he will play nicely (cooperatively) is an irrelevance, since he will play nicely or not, regardless of his prior promise, depending solely on which of the two strategies offer the greatest expected payoff. His promise will be ignored by the other rational players, who will never expect him to play nicely, if they see that he must see that the pair of possible payoffs from non-nice play (i.e., best and third best) are both superior to those from nice play (i.e., second best and fourth best), no matter which of their two possible strategies they adopt, the nice or the non-nice one. Consequently, their own strategy choice will not be affected by his prior promise. He will know that this is so, and they will know that he knows. The non-nice strategy will dominate regardless of who promised what and regardless of the dominant strategy being poorly rewarded with the meager third-best payoff.

Obviously, if commitments to strategies could be made binding, each rational player could offer a pregame commitment to nice play in exchange for a like commitment by the others. A contract could be profitably executed, securing for all the highest copossible payoff, that is, the second best. Since the binding commitment cancelled the noncooperative move from the set of two available moves, the game will have changed from Prisoners' Dilemma to, say, social contract.

The charm of Gauthier's alternative to this received theory is that it aims to produce the same cooperative result without creating a contract enforcer. The pity of it is that his way of producing it rests on implausible premises. His rational players, annoyed by their inability to make their promises to cooperate credible to others, will as the next-best thing adopt a cooperative disposition. Personalities are transparent or, what is less of a strain to accept, translucent.[28] Consequently, their dispositions show,[29] enabling others with a like disposition to rely on them; but relying on them does not include exploiting them by not cooperating in turn and leaving them the ungrateful role of sucker.

If Gauthier's players can achieve the mutual cooperation the orthodox theory of the single-play Prisoners' Dilemma shows to be impossible among fully rational beings, mutual dispositions must be able to achieve something that mutual promises cannot. They must be valuable to have. How does one come to have a disposition? Can one simply choose to have one that others will discern? And what does it mean to have one? Clearly, a disposition to act in a certain way is something deeper and more than a discernible frequency, a statistical probability to act in that way. The latter can perfectly well be the result of decisions taken on the merits of each case, if the cases happened frequently to call for acting in that way. A disposition is nothing if it is no more than a tendency to act on the merits of cases.

What, then, is a disposition, if it is anything? I can see only two interpretations; both are possible and could hold together at the same time, though the second cannot hold under instrumental rationality. By the first interpretation, a person can select ends by following a disposition that privileges certain ends over others. More pedantically, his preference ordering of a given set of feasible outcomes will systematically deviate from the preference ordering of the same set by another person, and the systematic deviation can, without risk of contradiction, be imputed to his disposition to favor certain outcomes more than the other person does. If he therefore ranks morally commendable outcomes more highly and "selfish" satisfactions or material riches less highly than do his neighbors, we may say that he has a distinctively moral disposition. This disposition, however, is already incorporated in his payoffs if payoffs are defined as they should be, namely, as maximands, that is, to be chosen according only to their magnitude.

It may then be that a person's "moral" disposition weighs so heavily on his evaluation of outcomes that, for him, the payoff from mutual cooperation is actually greater than that from free riding, first best rather than second best. To say that this is so, however, is to say that for this player the Prisoners' Dilemma does not exist; it has not been resolved, rather it has been replaced by another game with a different, more innocuous payoff ranking. To say instead (as Gauthier seems to suggest that we should) that payoffs are indeed maximands and incorporate all that we are disposed to value or deplore about them but that people with a cooperative disposition will feel constrained by the disposition from maximizing them (albeit with felicitous results if others feel likewise) is to say that these people first rank the payoffs according to their disposition and then are prevented by the same disposition from acting as the payoff ranking dictates. This would be double counting and an incoherent interpretation of "disposition." Gauthier has too fine a brain to mean this.

The second interpretation deals not with ends (payoff rankings), but with means to the ends, with the actions that gain the payoffs. The rational man will, of course, select the course of action that, on the balance of reasons, appears to lead to the best payoff. Neither cooperation nor noncooperation must be privileged as a matter of disposition. One or the other must be chosen on the merits of the case.

Indeed, to have a disposition at all, in the sense of systematically favoring one type of action over and above what the balance of reasons tells us, is to be making a systematic mistake. Deliberately to adopt such a disposition is to seek to be systematically mistaken. As Julian Nida-Rümelin more cautiously puts it, "it is an essential attribute of a rational person to be relatively free from dispositional determinants."[30]

It is bona fide theory to postulate that, as man does not live by bread alone, preference orderings are influenced by moral tastes, dispositions for and feelings of rectitude, honor, pride, shame, or sympathy and also that the prevalence of preferences formed under these influences will, at the end of the day, produce social outcomes that are superior not only in terms of these ennobled preferences, but even in terms of some narrowly material measure, say "wealth," as well as in terms of "selfish" individual interest (whatever that is taken to mean). It is also bona fide theory to explain the world by affirming that people systematically act more cooperatively than they should if they were aiming at the maximum fulfillment of their preferences (however, the latter may be influenced by cooperative or other dispositions) and also that this, too, will lead to superior social outcomes, but it is an inconsistency to uphold both the latter theory and the instrumental conception of rationality that underlies the only positive theory of choice we have. Game theory and social contract theory, as well as a lot else, are built on it. If it were discarded (and Gauthier would probably be among the last to want to discard it), perhaps in favor of categorical imperatives, in order to circumvent the problematic or even paradoxical nature of such institutions as the contract or the state, the paradoxes might be left by the wayside, but this would not make the respective theories less problematical; it would abolish them by ruling out the problem they are intended to illuminate.

*   *   *

What happens to the dilemma of contract if the necessity of enforcement by a third party, extraneous to the contract, is not assumed? Why should enforcement have to depend on the will of an enforcer, rather than on the opposing wills and interests of the parties themselves? Because a third-party enforcer is disinterested and impartial—goes the conventional answer. It is perhaps too quickly taken for granted, however, that it is possible for a supreme enforcer to be disinterested and impartial in the manner in which the conventional view sees these qualities and that these qualities, assuming that they could be had, really represent some kind of necessary condition for contracts to be enforceable. The assumptions seem to me unwarranted. Instead of making them, it is surely better to renew the analysis of the dilemma of contract without them. By rights, it should reveal to what extent, if at all, they are needed.

Recall, first, Hobbes's very proper and logically impeccable insistence, remarkable in an alleged contractarian, that while men contract with each other to found the city, and their contract is enforced by the sovereign, the sovereign is bound by no contract to them and none could be enforced against it. As he puts it in *De Cive*, citizens submit to such bodies as "companies of merchants, and many other convents . . . on such terms as it is lawful for any of them to contend in judgment against the body," but they submit in all things to the city; there are no terms to the submission, and it "is by no means allowable to a citizen [to contend] against the city."[31] The enforcer is not enforced by another enforcer.

The sequel, albeit implicit, is clear and almost writes itself. The transfer of legal power to the sovereign remains "vain breath" unless accompanied by the transfer of material power—arms or a lien over income and wealth. This is, so to speak, a pregame move that opens a noncooperative game (i.e., one without binding contract) between the sovereign and the subjects. There is an underlying intent to exchange—the sovereign is to use the power and consume the resources given up by its subjects to overcome their social dilemmas that would otherwise render their coexistence inefficient at best, intolerable at worst—but this exchange is not itself a contract. Its terms are poorly defined, not binding, and subject to at least partial nonperformance by one side or the other. No side has an advance commitment to, and nor will it do, anything that it is not in its interest to do, either because it is beneficial not to act or because it is enjoined by a threat of the use of force by the other side. Force can be resisted by force, successfully or not.

These alternatives can be translated into net payoffs, and they dictate the choice of mutually consistent equilibrium strategies by the two sides. If the cost of rebellion is high, if the expected ("risk-adjusted") value of its success is not very much higher, and if the very possibility of collective action against the sovereign is problematical (at least in normal peacetime conditions), then two plausible conjectures suggest themselves. The equilibrium strategy of the sovereign will be to use its discretionary power to satisfy its preferences, perhaps by exploiting all its subjects in the service of some holistic end, perhaps by exploiting some of them to benefit others. The equilibrium strategy of the subjects will be, not to resist, but to obey, adjust, and profit from the opportunities for parasitic conduct that coalition forming with the sovereign[32] at the expense of the rest of society may offer.

While a contract-bound contract enforcer, constrained to play a cooperative game, could be a rational social goal if it were not a logical contradiction—and I apologize for suggesting, albeit as a manner of speaking, that it could be rational to pursue an impossible goal—it takes courage to affirm that rational people could unanimously wish to have a sovereign contract enforcer bound by no contract. Such courage is either one of innocence or of the despair that the lack of any other alternative would inspire. The lack of alternatives has all too often been prejudged, typically by the very argument that we are contesting on the ground that it is either self-contradictory (contract can remedy the impossibility of contract) or circular (cooperation requires contract which requires cooperation). It is to this type of argument that we owe the proposition that the state is "prior to the market," because cooperation, including, of course, exchange, presupposes a legal infrastructure. If true, this would establish the impossibility of ordered anarchy. If untrue, ordered anarchy is perhaps possible. The question of whether it is ultimately boils down to the question of the enforcement of mutual promises without a final specialized enforcer. It is to this rock-bottom question that I now propose to turn.

The key is to find the characteristic elements of a noncooperative game where the strategy sets include the exchange of nonsimultaneous performances and where default by the second performer is not dominant. I will take it that a variety of actions—actual and potential, persuasive and punitive, ranging from self-help to mutual aid, and bought or hired help, and including information to be used in the selection of contract partners—can be taken by a potential plaintiff to induce performance and to reduce the probability of default. These actions (and forbearances) have resource and opportunity costs, and I will assume that the probability of default is inversely proportional to the total of such costs that the plaintiff incurs or is expected to incur. In similar fashion, actions to resist enforcement are available to the prospective defendant, and the effectiveness of resistance, hence the probability of default, is directly proportional to the cost that the defendant is expected to incur. The strategies of the parties are independent of any advance promise or commitment made in the past. Each side will do only what its interest, expressed by the expected payoff, dictates. In such a game, for contract to be an equilibrium the payoff from performing must be at least weakly superior to the payoff from defaulting. Several sufficient conditions can be imagined for this to be the case. One is that the expected cost of default is raised high enough by enforcement or its threat; a sufficient condition for this to happen is that the marginal cost of enforcement incurred by the first performer (the plaintiff in the event of default) is seen by both parties as no greater than the expected marginal benefit from specific performance or its equivalent in remedy.

At first glance, this looks a hopeless case, for once a first performer has performed, the (gross) payoff from not reciprocating is equal to the value of the contract, so that it pays the defendant to hang on to this gross payoff and resist enforcement by incurring resistance cost up to the contract value, that is, resist as long as his net payoff from defaulting is not negative. Likewise, it pays the plaintiff to incur enforcement cost up to the contract value, short of which his net payoff from enforcing is not negative. Both enforcement and resistance cost have the same upper bound within the same contract. Up to the upper bound, it looks as though it always pays to match enforcement with resistance, while beyond that it looks as though it never pays to enforce, and this must be common knowledge among the parties. Unless a unit of resources spent on enforcement is more effective than one spent on resisting it or unless the value of the contract is greater to the plaintiff than to the defendant, enforcement and resistance must cancel each other out. The threat of enforcement, then, must lack credibility, and the game reverts to the dilemma of contract. Its equilibrium is "no contract."

The gross and net payoffs change drastically, however, when calculated over a set of more than one contract, and they change in favor of performance rather than default by the second performer, for in such a set, the gross payoff that the second performer can gain by defaulting is at best the same as in a single contract, namely, the value of that contract. This best case, however, applies only to the last contract in the set. If the contract is not the last, the second performer loses some or all of the expected benefits from future contracts that he might have enjoyed if he had not defaulted on the present one, for other parties will either not deal with a known defaulter or will do so only on worse terms. This reduces the upper bound of the resistance cost that he will be willing to pay in order to succeed in defaulting and withstand enforcement. The enforcement cost that the first performer is willing to pay, however, now has an upper bound heightened by the effect that he expects successful enforcement in the present contract to have on the payoffs from future contracts. Reduced future enforcement cost is likely to be one source of this benefit. Only if the present contract is the last in the set will the enforcement cost that it is worth incurring not exceed the value of the contract. The long and short of it is that the opposing interests, evenly matched in the single contract, are tilted in the multicontract case: the resources it pays to spend on enforcement are increased, and those it is worth spending on resistance to it are reduced. This ceases to be true only for the last contract—a concept that is in urgent need of a close inspection.

It is easy to see, and well known from game theory, that if the last contract cannot be profitably enforced, and therefore will not be concluded, by jobbing backward, the parties will see that the last-but-one contract automatically becomes the last one and will not be concluded, and so forth, right back to the first contract, which will not be concluded either, so that the whole set unravels. This, if it were the case, would put paid to the prospects of ordered anarchy.

Reflection will show that there is in the relevant sense never, or hardly ever, a "last contract." In formal game theory, one postulates a probability of some event occurring or not occurring again in a consecutive series of events. A repeated game may be defined in terms of some probability that it will end before the nth repetition. Since each repetition brings n closer, the probability that the next game will be the last one keeps rising (along the lines of Laplace's "rule of succession"), and the strategy appropriate for the last game becomes progressively more attractive; a mixed strategy between performance and default may replace the cooperative strategy equilibrium that is best in an indefinitely repeated series of contracts. A rising probability that the last contract is near must act rather like a belief that the end of the world is nigh and there is no thereafter. If there is no reason to suppose that the world will ever end, however, or the likely end looks too far away for one more step toward it to matter, the parties would mislead themselves if they formulated a crucial determinant of their best conduct in such terms that the imminence of the "last contract" would be looking more probable with each successive contract, bringing a "take all you can while the going is good" strategy optimum ever closer.

If, instead, the parties reason in terms of a probability of the next game (i.e., the next contract) being the last one, and they do not take the probability in question either for high or (what comes to the same thing in the end) for rising, mutual performance is an indefinitely repeated equilibrium if it is an equilibrium in the present.

The next step in refuting the alleged threat to enforcement held out by the prospect of the "last contract" is to consider when a contract is really the last. In a contract where A is the first performer and B the second, if it pays A to incur enforcement cost in excess of the value of the present contract in view of the higher net payoff (lower enforcement cost) that the excess will secure in the next contract, incurring the excess may still pay even if there is no next contract with B, as long as there is a next contract with C or D. For symmetrical reasons, it may not pay B to default and incur resistance costs up to the value of the contract, even if it is his last contract with A, as long as he aspires to conclude another one with E or F. The tilt in favor of enforcement and/or to the detriment of resistance continues to and beyond the last contract between two parties, provided that one party expects to be contracting again with a third party and there is a significant probability of the best strategy of this third party being influenced by the strategies adopted in the earlier contract by the first two parties.

Stepping ashore from the cruise ship, the passing visitor to the exotic port is cheated, sold fake artifacts, and served an overpriced meal by a surly waiter. He leaves without tipping, having no more potent means for getting his own back. Whether he would have left a tip even if he had been better treated is a large question. In any event, he will lend no money to the natives and they will not sell him goods on credit, for everybody's contract with him is a "last contract"; he will not come back again, and if he ever did, he would not be able to tell who he had dealt with the first time round; he knows it, everybody knows that he knows, and if he does not, he should. If he acts as if he did not, however, and enters into "last contracts" where the other party has little interest to deal squarely, it is because it does not matter all that much to the transient tourist whether the deal is square or because he has no clue and no easy means of finding out, while the other party has little to lose if he did find out. Thus we derive the Transient Tourist Theorem: a last contract has a transient tourist as one of the parties, and neither party has much at stake. Unless both these conditions hold, it is unlikely that a contract should be the last within the game-theoretical meaning of the word.

Where parties can expect to deal again or can expect to deal with someone who has dealt or may yet deal with the other party or who is related to him by ties of blood, friendship, solidarity, or expected reciprocity or who has access to the same network of information and hears the same local gossip or trade talk—in short, where the parties live in a real society—a contract between them is most unlikely to work according to the pure logic of the abstract last contract. The latter may figure importantly in Hayek's "great society" with its "extended order" and in the "large group" of anonymous members who act in isolation, unnoticed by others, though it is not clear how, in that case, they can find anyone who will deal with them. It can rarely hold good among people who have names, live in particular places, make a living in particular occupations, have a past, and hope to have some kind of future.

Anyone who has a name, lives in a place, does something for a living—that is, anyone tied into the fabric of a society—would think twice before treating mutual promises as the single-play Prisoners' Dilemma says he must. He would have to look very carefully at all his affairs and tie up all his loose ends before defaulting on a contract, as if it were the last one he will ever enter. Feeling tempted, he would have to consider Hobbes's famous and un-Hobbesian answer to the rather Hobbesian Foole, who thinks that reason may dictate breach of promise and default.

> He therefore that breaketh his Covenant, and consequently declareth that he thinks he may with reason do so, cannot be received into any society, that unite themselves for Peace and Defence, but by the errour of them that receive him; nor when he is received, be retayned in it, without seeing the danger of their errour.[33]

*   *   *

Though it is but the merest sketch, the schema of the expected payoffs from performance and default and of the tilt of repetition that favor enforcement over resistance to it point to the direction where a full-bodied theory of ordered anarchy is most likely to be found. The sketch seems to me sufficient for predicting that the weight-bearing main arch of the theory would prove to be a complex convention, having perhaps unexpected self-enforcing properties about the keeping of mutual promises.

If there were a primary convention that mutual promises are contracts binding the promisors to performance, it would obviously be a conflictual one. As long as enough others adhered to it, it would seem best for each to violate it whenever he thought, with Hobbes's Foole, that the balance of reasons spoke in favor of his breaking a particular promise. Like all such conventions, the one about honoring contracts would therefore be fragile, unstable, and in need of stiffening by an adequate sanction. Whatever vocabulary it uses, it is at bottom always by this unmet need for sanctions that standard political theory explains the passage from convention to law enforced by a sovereign and justifies the replacement of anarchy by the state. We have paid what may seem more than enough attention in this essay to the logical and other difficulties involved in this passage, why it cannot be a contractually agreed one, and why it generates a principal-agent problem of limited government that is intrinsically insoluble, but if the primary convention about reciprocal promising were somehow to be coupled with a secondary convention about enforcing promises, the primary one would gain stability if the secondary one held stable. The two together would function as a single, complex convention that enforced itself as if it were a pure, nonconflictual one that it was in everyone's interest not to violate.

This complex convention, then, must be one that reason never, or hardly ever, dictates to violate. Such would be the case and everything would fall into its proper place without too much further ado if most people saw reasons as mutually compatible Kantian categorical imperatives. Perhaps they ought to, but we have no plausible theory predicting that in fact they will, ex nihilo, without good prior cause in education or experience: morality may well not impose itself. Happily, however, a lesser requirement will do nearly as well to start with. The primary convention will be stable if instrumental reasons seldom, if ever, dictate its violation, that is, if the Hobbesian hypothetical imperative, "If performing brings you a better payoff than defaulting, then perform; if it does not, do not," generally counsels adhering to the convention.

In a set of contracts with nonsimultaneous performances that are interrelated, however loosely, by having some of the same parties and being the object of some common information, the cumulative payoff sum accruing to performers is (at least weakly) superior to the sum accruing to defaulters. From this can be derived the predominance of the maximum of resources that it pays to devote to contract enforcement in the set over the maximum that it would pay to devote to resisting enforcement. This means, putting it summarily, that enforcement must potentially have the upper hand and hold out the more credible threat. Default, therefore, will tend to have the inferior payoff and the threat of resisting enforcement will be less credible.

The sum of the payoffs from performance being greater than that from default (or from a randomly mixed strategy) merely means that performing is collectively rational. This is tantalizing but beyond the reach of voluntary action, unless it is individually rational, too. It is rendered such by the rationality of enforcing any single contract if it is part of an interrelated set and is not the last one.

Collective rationality underlies the behavior norm of the primary convention, "Always perform what you promised in exchange for another's promise." Individual rationality motivates the secondary or satellite convention that takes care of the conflictual character of the primary one: "Always enforce performances due to you" (eventually, "including performances due to others as well, if that is a cost-effective way of enforcing performances due to you"). Accessorily, "Always punish default."

These norms are stated without reference to the cost of adhering to them, since the theory tells us that the costs generally will not exceed what it is worth incurring. I am not dealing separately with adjudication, treating its cost as included in enforcement cost. Although the two functions are separate, or at least separable, the analysis loses nothing by lumping them together, nor would I attempt to prejudge the source of adjudication. It is hard to judge toward what kind of institution the task of adjudication would gravitate within the framework of a convention of honoring and enforcing contracts. Panels of the parties' peers seem a not-unlikely solution, but *pace* Robert Nozick and his "dominant protective agency,"[34] I see no intrinsic reasons why either adjudication or enforcement would naturally end up in the hands of a single agency (or of a few specialized agencies, for that matter). Neither in efficiency nor in impartiality does scale seem to bring increasing returns and monopoly to possess a comparative advantage.

The secondary, satellite convention protects the superior payoff sum justifying the primary one and allows the collectively rational solution, that is, binding contracts, to be realized.

It is important to grasp the sense in which this complex convention is self-enforcing. A typical conflictual convention, for example, "wait in the queue" or "no littering," is stabilized by a satellite convention whose norm is to sanction queue jumpers and litterers, but if sanctioning is costly, it is not clear that it is in anybody's interest to assume the task at his own expense. It is thus not clear that the satellite, enforcing convention is itself self-enforcing. Many such are probably not, and if they nevertheless survive, they do so by depending on binding contracts that reallocate benefits and costs. They may also depend on yet another convention, such as "do your civic duty," sanction queue jumpers and litterers regardless of whether it pays you to do so and without having agreed to do it against due compensation. The contract-enforcing satellite convention, on the other hand, is self-enforcing because it is, most of the time, in the individual contractor's interest to devote such resources (whether his own or borrowed) to the enforcement of his own contract as are adequate to deter default. The primary convention, prevailing over a set of contracts, ensures that adequate resources will in fact be generated and can be made available in case of need. These interdependent functions are all built into the complex convention.

There is no guarantee—there never is—that this theoretical construct would withstand the tests of reality if the occasion for such tests could possibly arise, as no doubt it cannot. Its rival, however, the theory of the state as a necessary condition of contract enforcement and of the solution of social dilemmas, suffers from this disability to a perhaps even greater extent, for how do we test the necessity of the state if we cannot remove it and, ceteris paribus, see what happens? For what it proves, we may recall the prevalence of a respect for reciprocal, protocontractual commitments in primitive societies and for contracts in extraterritorial trade and in international relations devoid of a sovereign enforcer. These are telling us that the construct of conventional enforcement could find a place in a possible world and has at least some outward resemblance to experience.

Having said all this, most of what is needed for recognizing our own much-neglected, belittled, and underused capacity for circumventing (not solving) social dilemmas by binding agreements has been said. Collectively rational arrangements can be reached, if reaching them is worth the trouble, without benefit of states and the constitutions meant to bend them to our service. The whole social order has self-enforcing properties that, like muscles, develop with use or atrophy with disuse. They are imparted to it, in the last analysis, by the self-enforcing properties of the complex convention that upholds contracts. States are an imposition, sometimes useful, sometimes a millstone, always costly, never legitimate, and never a necessity for binding agreements. If they were, it is hard to see how a state could ever be created, as if by agreement, before it existed. Theories that dwell with apparent ease in logic traps of this type in arguing for its legitimacy can be redeemed, if at all, by their placatory qualities only as some lay opium for the people.

Notes

1. The proportionality condition is ambiguous, and purists would say that it is meaningless, unless all contributions on the one hand and all benefits on

the other are homogeneous. This will be the case, for example, if all contribute sums of money and all get back quantities of one and the same good in proportion to the money. If, however, contributions consist of labor, the good, bad or indifferent, clever or clumsy work of the several contributors must first be converted to a common unit, and the conversion is problematical. The same is true of any other contribution or benefit in kind. In perfectly competitive markets, contributions can be compared and measured in terms of their marginal value productivity and benefits in terms of their price. Plainly, however, this solution is not available in every case, and proportionality can at best be a matter of commonsense judgment. The same ambiguity pervades problems of distributive justice where it is often desired to apply some equality postulate, but it is not always clear whether any two magnitudes are equal or not.

2. Unless the state is there to decide this, we are told, "access to goods, services and life itself will be decided on the basis of 'might is right'—whoever is stronger and shrewder will win" (G. Calabresi and A. D. Melamed, "Prosperity Rules, Liability Rules, and Inalienability: 'One View of the Cathedral,' " *Harvard Law Review* [1972], reproduced in S. Levmore, *Foundations of Tort Law* [New York: Oxford University Press, 1994], 251). The view that property relations must be decided by the state and remain ill-defined if they are not is a widely used tacit assumption in many branches of the social sciences, not least by the law-and-economics school. It is warranted by neither theory nor evidence.

If it is true that people in the state of nature cannot make agreed bargains (because their agreements are unenforceable), then they cannot have division of labor, markets, property, and all the rest either, and the argument in the paragraph above is redundant. Its addition to the basic promise-fulfillment and agreement-enforceability argument is double counting. The text by Calabresi and Melamed, unlike many other law-and-economics texts, does not make this mistake. What it asserts is that agreements in the state of nature are possible, but since their terms would be decided by strength and shrewdness, they would be unfair. This, of course, is a matter of opinion and cannot usefully be discussed, except perhaps in very roundabout ways, starting way back from first principles.

3. David Hume, *A Treatise of Human Nature* (1740; 2d ed., Oxford: Clarendon, 1978), 539.

4. In David Hume, *Essays Moral, Political, and Literary* (1748; Indianapolis: Liberty Classics, 1985).

5. Hume, *A Treatise of Human Nature*, 541.

6. Ibid., 543.

7. Ibid., 540.

8. Hume, "Of the Original Contract," in *Essays Moral, Political, and Literary*, 471.

9. Cf. Leo Strauss, *The Political Philosophy of Hobbes* (Chicago: University of Chicago Press, 1952).

10. Jean Hampton, *Hobbes and the Social Contract Tradition* (Cambridge: Cambridge University Press, 1986), chap. 2.

11. For a valuable juxtaposition of the hypothetical and the categorical imperative and the idea of a noninstrumental rationality, see Robert Sugden, "Rational Choice: A Survey of Contributions from Economics and Philosophy," *Economic Journal* 101 (1991): 753–56. Cf. also M. Hollis and R. Sugden, "Rationality in Action," *Mind* 102 (1993).

12. Hume, *A Treatise of Human Nature*, 489.

13. What is one to make of the story of the gang of Chinese workmen straining on a rope as they pull a barge upstream on the Yangtze River? An overseer walks alongside the team, cruelly whipping now one, now another, when they do not pull hard enough. One of the barge's passengers is an American lady much preoccupied by human rights who protests at the treatment the workmen are subjected to. She is told that it is they who employ the overseer and pay him to whip them so that the boat should get pulled to the place where they will be paid.

Is this a story of the contractarian state? One pertinent observation suggests itself: the overseer is no stronger than any one of the workers, let along any subgroup within the team. He has a whip, but they have a rope end, which can hurt almost as much. In addition, even a coalition of the overseer and a subgroup of workers could not profitably subjugate and exploit the rest of the team, because the whole team's strength is required to move the barge at all, hence, no redistribution of effort and no parasitism is feasible. None of these favorable conditions seem to obtain when the team is the whole society and the overseer is the state. One fundamental reason is that the teamwork of pulling the boat has a binary result: the boat either gets pulled to her destination or there is no payoff at all. By contrast, the social product is continuously variable: though some may shirk, something still gets produced as long as others work. There are gains to be had for a coalition of some against the rest, both in the allocation of burdens and in the distribution of benefits.

14. This, one might surmise, is a rational choice-type foundation for the Lockean ideal government and for the right of rebellion, both of which are difficult to understand if only the government is armed.

15. See pp. 146–48, above.

16. Leslie Green, *The Authority of the State* (Oxford: Clarendon, 1990), 147–49.

17. Hampton, *Hobbes and the Social Contract Tradition*, 268–84.

18. Ibid., 275.

19. Ibid., 276.

20. Ibid., 280–83.

21. Ibid.

22. Ibid., 284.

23. Ibid., 283.

24. David Lewis, *Convention: A Philosophical Study* (Cambridge, Mass.: Harvard University Press, 1969).

25. Edna Ullman-Margalit, *The Emergence of Norms* (Oxford: Clarendon, 1977).

26. If "transgress" were not preferred to "obey," would there be any point in empowering a ruler to enforce obedience to norms?—though it might be useful when making a fresh start to appoint a prophet or a judge to suggest what norms we should all willingly choose to obey. In existing societies these choices have mostly been made long ago.

27. See David Gauthier, *Morals by Agreement* (Oxford: Clarendon, 1986). Gauthier's attempt is a double one: to show why voluntary cooperation in apparent Prisoners' Dilemma situations is rational and how rational people would agree to share the resulting cooperative surplus. For the present purpose, I shall ignore the second of these two elements.

28. There is a parallel, though not a meeting, between Gauthier's assumption of a disposition being discernible and the harnessing of "signal detection theory," the reading of minds from visible or audible signs, to advance a hypothesis of rational cooperation in single-play Prisoners' Dilemmas (R. A. Heiner and Dieter Schmidtchen, "Rational Selfish Cooperation in One-Shot Prisoners' Dilemma Situations," unpublished, 1994, and Heiner and Schmidtchen, "Rational Cooperation in One-Shot Prisoners' Dilemma Situations," unpublished, 1994. Cf. Robert Frank, *Passions within Reason: Prisoner's Dilemmas and the Strategic Role of Emotions* [New York: W. W. Norton 1988]). The hypothesis states that if one player forecasts that another will play cooperatively, the latter is more likely to do so. The relation is statistical and does not specify the direction of causation. Does the cooperative intention generate the forecast, or the forecast the intention?

Suppose player A expects player B to cooperate, and he is right for either reason. A can always earn a better payoff by defecting than by cooperating. To make cooperation nevertheless the payoff-maximizing move, A must assume that B's intention, or indeed his decision, to cooperate was dependent on B's correct forecast that A was going to cooperate; B would not have decided to cooperate today if he, A, were thereupon to decide to defect tomorrow.

This solution of the Prisoners' Dilemma follows the strange assumptions of Newcomb's paradox (as James Buchanan has pointed out in a personal communication). Significantly, one of the two players (player B) in Newcomb's paradox is God, who knows today what the other player will do tomorrow. The interaction of the players involves questions of foreknowledge versus free will. Pursuing them would take us far from game and contract theory in general and Gauthier's in particular. Molina of Salamanca proposed a solution, the *scientia media*, that depends on God's foreknowledge of man's will to accept his grace. Man, then, is in some sense free to cause God to withhold his grace, for God has foreknowledge of man's lack of will to accept it.

29. Gauthier, *Morals by Agreement*, 173.

30. Julian Nida-Rümelin, "Practical Reason, Collective Rationality, and Contractarianism," in David Gauthier and Robert Sugden, eds., *Rationality, Justice, and the Social Contract* (Hemel Hempstead, Herts.: Wheatsheaf, 1993), 56.

31. Thomas Hobbes, *De Cive, or the Citizen* (1642; Westport, Conn.: Greenwood Press, 1982), 68.

32. "Coalition-forming with the sovereign" is old-fashioned language imposed by the Hobbesian context. "An alliance of articulate, organized and self-serving groups in control of the state's agenda" calls the rose by another, more modern name.

33. Thomas Hobbes, *Leviathan* (1651; Harmondsworth, Middlesex: Penguin Classics, 1985), 205.

34. Robert Nozick, *Anarchy, State, and Utopia* (Oxford: Blackwell, 1974), 110–15.

9

The Rights of Chickens: Rational Foundations for Libertarianism?[1]

Peter Danielson

Hobbes in, Locke out?

In *The Libertarian Idea*[2] Jan Narveson defends what I call rational libertarianism. The libertarian idea posits individual liberty as the sole political value; "the libertarian thesis is that *a right to our persons as our property is the sole fundamental right there is*" (66). "Following the respectable tradition of Locke," many libertarians defend this morality directly by appeal to moral intuition.[3] In contrast, rational libertarians hope to reach these Lockean conclusions indirectly by working through a Hobbesian contractarian argument. This change in method is appealing. As Narveson points out, moral intuitions are poorly suited to overcome serious conflicts of interests. In contrast, the Hobbesian method builds on the solid—at least social scientifically respectable—foundation of rational choice social theory, known for its realistic assessment of conflict.[4] It offers the philosophically exciting prospect of putting the largest questions of moral and political philosophy—Is it rational to be moral? to accept coercive political authority?—to a simple test: what kind of agents can solve the state-of-nature problem? Narveson thinks that moral agents suffice. Amoral rational agents would reject Thomas Hobbes's authoritarian political solution in favor of a libertarian moral solution to their social problem.

This bold argument—the distinctive contribution of Narveson's

171

book—deserves attention. To focus on it, I grant several key assumptions—the appeal to simple game models of social interaction and the possibility of rationalized moral constraint—and criticize Narveson's main argument in its own terms. I show that by modeling the state of nature as a Prisoners' Dilemma, he begs questions at issue between moral and political philosophy. The Prisoners' Dilemma model abstracts away crucial features found in real situations and required by Narveson's own account of morality. When we construct a game that begins to model these features, the game of Chicken, we find that a libertarian morality of negative rights does not solve some state-of-nature problems.[5] It appears that rational agents still need a state, so contract arguments should reflect this fact. Hobbes in; Hobbes out.

Rationality: States of Nature

The Libertarian Idea begins with Hobbes's state of nature, a social situation where amoral agents could benefit from cooperation but such cooperation is unstable, and argues that such agents would agree to libertarian rights instead of to Hobbes's authoritarian state. How can Narveson start with Hobbes's method and premises and reach such different conclusions? The answer is: there is a moral solution to the state-of-nature problem as Narveson conceives it.

The Prisoner's Dilemma

Narveson addresses the state-of-nature problem with tools derived from the theory of games, an approach that has become widely accepted.[6] More controversial is his use of the Prisoners' Dilemma (PD; see figure 1) to model the state of nature.[7]

	C	D
C	2, 2	0, 3
D	3, 0	1, 1

Figure 1: Prisoners' Dilemma

This game does model many situations in which social cooperation is unstable. For example, consider how it applies to a simple case of exchange.[8] I can give you my potatoes (*C*) or not (*D*); you can give me your wheat (*C*) or not (*D*). Trade is cooperative when there are mutual gains to be had; I want your wheat more than I want my potatoes and conversely for you: each of us prefers *CC* to *DD*. I can cooperate (*C*) by giving you my potatoes, you by giving me your wheat, but I would prefer receiving the wheat and keeping the potatoes (*DC*; I choose to defect while you cooperate). Finally, no trade is better than losing my potatoes and getting no wheat; I prefer *DD* to *CD*.

Social cooperation (the *CC* outcome) is better for both of us than the *DD* outcome. It is also, however, unstable. Each of us prefers to defect, whatever the other chooses. Therefore, unless we can arrange to trade instantaneously or engage in iterated trades, rational agents will end up not trading. In a one-play PD, *DD* is the stable equilibrium. When *D* is a deadly aggressive act, instability is almost certain and rational agents will end up in a state of war.[9] From this Hobbes concluded that rational agents should create an institution, the coercive state, to change the payoffs. In contrast, Narveson builds on David Gauthier's argument for a moral solution to the PD. Following Gauthier,[10] Narveson proposes that agents "re-wire" themselves (or their children) for cooperative self-constraint (145). This conception of moral artifice[11] is a major modification of the marriage of Hobbes to game theory, as agents with the ability so to constrain themselves deviate from the received theory of rational choice. This change is what makes a rational morality possible.

I agree with Narveson that Gauthier's moral solution to the problem modeled by the PD is broadly correct.[12] Very roughly, the solution is to introduce a new conditional strategy, constrained maximization (CM). CM is disposed to cooperate with similarly disposed agents and not to cooperate with straightforward maximizers (SMs). CM can achieve stable mutual cooperation and avoid exploitation by SM. Figure 2 shows that the availability of the CM strategy changes the Prisoners' Dilemma into a simple coordination problem where mutual cooperation is the expected outcome. This is a solution because the constrained maximizers each do better than the straightforward maximizers favored by the received theory of rational choice. Constrained maximization is a moral solution because the result is mutually beneficial and achieved by self-imposed constraint (each CM chooses *C* although she prefers *D*). Let us therefore accept that constrained maximizers can solve the Prisoners' Dilemma.

	C	*D*
C	*2, 2*	*1, 1*
D	*1, 1*	*1, 1*

Figure 2: A Moral Solution

We thus allow that it can be rational to be moral in a Prisoners' Dilemma. While this conclusion is crucial to ethics, it leaves open Hobbes's question about the rationality of the state. A morality that rationally solves some of our social problems (namely, those that can be modeled by the two-player Prisoners' Dilemma) does not answer Hobbes's challenge. We might still need the state for any remaining (now: morally intractable) problems. The bridge between the (minimally) moral and the political is Narveson's main concern: "[T]he relation [of Gauthier's solution] to political structures . . . [is] the main question dealt with in this book" (149). This question requires that we ask, "Is life in general, for essentially everyone, enough like a Prisoners' Dilemma . . . for this model to work?" (146) Narveson answers his question in the affirmative; I disagree. The Prisoners' Dilemma is not the only problem of partial conflict that rational agents face in the state of nature, as we shall see when we consider the evidence.

Better Bled than Dead

Gauthier's solution is good news for rational moral theory; indeed, I shall argue that it is too good to be true. According to Hobbes, an unconstrained agent remains at war with the rest of us. From this Narveson concludes that an amoral agent faces a "battle with what will certainly be the vast majority of" us (181). This second claim, however, does not follow from the first. It does follow that when we are attacked (*D*) we should defend ourselves (*D*) in a Prisoners' Dilemma, but sometimes we are forced to play other games where defense is not rational. I begin with Narveson's own examples.

According to Narveson, the alternative to moralized cooperation is unconstrained predation met by unconstrained defense. This state of war is very costly. On this point Narveson illustrates his argument (177ff.) with pertinent historical examples. He notes that the forebears of today's peaceful and wealthy Scandinavians were aggressive Vikings. Peace evidently pays. This slogan puts me in mind of Neville Chamberlain, who remarked, "In war . . . we are all losers," and, more recently, the Toshiba Corporation.[13] Since peace pays, then it may be rational to conclude "give me peace for our time, and failing that, let me make a profitable separate peace with the warriors."[14] If peace pays, why assume that aggression will be met with organized or even widespread resistance? Narveson cites Cambodia and Afghanistan; he neglects Austria and Czechoslovakia. By appeal to the same sort of impressionistic history Narveson uses, I conclude more modestly that since peace pays, sometimes people resist and sometimes they do not. Correspondingly, sometimes aggression does not pay and sometimes it does.

I hasten to add that Narveson is aware of the increased likelihood that for "sizable groups" aggression may pay (179) and to offer a small-group example of my point.[15] Some years ago I found myself in a Toronto subway car with two hefty "white" male teenagers who began spitting at two Asian female teenagers while muttering racist epithets. Like all the other passengers within sight and sound of this incident (perhaps ten of us), I did nothing. I conjecture that each of us did the rational thing. That is, twelve of us chose peace in our (travel) time and the two toughs chose unresisted aggression. I conjecture that this sort of thing has happened to most of us.[16] Civilized wimps like us are a natural breeding ground for bullies; doves encourage hawks both in small groups and large. These stories are not intended to elicit moral intuitions, but rather to remind us that not all state-of-nature situations result in a war of all against all. Sometimes some of us choose to cooperate even when others do not, resulting in outcome *CD*. (I call this *acquiescence*.) The point is that this should never happen in a Prisoners' Dilemma, where only *CC* and *DD* are accessible to rational agents.[17] If Gauthier is correct, moralized rational agents should reach outcomes *CC* among themselves and *DD* when facing traditional straightforwardly rational agents (who should reach outcome *DD* among themselves). It is never rational to acquiesce in a Prisoners' Dilemma, but as a matter of fact, acquiescence is not uncommon. There are two possible explanations for this deviation between the prediction of the model and reality. Either people are irrational or their situation is not a Prisoners' Dilemma.[18]

Chicken

I believe that the second explanation is far more plausible: acquiescence is rational in some situations. As M. Taylor and H. Ward[19] and A. de Jasay[20] have argued, if it is irrational to allow one-sided defection in the PD, yet we experience free riding in the world, this shows that the PD does not model our social situation. In particular, when we see that the Prisoners' Dilemma is not the only model of partial conflict, we understand how it could be rational both for one player to defect and for the other player to allow the first to aggress. In the Prisoners' Dilemma each player considers acquiescence to be her worst outcome, but we do not always have such preferences. For most of the second half of the twentieth century most citizens of "captive nations" evidently preferred to be red than dead. I preferred to be intimidated by bullies rather than to be beaten or humiliated by them. When each of us prefers acquiescence (*CD* or *DC*) to joint defection (*DD*), we find ourselves in a game called Chicken (see figure 3).

	C	D
C	2, 2	1, 3
D	3, 1	0, 0

Figure 3: Chicken

In the Prisoners' Dilemma *DD* is the equilibrium outcome because each player has a dominant strategy, *D*; but in Chicken, if you choose *D*, I do better to acquiesce by choosing *C*. There are therefore two equilibria in pure strategies: *CD* and *DC*. Morality and rationality seem to diverge, the former directing us to *CC* and the latter to one-sided acquiescence and domination.[21] Rather than fighting (at *DD*), it is rational for one of us to switch to unilateral disarmament (the *C* strategy). If either is a hawk (who chooses *D*), then the other should choose to be a dove (who chooses *C*). I shall put off the question of morality until the section titled "Morality: Enforcement and Rights"; my point in this section is to argue that the facts of tyranny and acquiescence show that Chicken models some state-of-nature situations better than does the Prisoners' Dilemma.

I should add that I realize that Chicken is a difficult model.[22] In contrast, the Prisoners' Dilemma makes clear the partially opposed vectors of conflict and cooperation and facilitates a rational choice argument for morality. Clarity and tractability, though, are not arguments for choosing a model. We cannot select models because we understand and have solutions for them. Chicken better models situations where we find neither mutually beneficial cooperation nor a state of war, but one-sided acquiescence instead.

Refinements

This section clarifies and refines the argument for using Chicken rather than the Prisoners' Dilemma to model aggression in the state of nature.

Many Players

Disputing Chicken versus the Prisoners' Dilemma may seem to miss something more important. Any real state of nature contains many agents; why suppose that either of these two-player games could adequately model multiplayer situations? We must accept this point; better models are preferable. Nonetheless, there are two reasons to press our case for (two player) Chicken over the PD. First, as evidenced by the impact of the PD in the field, moral and political theory needs and can learn from even grossly simplified models. Second, and more important, given agents capable of conditional strategies appropriate to multiplayer situations, multiplayer Prisoners' Dilemmas will have the strategic structure of Chicken, so Chicken will be the better simple model of these situations than the PD.

Consider an example of a five-player PD; each player gets the original payoffs (see figure 1) from his interaction with each of the four others, but none can discriminate cooperative from noncooperative partners individually. Each can distinguish only degrees of group cooperativeness: four cooperate, three cooperate, and so on. Each can choose a threshold strategy to cooperate, given some degree of group cooperativeness; call these *Coop-4*, *Coop-3*, and so on. *Coop-4* demands that all the others cooperate; *Coop-3* allows one of the others to defect.[23] In this way, the higher the threshold T in *Coop-T*, the less disposed the agent is to cooperate.

Figure 4 shows the situation where would-be cooperators (playing row) are choosing a strategy to deal with one player's (column) temptation to defect.

	C	D
Coop-3	8, 8	6, 12
Coop-4	8, 8	4, 4

Figure 4: Five-Player Prisoners' Dilemma

If the cooperators choose *Coop-4*, they make D unattractive, since column's choice of D makes him worse off; but it also makes the would-be cooperators worse off than they would be had they tolerated his defection, by choosing *Coop-3*. Therefore, the choice of *Coop-4* is a threat, because the punishment must be inflicted on three would-be cooperators, and the game induced by the availability of these conditional strategies has some of the strategic structure of Chicken.[24] Finally, this mapping of multiplayer PDs onto two-player Chicken is asymmetrical; conditional strategies do not turn multiplayer games of Chicken into a PD.

Pure Conflict

I have suggested Chicken as a model for aggression in the state of nature. This suggestion might be misleading in two ways. First, it might seem stronger than it actually is. Chicken does not model all conflicts; in particular it does not model pure conflicts of interests. In Chicken, as in the Prisoners' Dilemma, interests are only partially opposed; we can both do better at *CC* than *DD*. Unlike the PD, however, *DC* and *CD* are also mutually better than *DD*, so our interests conflict over these three outcomes.

External Preferences

Finally, the game of Chicken might suggest that the opposed preferences are caused by special external preferences. This is true in dramatic instances of the game, where the prize is superiority over the opponent who "chickens out." Such motivations, including envy, honor, or spite, can make a partial conflict game into a pure conflict game, as Narveson correctly points out. (See his discussion of "the 'nasty' theory" of motivation on p.136f.) First-order, mutually disinterested preferences can, however, create a game of Chicken; compare Gauthier's discussion of nuclear deterrence.[25] We need not assume extra sources of conflict.

Morality: Enforcement and Rights

I have argued so far that Narveson suffers the common affliction of seeing the world as a Prisoners' Dilemma. It is not always so, nor is it clear how Narveson can use Gauthier's moral solution to the Prisoners' Dilemma for situations that require a different strategic model, namely, Chicken; but it may be possible to extend Gauthier's solution to Chicken. In fact, Narveson stresses two features of morality, enforcement and rights, that appear specially relevant to Chicken. Therefore, in this section I focus on Narveson's libertarian extension of Gauthier's solution and argue that the focus on enforcement makes

Chicken unavoidable and that a morality built on negative rights is particularly inadequate to the problem that Chicken presents.

Enforcement[26]

Gauthier's account of constrained maximization stresses the psychological aspect of constraint. Narveson makes social enforcement equally important.

> Moral rules *overrule* us. . . . What does this mean? . . . First, that a conscientious individual, when confronted with a choice between what morality tells her she must do and what she might otherwise like to do, will do what morality says. Somehow, we must be capable of having moral motives that are stronger than any inclinations to the contrary. And second, we may point to the social aspect. If someone proposes to do something wrong, even though it may be highly beneficial to the doer, the *rest of us* should exert ourselves to steer him back to the . . . path prescribed by morality (124).

Roughly, enforcement is a social analog of counterpreferential principles. We should notice, incidentally, that social enforcement and self-constraint are also complementary. For example, in the limiting case of the iterated Prisoners' Dilemma, enforcement by others using the tit-for-tat strategy obviates the need for any moral self-constraint.[27] This suggests that we ask about the converse possibility. Are there cases where there is no need for social enforcement? I think that there are. Indeed, the one-shot Prisoners' Dilemma itself leaves no room for enforcement, strictly speaking. Recall that I do better defecting on a defector than cooperating with her (because D is dominant). Enforcement by defection in the Prisoners' Dilemma never calls for any exertion on the agent's part because it never costs anything. In the Prisoners' Dilemma moral agreement is self-enforcing in this sense: no new sanctioning motive is needed.[28] In general, unless $DC > CC$ there is no need for self-constraint, and unless $CD > DD$ there is no need for a special moral motive to drive enforcement. In the one-shot Prisoners' Dilemma, defecting on a defector does not hurt us; the PD calls for self-constraint but not social enforcement.

Enforcement is needed where joint defection (DD) is worse than one-sided cooperation (CD), that is, in Chicken. Narveson's addition of enforcement to his conception of morality is motivated only for situations with Chicken's strategic structure. Therefore, Narveson cannot dismiss my focus on this situation. Enforcement is important because rational agents are tempted to acquiesce to amoral threats just as they are tempted to defect. If the state of nature is never structured as a game of Chicken, Narveson's stress on the enforcement of morality lacks a point.

Moral Failure

Can moral agents use enforcement to solve Chicken? I now turn to the question of whether Gauthier's moral solution to the Prisoners' Dilemma can be extended to Chicken. This will be an extension because in the PD a moral agent need only promise *C* if *C*, without also threatening *D* if *D*. (There is no need to threaten what follows from straightforward rationality.) Should we extend constrained maximizing (cooperate with and only with cooperators) to require threats and resistance to threats? Narveson appears to think so: "bullying is itself one of the very things that any reasonable morality will decry" (128). More generally, the contract perspective asks what "principles of morality . . . it is reasonable for everyone to accept" (131). Surely that principle is to resist threats. Consider the situation in figure 5. Resisters—who cooperate with each other, threaten hawks, and resist hawks' threats—do better than hawks. The case for the rationality of a morality of threat resistance appears to parallel Gauthier's solution to the Prisoners' Dilemma; see figure 2. Rational contractarian morality therefore seems to demand resistance.

	Resister	*Hawk*
Resister	2, 2	0, 0
Hawk	0, 0	0, 0

Figure 5: United We Stand

This account, however, leaves out a third alternative strategy, acquiescence (see figure 6).

	Dove	*Resister*	*Hawk*
Dove	2, 2	2, 2	1, 3
Resister	2, 2	2, 2	0, 0
Hawk	3, 1	0, 0	0, 0

Figure 6: Divided I Fall

Doves cooperate with resisters but acquiesce to hawks' threats. Which of these three strategies, hawk, resister, or dove, is rational? Doves always do as well as resisters with doves and resisters but do better by chickening out when faced with a hawk. The dove strategy (weakly) dominates the resister strategy but doves are not uniquely rational. Doves make hawks rational and hawks make doves rational.[29] This is an unhappy result for rational moralists. Their solution to the Prisoners' Dilemma (cooperate with and only with cooperators) fails to be rational in the game of Chicken.[30]

Constrained maximization converts the Prisoner's Dilemma into a benign second-order coordination problem, but constraint in Chicken gives rise to a second-order game of Chicken (where C is dove and D is hawk) precisely as nasty as the first. A gap between moral resistance and rational acquiescence looms.

Narveson and Gauthier Distinguished

We have shown that a morality of commitment to mutually advantageous principles will not solve games of Chicken, but this is the weakest version of rational morality: pure constrained maximization. Gauthier's own account (morals by agreement) has more content—in particular, a principle of distributive justice—so it remains an open question whether it can solve the problem posed by threats.[31]

Narveson does not accept all of Gauthier's moral conclusions, however; he emphasizes a libertarian morality. We have noticed two features of this morality, the stress on negative rights and social enforcement. A third feature plays down the role of public goods and the consequent role of a principle of distributive justice.

> Gauthier's principle of fair distribution, in short, is very confined in its application. From the point of view of broad social theory, I would argue, it is essentially dispensable. Justice respects the agreements people make; if potential parties to agreements perceive proferred [sic] terms as distributively unfair, then they should not enter into those agreements. (196)

Narveson thus departs from Gauthier in two respects: stressing individual agreements over a social contract, and stressing the minimal morality of mutual advantage over morally more demanding principals such as impartiality. As we shall see, these two features make it less likely that Narveson's moral proposal will be able to deal with Chicken.[32]

Rights

I have assumed that morality requires resistance, but we should consider how Narveson specifies the morality of enforcement.

> Morality is (to be) *enforced.* Not in the sense in which the Law of the Land is enforced, with specially appointed enforcers, . . . but rather by . . . "informal" means. Verbal means are preeminent among these. . . . But we each do this, as it were, on our own time. Each individual can *decide*, not only whether she herself will do *x* when called for by Morality, but also what if anything she will do about getting others to do or not do *x*. (125)

This is a morality of rights; in particular, these are negative rights. There is a correlative duty not to violate a negative right but no additional duty to provide the object of the right. Positive rights add this second duty.[33] For example, according to Narveson, there is no duty to provide protection by enforcing morality, only a right to do so or not. Enforcement is optional. Perhaps this is Narveson's attempt to save enforcement from the charge of irrationality. He does not present it that way; he uses the language of freedom. Rights of enforcement preserve agents' freedom of action at the second level; they embody moral freedom.[34]

In any case, enforcement rights unfortunately do not solve the problem posed by Chicken. As we have seen, were all would-be doves required to resist, the resisters would do better than hawks; but if a would-be dove has the right to acquiesce, rationality leads her to her individual local optimum of concession.[35] The right to withhold moral enforcement undermines the collective regime of moralized resistance to threats and makes doves and hawks rational. It is never rational for any agent to be a resister rather than a dove, but it remains rational for a population to require all to be resisters rather than doves.[36] If rational contractarianism proceeds by way of the several "agreements . . . made by individuals," as Narveson stresses (195), it will often not produce the "public good of peace" (196) as he supposes, but one-sided oppression instead.

Informality

We need to see that no definition of morality as informal (125) can block this conclusion. Hobbes's point was that since morality was insufficient to solve the problem of social instability, rational agents should turn to politics. Politics is not morality—it is formal and organized—as Narveson stresses in the quote above about the informality of moral enforcement.[37] Of course, this does not show that politics is immoral; once Narveson commits us to rational justification, whatever it is rational to agree to acquires the justificatory warrant that morality sought. Rational contractarianism thus carries the risk that it might not justify morality at all, but some other means of securing order.[38] This risk brings a methodological benefit; it indicates questions that rational contractarians do not beg. So, while "moral" might classify some of the contractors' alternatives, it cannot serve to limit their agenda by excluding weaker or stronger principles as non-moral. Narveson notes that "violence, turmoil, and war . . . await . . . a group which cannot resolve its problems by adopting internal constraints on behavior" (162); it may also await those who rely on libertarian moral means (self-constraint plus informal enforcement) to solve problems that require more powerful constraints.

In this section I have argued that Narveson's stress on enforcement is important since states of nature modeled by Chicken have a place for moral enforcement by means of threats and threat resistance. We have seen, though, that Gauthier's solution to the Prisoners' Dilemma cannot simply be extended to Chicken: the morality of resisting amoral threats is not rational; nor does Narveson's principle of negative rights to protection solve the problem that Chicken poses. The rights of chickens let them choose, individually, to be exploited.

Beyond Rational Morality

So far we have criticized Narveson's proposed libertarian principle as inadequate without exploring the resources of his contractarian argument. In this section we broaden our argument to consider what difference it makes that rational agents can choose the libertarian principle or some other.

Peace-loving oppressed people face a serious problem. They find themselves in a game of Chicken where it seems to be rational to commit themselves to something stronger than libertarian rights. This leads me to take up Narveson's challenge of whether we can improve the libertarian option: "Could I bring it about that you are at least as well off as you would otherwise have been by performing actions that violate your libertarian rights?" (181) To many the answer will be obvious; we all would be better off by restricting each agent's right not to enforce the rights of others. I do not wish to press this stronger criticism; it is not obvious to me that the positive duty to protect (*P*) is better than the negative right to protection (*N*), but it is clear that rational agents in the state of nature have at least these two alternatives. It seems to me that the crucial question for the rational contractarian method is to resolve this dispute, leading as it does to moral anarchism on the one hand or a defense of the state on the other.

Narveson has difficulties recognizing that there are alternatives here. This is related to his overemphasis of the Prisoners' Dilemma. I argue that questions of distribution are unavoidable, that they lead us back to the game of Chicken and, finally, away from libertarian morality to the state.

Who Should Pay the Price of Liberty?

Another problem with modeling the basic social problem with the Prisoners' Dilemma is that this model eliminates any problem of distributive justice. Therefore, while Gauthier's solution to the compliance problem modeled by the Prisoners' Dilemma is extremely important, we must keep its limitations in mind.[39] Roughly, securing compliance with cooperation addresses and solves only half of the contractarian's problem.

> There is an identity of interests since social cooperation makes possible a better life for all than any would have if each were to live solely by his own efforts. There is a conflict of interests since persons are not indifferent as to how the greater benefits produced by their collaboration are distributed, for in order to pursue their ends they each prefer a larger to a lesser share.[40]

In the Prisoners' Dilemma there is no conflict over distribution because there is only one accessible Pareto-optimal alternative, namely, joint cooperation. Once there are alternative ways to cooperate, which benefit the would-be cooperators differently, the situation changes. Narveson is wont to deny that there are alternatives here, but as we have seen, there is at least one pair, namely, the negative (*N*) versus positive (*P*) right of protection. These two regimes can be seen as two different ways of distributing the " 'price' of liberty" Narveson mentions on page 322 of his book. Even among agents who all agree that liberty is worth its price there will be disagreement about ways to pay this price.

Nonviolence as a Public Good

Before we address the choice between these alternatives, we must consider Narveson's attempts to deny us this choice. My proposal of a positive right to protection can be seen as a second way of distributing the public good of nonviolence.[41] Narveson argues, contrary to Braybrooke, that nonviolence is not a public good of the ordinary kind, about which questions of proper distribution arise.

> But there is not a reasonable question about the division of the benefits of the original agreement between us to refrain from further violence, for those benefits, consisting as they do merely in the possibility of each of us actually realizing the fruits of our separate labors, are abstractly equal and nondivisible. . . . But there are no other problems about the division of *this* "public good," the good of nonviolence, to which a reasonable theory can address itself. (194)

Narveson argues that protection, in particular, is not inherently a public good. This may be true of the good of nonviolence, but what about the costs of protection? Evidently, these can be divided in different ways, as Narveson himself proposes a new division, shifting costs from the public (punishment) to the criminal (compensation) in his chapter 16. In particular, he proposes that the costs of protection be internalized, that is, borne by violators and victims. He seems not to notice that this particular scheme is also not inherent to protection. Why, we might ask, should the victim pay? Of course, there are market-based benefits from users' fees for protection; they encourage would-be victims to seek cost-minimizing means of self-defense and the like. These benefits, however, must be considered against the costs. Under Narveson's proposal (*N*), the "weak and mild" end up paying more (because they need to pay for defense) than they would under my proposal (*P*) of a positive duty of protection paid for by all.[42]

Narveson also argues against Braybrooke that the market is the sole alternative to the state of nature. "[T]he alternative of socialist arrangements . . . is not available because everyone has a veto on everything in the Social Contract" (195). Even if this works against socialism,[43] it does not work against my alternative. I agree that anything can be vetoed—including Narveson's proposed negative right to protection.

I conclude that protection of rights is a divisible public good. We must decide who is to pay its costs. I have proposed the alternative (*P*) of a positive duty to protect, which shifts some costs from victims to the general public. The question is: which of these two ways would be rationally chosen?

Logic Cuts Both Ways

At this point the relation of part 3 to part 2 of *The Libertarian Idea* is troublesome. Narveson assures us that part 3 will fill out part 2's prima facie argument (175). We would expect to see how alternatives such as *N* and *P* would work out in practice prior to deciding which (rationally) to choose—but this is not what we find in part 3. For example, here is Narveson on a point relevant to the question of positive versus negative rights of protection.

> It is important to be clear that the right to protection that follows from our fundamentally negative right to liberty is also, therefore, fundamentally negative. Thus, if by the "right to protection" is meant the *positive* right that other people protect you, then it is not automatically on the libertarian agenda. What is on it is the right that others not, in various ways, molest you. If people threaten to molest you, then there is a practical question what to do about it. This may be answered by enlisting the aid of others, who may help you for various reasons: out of their own free wills, because they like you, or perhaps because they have a touch of Wyatt-Earpism and like a good fight so long as they are siding with the good guys, or. . . . (217)

I interrupt this ode to voluntarism because at this point one rational agent (me) is persuaded that we got the wrong agenda. That is, when these consequences of the libertarian commitment to a monism of strict negative rights are spelled out, I suspect that there must be a better—more rationally attractive—alternative available for choice in the social contract.

John Rawls is helpful here in two respects. First, his argument from the strains of commitment reminds us of the way contract arguments work. Untenable consequences of a proposed principle—his target is (average) utilitarianism—are reasons to backtrack and reconsider not making the (now) offending choice.[44] Narveson seems to employ a simpler, unidirectional logic, where *modus ponens* prevails; but deriving repulsive *Q* from *P* only sticks us with *Q* when *P* has some independent basis.[45] Otherwise, what we have is just as much an argument against *P*. For those of us committed to a contractarian methodology, logical derivations always cut both ways. Once I find that libertarianism leaves some—the peace-loving who are poor or unphotogenic—to mercenaries or romantics, I want to reconsider my options.

Second, Rawls lays out a reasonably long agenda of traditional alternatives for the contractors to choose among.[46] His rejections of utilitarianism and perfectionism show the contract argument at work. Narveson's use of "agenda" for an already trimmed list of alternatives raises the question: why should the social contractors' alternatives be limited to negative rights, since they are not committed to anything yet? I suspect that Narveson confuses the exposition of his book with its contractarian argument. He argues as if our choice in part 2 of the book binds us in part 3.

Problems with Positive Rights

While I have accused Narveson of one-sidedness, I should immediately add that he provides exactly what we need to know about the libertarian option in order to make a rational choice. His elaboration of libertarian possibilities, the way voluntary arrangements might improve our situation, is impressive and inspiring. A rational choice between positive and negative rights to protection would need to work out the practical consequences of the former. Obviously, I cannot do that here. I will grant that a regime of positive rights—even a minimalist regime limited to duties to protect—creates new problems. In particular, I agree with Narveson that there are coordination problems. I can see other problems as well. For example, a duty to protect is strongly intolerant of alternative ways to draw the line between morality and immorality; it requires one to be intolerant of the tolerant. For these two reasons, the minimalist regime of positive rights would likely require a state. I also grant that states are risky and costly, but we must face the central question dividing moral from political theory. Exclusive focus on the Prisoners' Dilemma does not serve us well here. Why we need the state is not simply because some would like to free ride, but because others are tempted to let them do so. The difficult problem is not punishing the amorally guilty, but punishing fellow moral agents who differ with us on the matter of tolerance.

Hobbes argued that moral constraints are not sufficient to solve the social problems that he called the state of nature. I agree. While it may be rational to be moral in the Prisoners' Dilemma, libertarian morality will not solve the game of Chicken. Something more constraining than morality, with its informality and freedom to enforce, is needed. I would argue, with Hobbes, that rational agents would choose a coercive political authority. A coercive political authority solves the problem of Chicken by spreading the costs of enforcement over the whole population.

Conclusion

I do not believe that Narveson has provided a foundation for libertarianism. He correctly sees that the most distinctive and attractive form of libertarianism challenges the state as an ordering device, proposing instead that we rely on property rights and market relations. Moreover, he correctly sees Hobbes both as a methodological model and as the most able defender of the rival claims of the state. In these terms, Narveson's argument fails because it ignores aspects of the state-of-nature conflict that require a state. States of nature are not all Prisoners' Dilemmas; some are better modeled by the game of Chicken. This nastier game is not amenable to the individualistic moral solution of libertarian rights even when enforcement is added.

Although my conclusions are negative, they are not destructive. I agree that rational contractarianism is the best hope for constructing nontrivial justifications in moral and political theory. This theory is quite young, with many alternatives and methods yet to be explored, so initial failures are no cause for despair.[47] In general, rational contractarians need to explore stronger and more institutionalized contracts, like Rawls's, that do not rely on informal morality alone, nor indeed on continuing rational appeal. This is to say that we still need a bridge from rational morality to rational political theory.

Notes

1. Earlier versions of this paper were read at the Canadian Philosophical Association and the American Association for the Philosophic Study of Society. Thanks to Jan Narveson, Chris Morris, Ken Hanley, and David Schmidtz for helpful comments.

2. Bare page references below are to this book, *The Libertarian Idea* (Philadelphia: Temple University Press, 1988).

3. See R. Nozick, *Anarchy, State, and Utopia* (New York: Basic Books, 1974), 9.

4. Cf. M. Cohen, "Moral Skepticism and International Affairs," in Charles R. Beitz, Marshall Cohen, et al., eds., *International Ethics* (Princeton, N.J.: Princeton University Press, 1985).

5. For explanation and further discussion of the Prisoners' Dilemma beyond what is offered in the present chapter, see above, pp. 121–35, and below, pp. 172–88. For Chicken, see below, pp. 207–8 and 265.—Ed.

6. Cf. J. Hampton, *Hobbes and the Social Contract Tradition* (Cambridge: Cambridge University Press, 1986), and G. Kavka, *Hobbesian Moral and Political Theory* (Princeton, N.J.: Princeton University Press, 1986), for more detailed application of these tools to Hobbes.

7. The payoff numbers represent individual preference rankings, with 0 = worst and 3 = best.

8. Cf. Narveson, *The Libertarian Idea*, 137f., and R. Hardin, "Exchange Theory on Strategic Bases," *Social Science Information* 21 (1982): 251–72.

9. Peace is a good not amenable to instantaneous trade, and iteration does not help if I am dead in the short run.

10. See David Gauthier, *Morals by Agreement* (Oxford: Oxford University Press, 1986).

11. Narveson may not like this description; see his discussion of rational morality as "natural law" in Narveson, *The Libertarian Idea*, 148ff.

12. I have criticized several components of Gauthier's theory in P. Danielson, "The Visible Hand of Morality," *Canadian Journal of Philosophy* 18 (1988): 357–84; see also Danielson, "Closing the Compliance Dilemma," in P. Vallentyne, ed., *Contractarianism and Rational Choice: Essays* (New York: Cambridge University Press, 1991), 291–322, and Danielson, *Artificial Morality* (London: Routledge, 1992).

13. The slogan in the text recalls Chamberlain's famous phrase after signing the Munich Agreement in September 1938. As I wrote the first version of this paper, the United States was accusing Toshiba of selling militarily crucial machine tools to the Soviet Union.

14. As Hobbes noted, international relations take place in a state of nature, and the affairs of states provide many examples of the failure of alliances to secure unanimous cooperation. Think of the Dutch trading with their enemy, Spain, in the seventeenth century, and U.S. neutrality before 1917. Indeed, such profitable defection plays a role in the rise and fall of great powers according to P. Kennedy, *The Rise and Fall of the Great Powers* (New York: Random House, 1987).

15. I should note as well other complications caused by shift in scale. For example, citizens may face a tyrant in a game of Chicken but still face each other (as potential revolutionaries) in a game of Prisoners' Dilemma. I owe this point to David Schmidtz.

16. Else why would urban resistance fantasies such as *Karate Kid* find a market?

17. I restrict attention to two-player games; many-player PDs admit of asymmetrical solutions. (See the section titled "Many Players.") Note as well that labeling actions (like *C*) with names (like "cooperation") that refer to intended outcomes is a handy shortcut in the PD that becomes a potential

source of confusion as we move to another game, where the constrained choice, C, need not lead to cooperation but to one-sided acquiescence.

18. Narveson sees the problem and tries to explain the deviation between the PD model and reality in terms of irrationality. His attempt has about it an air of desperation and violates the fundamental methodological dogma of social science: assume rationality for a little longer. It would be foolish to deny that people are sometimes stupid or irrational, but Narveson stretches the schema of rational explanation when he wonders on p. 224 of *The Libertarian Idea* why there are criminals and appeals to lack of information and rational advice. The simpler explanation is that in some situations crime pays.

19. M. Taylor and H. Ward, "Chickens, Whales, and Lumpy Goods: Alternative Models of Public Goods Provision," *Political Studies* 30 (1983): 350–70.

20. A. de Jasay, *Social Contract, Free Ride* (Oxford: Clarendon Press, 1989).

21. This is an oversimplification. As we shall see below, the morality needed to pick out CC in Chicken needs to be stronger than the morality of mutual advantage that suffices in the PD. One reason for this follows from the text above. In the PD, CC is better for both than the equilibrium DD. In Chicken, DD is no longer the equilibrium, and CC is not mutually better than CD or DC.

22. One can object to the use of Chicken on purely rational grounds. I have argued that it is rational for one to threaten and the other to acquiesce. At the least, there is a coordination problem here, and a fuller account would consider the introduction of mixed strategies. (S. J. Brams, *Paradoxes in Politics* [New York: Macmillan, 1976], section 5.3, provides a good account.) There are other problems as well. For example, one objection is that it is not clear whether straightforwardly rational agents of the received theory can threaten. This need not detain us, however, because we have accepted Gauthier's extension of the theory of rational choice. Therefore, agents can constrain themselves to make counterpreferential choices and they can communicate these commitments. As a consequence, agents who can make and keep promises in the Prisoners' Dilemma can also make and keep threats to defect in Chicken. The rational moralist's tools of communication and constraint can be turned to amoral advantage in the game of Chicken. I note, however, that Gauthier's defense of threatening (cf. Gauthier, *Morals by Agreement*, section VI.3.2, and "Deterrence, Maximization, and Rationality") is qualified, and more recently, Gauthier has further refined his account of constrained maximization to distinguish threats from assurances. See Gauthier, "Assure and Threaten," *Ethics* 104 (1994): 690–721, and Gauthier, "Intention and Deliberation," in P. Danielson, ed., *Modeling Rationality, Morality, and Evolution* (New York: Oxford University Press, 1995); for a criticism, see M. Bratman, "Following through with One's Plans," in P. Danielson, ed., *Modeling Rationality, Morality, and Evolution*.

23. Iterated versions of similar strategies have been discussed widely in the literature. Cf. R. Hardin, "Individual Sanctions, Collective Benefits," in R.

Campbell and L. Sowden, eds., *Paradoxes of Rationality and Cooperation* (Vancouver, British Columbia: University of British Columbia Press, 1985), 344f., for a compact and accessible discussion. In his terminology, k is 3, because a group of three cooperators is the smallest group that does better than the noncooperative outcome.

24. Only some, because in the left column the conditional cooperators make an offer or promise to cooperate; cf. figure 2. The right column, though, shows that *DC* remains tempting and *DD* costly; cf. figure 3.

25. D. P. Gauthier, "Deterrence, Maximization, and Rationality," in D. MacLean, ed., *The Security Gamble: Deterrence Dilemmas in the Nuclear Age* (Totowa, N.J.: Rowman & Allanheld, 1984), 101–22.

26. This discussion is taken from Danielson, *Artificial Morality*, section 9.1.1.

27. For this reason, Gauthier finds the iterated PD to be morally insignificant (Gauthier, *Morals by Agreement*, 169f.); Narveson does not say whether self- and social control are jointly necessary to morality. On p. 128 he argues that enforcement is not sufficient.

28. Nor need others be called in to aid an agent, and if they are called in (in some extension of the PD), they still gain by sanctioning.

29. The ecological equilibrium of such a population will see resister die out and dove and hawk form a stable predator/prey relation. Note, however, that this calculation depends on a stronger utility concept than I have used throughout. This example roughly follows J. Maynard Smith and G. R. Price, "The Logic of Animal Conflict," *Nature* 246 (1973): 15–18.

30. Can this conclusion be strengthened? In Danielson, *Artificial Morality*, chaps. 9 and 10, I argue that there is no way to threaten doves into acquiescing less. I no longer think that this claim can be defended; I overestimated the role of transparency. In any case, such a threat would violate Narveson's morality of rights, as we shall soon see.

31. Recall from note 18 above that Gauthier has an answer to this question. I discuss his answer in Danielson, *Artificial Morality*, chaps. 9 and 10, but here I am concerned with Narveson's extension of Gauthier's solution to the PD.

32. In addition to compliance and bargaining, there is a third feature of rational contractarian arguments, the setting of the contractual baseline, that might be relevant to solving the problem of Chicken. Narveson relies on an account of appropriation similar to Gauthier's to set the baseline for contracting. I will not be able to discuss these arguments here, except to note that in both arguments this is the feature most dependent on intuition. Cf. P. Danielson, "The Lockean Proviso," in P. Vallentyne, ed., *Contractarianism and Rational Choice: Essays*, 99–111, for Gauthier's baseline argument.

33. See the section titled "Logic Cuts Both Ways" below.

34. I admit to being somewhat confused on this because early on Narveson entertains the "thought . . . just to deny the 'rights of conscience' altogether" (Narveson, *The Libertarian Idea*, 36), while later he writes of the entitlement to think what one likes about rights (254).

35. The main line of Narveson's argument leads to rights of protection, but he does mention another way to deal with the problem in Narveson, *The Libertarian Idea*, 322, where he suggests that forcing people to pay for defense may be justified "if those defended would otherwise be dead or enslaved, then it is difficult for them to argue that your activity has made them worse off than they would be if they were instead forced to assist in the defense." This argument does not apply to Chicken, since forcing a dove to be a resister does make the dove worse off. (On the other hand, even when this argument does apply, it leads to unfortunate consequences, since it seems to license Lockean appropriation leading to property rights in people. Morris Cohen, "Property and Sovereignty," in C. B. MacPherson, ed., *Property: Mainstream and Critical Positions* [Toronto: University of Toronto Press, 1978], and B. Russell, *A History of Western Philosophy* [New York: Simon and Schuster, 1945], have challenged defenders of property rights to distinguish them from feudal rights to people; I sense that the answer suggested by the current line of argument is not the desired one.) Finally, in this same discussion Narveson notes the possible advantage of totalitarian states in "effective coordination" of defense; but forcing doves to fight does not address a coordination problem. The tendency so to classify it is perhaps because of modeling all partial conflict situations as Prisoners' Dilemmas and all non-PDs as (mere) coordination problems.

36. Lest one think that this point is without application, think of the right, rather than the duty, to resist threats of kidnappers. It is not in my interest, as the parent of the kidnapped child, to help the police—I risk my child—but all parents have an interest in preventing any parent from complying.

37. And also in J. Narveson, "At Arm's Length: Violence and War," in Tom Regan, ed., *Matters of Life and Death* (New York: Random House, 2d ed., 1986), 128.

38. Narveson quotes Buchanan on law and morals as "alternative means of securing order" in Narveson, *The Libertarian Idea*, 150.

39. I will focus on the politically most important limitation: the lack of bargaining in the Prisoners' Dilemma.

40. J. Rawls, *A Theory of Justice* (Cambridge, Mass.: Harvard University Press, 1971), 4.

41. Perhaps Narveson agrees that there are two such ways; market protection and minimal state protection are mentioned in Narveson, *The Libertarian Idea*, 190, without evaluative comment.

42. We run into a contextual problem with Narveson's exposition here. He notices that the alternative of bargaining about protection leads to the result I cite but rejects this because it is "not quite the result Braybrooke is presumably pressing for." This may be so, but it amounts to dropping an important point on the basis of the smallest context of argument. We should be concerned with the large question Braybrooke raises—whether protection is a divisible public good—not the smaller internal question of whether Gauthier's method of division (which Narveson rejects) would please Braybrooke.

43. It may not, because Narveson ignores the shift in context between part 1 of his *The Libertarian Idea*, where libertarianism is assumed, and part 3, where it is in question. He cannot import his (context-bound) argument from the former to the latter without begging the question.

44. Rawls, *A Theory of Justice*, section 29.

45. Given Narveson's rejection of intuitionism, one wonders what this independent basis could be.

46. Rawls, *A Theory of Justice*, section 21.

47. For example, Gauthier has yet to develop the political theory evidently needed to complete his *Morals by Agreement*.

10

The Anarchist's Case

Jan Narveson

Introduction

The anarchist is all but universally regarded as a wild-eyed, dangerous
character. Wildness of eye is imputed on the basis of conceptual
confusion and impractical utopianism: anarchism is thought to be
virtually self-refuting, impossible to expound clearly, and dependent
on obviously false estimates of the capabilities of human nature. The
ascription of danger has two sources: first, a perception that the
anarchist is out to destroy something of great value, something on
which the stability of society rests, which of course is assumed to be
or be due to the state; second, that some who have called themselves
anarchists did actually throw bombs and the like. These are not just
frivolous charges: certainly some purported anarchists are guilty on
both counts. Both must be refuted, at least in principle, if anarchism is
to be regarded as a legitimate option in social theory.

At the same time, however, the charges against the state that
motivate anarchism have a tendency to be swept under one or another
of several available carpets. We move the theory of anarchism out of
the dustbins of political theory if we can give decent replies to the
familiar claims against it, while at the same time pressing our complaints against the state in a clear-eyed way, both as regards its
theoretical claims and in the cold light of the empirical facts. And we
move it to the front of the desk if, in addition, we can supply positive
motivation for the anarchistic outlook.

The present paper undertakes sketchy, outline-level responses on

195

all of these fronts. The task is rendered more manageable by the perception that the critique of the state is largely coordinate with the positive construction required. What's wrong with the state is what's right with anarchy. More than that, it's also what's *good* about anarchy. However, the new case for anarchism requires complete repudiation of the older, utopian-socialist type of theory. No one in the history of social theory has been wronger about anything than marxists about the nonnecessity of telling us quite a bit about what their system would be like if the revolution succeeds.

To see this, of course, we must expound the moral outlook underlying anarchism. To do this, we must first make an important distinction between two general options in anarchistic theory, one of which fully deserves anarchism's disdainful view in the public eye, but the other of which is not only enormously plausible on the face of it but apparently feasible as well. The two are what we may call, respectively, the socialist versus the free-market, or capitalist, versions.

Anarchism 1: The Socialist Version

Anarchism is the view that the best state of society is the stateless state: society lacking centralized, authoritative decision-making and decision-enforcing agencies. Is this compatible with any sort of socialism? By the latter we understand what Marx understood by it: rejection of private ownership of the "means of production." It is useful to open our discussion by considering whether socialist anarchism—by long odds the historically most popular version—makes any sense. We begin by seeing why it does not.

States tell people what to do. They don't just *tell* them that, of course: they do so with "authority," meaning, in effect, that they make their directives stick by backing them with highly credible threats to use force against those who do not comply. States enforce uniformities across society: all are required to do things one way rather than any of an indefinite number of possible other ways. In a free-market or private-enterprise economy, productive resources are under the direction of individuals or voluntarily acting groups, acting on their own. If it is claimed that this is somehow morally wrong, because we do not approve of what those individuals do or fail to do with the products resulting from this uncontrolled activity, or to the manner in which they are produced, then there is a problem. For socialism imposes requirements on at least the disbursement and/or production of those products that are typically at odds with the interests of the producers. The socialist's proposed cure for the alleged deficiencies is to scuttle private control, thereby opting for an enormous range of what he takes to be "corrections" of voluntary activity. Since those activities are voluntary, the corrections in question must be markedly at odds with the intentions of the producers. A uniform system is imposed where what would happen otherwise can be expected to be quite nonuniform. Could this possibly be done in the absence of central authority? The short answer is that it cannot.

At this point, to be sure, the socialist will opt for democracy—in the workplace, in the committee rooms, and in society at large—but democracy cannot bring about societywide changes of heart; it merely settles things by voting. Any expectation of unanimity regarding such things as what to produce and for whom deserves the name "utopian"—assuming what we should not accept anyway, that a society in which uniformity of production and consumption prevails is such a good thing that an extreme state of it deserves the adjective "utopian" rather than the reverse. The majority, then, will simply overrule the minority, just as it does at present. There is, then, no possibility of achieving socialist goals without a state or what amounts to one. Those who hope for it without the state are starry-eyed; those who prefer the state to the nonattainment of those goals are not anarchists; and those who suppose that decision-making methods coercively enforceable over all do not amount to a state are confused.

It is regrettable that so much and so interesting a stretch of intellectual history should have to be dismissed so briefly, but there is no way around this result, and nonmarket anarchism will accordingly be ignored hereinafter.

Anarchism 2: Market Anarchism

The alternative version is what is now called "market" or sometimes, if misleadingly, "capitalist" anarchism. The moral of my story so far is that if anarchism is possible at all, it must be in the market version. There, production is always under the control of individuals or groups acting on their own, and distribution likewise is effected only by voluntary exchange, which may be assumed to consist typically of commercial exchange. In short, it consists precisely of that very "anarchy in the system of production and exchange" that Marx deplored. On the face of it, then, the market system is such that everything that is done is done because somebody wants to do just that, rather than because someone has threatened the doer with evil if he does not.

So, at first sight, it looks as though, at one stroke, we have the reason both why the market system should be feasible and why it should be desirable. But that would be too quick. Some theorists, of course, will insist that people getting what they want has nothing to do with whether it is a good society anyway. In the present discussion, we will ignore such complaints. But even granting liberal premises, it is still too quick. For perhaps a society in which people *do* what they want is not necessarily a society in which people *get* what they want. Some will be inclined to get what they want by doing what others do *not* want: by using force, in short. And many will no doubt complain that a society in which everyone does only what he wants will fail to bring it about that many get what they not only want but need. To say that a market-anarchic society is one in which people do what they want is thus cheating. The *idea* of a market society is that people do what they want, yes; but what do we do about all the people who won't *let* some of them do what they want? Anarchism in the sense in which they do what they want would seem to have to be the result of the operation of a normative system in which people *may* not use force: interferences with voluntary activity are forbidden. But surely, it will reasonably be said, at least some of those people, in turn, will not be put off from using that force except by the prospect of force being used against them. Does this not bring us back to the state? And if the case is accepted that the needy must be helped regardless, then similarly a role for the state may seem to be assured.

It would take more space than is available here to respond to the latter group. If it is accepted that one may permissibly help the needy by coercing one's neighbors to do so, then lessons in both economics and morals are required before the discussion can resume on a reasonable plane. However, the anarchist's case that the needy will almost certainly do better without the state would at least have to be regarded as plainly relevant by all concerned, if it can be made out. But if the answer to the former question about private violence were to prove to be, as Hobbes and his successors all insisted, in the affirmative, then it would be game over for anarchism.

Fortunately, that answer is by no means certain. It turns out that there are very good reasons for thinking that the private allocation of force, without central control, is indeed possible, both in principle and, on the basis of ample evidence, in practice.[1] Careful attention to both evidence and analysis will make this clear beyond peradventure; yet it is quite understandable why people should believe the contrary. Their governments, after all, have been telling them for several millennia that it is not. And should we not believe everything our governments tell us?[2]

In a real society, some people will resort to force. For that matter, to speak of "resorting" to force may be to understate the case: some people may positively relish the idea of using force. Whatever their motive, the use of interpersonal force inherently conflicts with market liberty. More precisely, it is the use of coercive force that does so: the ballet dancer who lifts his partner in a graceful maneuver uses force but does not coerce. The coercer, on the other hand, uses power, which often enough is force, in order to get his victim to do what the victim would have preferred not to do. Let us understand this to be the sort of force we intend in present contexts. We may thus say that a libertarian society is one in which force may not be used against those who, in their turn, do not use it against others. The word "may" is a moral one: the sentence containing it says that the use of force against the innocent is wrong. The status of this prohibition as a moral claim raises several questions. I shall address two in particular, one essential for present purposes, the other important for wider purposes of social theory.

Defining Libertarian Rights

The first question is, just what is meant by "may"? Fortunately, it is also fairly easy to answer: to say that someone "may not" do something is to say that he is prohibited from doing it. But doesn't that just mean, in turn, that he *may be prevented* from doing it?—there's that word "may" again. Have we made any progress, then? Indeed we have, as I shall now explain.

Someone, S, who believes that a person, A, "may" be prevented from doing something, x, envisages that some person B (who may or may not be identical with S) is such that if B acts to prevent A from doing x, then S will be inclined, in turn, not to intervene to prevent B from so intervening. If, on the other hand, S believes that A may not be so prevented, then S will incline to disapprove of B's intervention and will be inclined to do, or at least to support the doing of something, to see to it that B does not do that. Moral attitudes, attitudes of approval and disapproval, are directed at two sorts of activities, not just one. First, they are directed at the actions of people in general, people having no particular relation to the activities of further people. But second, they are directed at activities that, in their turn, are intended to control or influence people's actions, not necessarily consensually. In other words, we may distinguish between simple approval and disapproval, on the one hand, and approval or disapproval of reinforcing activity on the other. A theory of right and wrong, insofar as it is relevant to political theory, is a theory about the latter: about the use of methods of social control or influence, including force. Qua political theory, it is essentially about the use of force in particular, for a state is just a monopoly of control over the use of force.

A libertarian morality, then, holds that force may be used only to counter[3] force. Many put this in terms of "initiating" or refraining from initiating force, and we will accept that terminology as broadly appropriate. The innocent do not initiate force against anyone; the guilty initiate force against the innocent; and a libertarian morality says that we are not to use force against any except the guilty. Market anarchism is really just the instantiation of the libertarian moral theory.[4]

It is of fundamental importance to note that force may be used only to counter aggressive force, but it does not follow that we must use it. The misconception that libertarianism says the latter is perhaps the major source of supposed support for statism from within what is claimed to be libertarian theory. Some will think this nonobligatoriness of using force even when justified the Achilles' heel of anarchism; others will think it liberating and right. Whichever, only the weaker view is really consistent with the libertarian idea.[5]

The idea of a market is the idea of people who are free to make exchanges and, in practice, often do so. No one is to intervene to prevent initiation or completion of an exchange, so long as it is a free exchange in the sense that both parties to it voluntarily agree to that exchange. (How much information they must supply each other in order for it to be accounted "voluntary" is, of course, an important question; but the information supplied must be, literally, information, not *mis*information. Fraud, in other words, is ruled out.[6]) Importantly, there is no assumption or presumption that the parties to exchanges are antecedently equal in any respect other than that each is under no coercive pressure from other persons to choose one way or another: no one acts under threat of force by another. They may act under self-imposed compulsions, of course—that is quite another matter. They may well act under threats of withdrawal of love, companionship, or other services previously voluntarily supplied by spouses, friends, or associates. But they do not act under threats of force, unless there is a previously accepted arrangement calling for such means in the case in question. (Boxers in the ring have agreed to attempt to hit each other. Plenty of force is employed, but no coercion.)

Moral Reinforcement

The second question to address, then, is: What resources for enforcing market arrangements could there be in an anarchic society? May we expect such arrangements actually to be made when needed and to be effective? Putting the matter this way might suggest the need to alter our definition of "market society" as one in which people do not initiate force. But if we are to have a useful definition, applicable to real-world society, we shall have to say instead that a market society is one in which the rule is not to initiate force. In what sense, though, may a society be said to "have" a rule? The answer lies in the prevailing pattern of attitudes among its people. If virtually everyone in the society has the appropriate attitudes and generally acts on them, then we have a market society in about as full a sense as could be realistically hoped.

The societies that we live in are not fully market societies. There is a good deal of the market attitude in many people, and yet most people are not anarchists. They think, or at least think they think,[7] that it is just fine to have a centralized authority with the power to enforce rules. And most of them perhaps think that that authority may do much *more* than that. It is, to be sure, unsafe to speculate about what people "really think." Much of what they think, after all, is heavily influenced by information, much of which may well be misinformation. It is the job of a theorist who thinks that what appear to be the prevailing attitudes on some matter are wrong to identify the errors that lead people to make the professions they do, in hopes that recognition of those errors will revise those professions. And when this is done, the market theorist supposes that every reasonable person will wind up accepting the market idea rather than some other. His claim, in short, must be that anarchism is *reasonable*.

The informal enforcement of morals consists in the main of two things. One is that expressions of approval and disapproval are marshaled on behalf of the type of behavior called for by the principles under consideration. Strongly supplementing these are a range of more robust responses to behavior, including such things as "admission to the society" of the persons in question. Our dealings with those who adhere to those principles are likely to be more extensive and more profitable than with those who do not; withdrawal of opportunity for such dealings is a considerable inducement to deal honestly if one deals at all.

The other sort of enforcement, of course, is by outright employment of coercive force. Precisely what it may be used for is an important question, to which the market anarchist answers, broadly, that it may be used when necessary for the defense of oneself or legitimately acquired property or of anyone else or their property, provided the others are willing to be defended in that way by you—and for nothing else. The question of the viability of anarchism is open precisely because such force, which we may assume would sometimes be necessary, is not and need not be wielded exclusively by governments. Is there anything about power that inherently drives us to statist control over its use? The tendency has been to assume this, but that assumption is in question here.

Forcible Enforcement

Many agreements among individuals are not enforced, or at least not overtly so, and yet these agreements are effective. Friends and acquaintances, colleagues, relatives, and even random strangers often enough make agreements that the parties to them keep, feel obliged to keep, and moreover, keep because they feel thus obliged. How is this possible? Hobbes argues that agreements in the "state of nature," the stateless state, would not be valid, citing the frailty of "mere words." But he overlooks the fact that much "enforcement" of agreements is internally monitored by the parties to them. The costs of reinforcement in such cases are very low—or at least, those costs are psychical rather than physical. Many other agreements, to be sure, are enforced, or at least are agreed to be enforceable. This brings up the question, Which are which? How do we decide whether an agreement is enforceable?

The terminology in which this last question is formulated is, however, insufficiently discriminating. For there are many means of enforcement. If a loved one will receive you coldly unless you do x, that is likely to induce your performance of x; but between persons who scarcely know each other or who do but do not particularly care about each other, that is unlikely to be effective. We must distinguish, at least, between, on the one hand, enforcement that consists in effective threats to punish or to forcibly restrict the party's freedom and, on the other, enforcement confined to withdrawal of previously supplied services or alteration for the worse of previously held attitudes. Since we are talking about social arrangements, arrangements to prevail in a sizable society with many members who are unfamiliar or not particularly friendly with each other, it is the former that requires special attention in the present context. Politics is about the use of force. The market anarchist's thesis is that force may be used only to counter force and not for any wider purpose. We assume that force against people's property is included in the proscribed uses of force.[8] Clearly, the libertarian view entails the market anarchist's: we may make whatever agreements we wish, such as that if I don't do x, you may hit me, or I shall pay a fine of $X to your solicitor, and so on.

A market society, then, may now be described as one in which the accepted rule is that one refrains from using force just to get one's way, confining the use of force instead to defensive activity or to any employments agreed to by the parties against whom it is used. There are then two questions to ask. One is whether we can expect a society so organized to work—granting that it is very unclear just what "working," in the relevant sense, consists of. One aspect that seems clearly relevant is stability. Would any such society be able to achieve stability? That is, would such a society persist in that form, or would it be crucially suskeptible to takeover by a state-type agency? Would an anarchy inevitably turn into an "archy" of some kind? Why should or would everyone accept that rule—the rule of liberty, as we might call it—and not some other? Why should we accept a principle that restricts use of coercion so narrowly?

The first question sounds like one for or against which it should be possible to assemble empirical evidence. If that is so, then the evidence certainly looks to be entirely against the anarchist. There appear not to be or to have been any anarchies amongst sizable and enduring societies on earth. But that is much too quick; a distinction must be made here. A state assumes power over all, and in principle it assumes unlimited power—power in all respects; yet, the extent of power actually wielded or even merely claimed by states, though it has varied a great deal, has never been totally unlimited. Within the boundaries of political states, there are and have been many areas of life within which anarchy is the order of the day. People frequently interact in

various ways without evident leaders and in the absence of acknowledged central rule makers among the group of participants. This,
indeed, is what makes sociology and economics possible. People relate
to each other on their own various terms, and structures and patterns
result that are of interest to the social scientist. The question is
whether these innumerable constellations of independent actors are
dependent for their existence on an overarching state, as some appear
to think, or at any rate whether an anarchic condition would inevitably
be such as to evolve into statelike arrangements.

Market Enforcement

At the level of logic, at least, the anarchist seems to be on solid
ground. Market interaction requires that people predominantly respect
the property rights of those with whom they interact. The occasional
violator either gets away with his violation and is subsequently ignored, or something is done about him and he gets punished or his
victims are suitably compensated. Those who administer the punishment or compensation can be acting on behalf of the victim exclusively
and need not have assumed a general duty to rectify all situations in
which violations of rights have taken place. There is certainly no
strictly logical necessity that any centralized agency possessed of
statelike powers perform such functions.

It seems to be true, nevertheless, that constellations of independent
actors readily succumb to statelike arrangements. We may describe
this either (1) as a matter of participants seeing advantages in, or a
"need" for, such an agency, or (2) as their falling prey to the wiles of
the power hungry. Which of the two it is, though, is an important
question. People will likely see the need for such an agency if there
really is a need for it, but it does *not* follow that if they profess to see
such a need, then there also *is* one. Whether there is would seem to be
a matter of logic, conceptual analysis. Either there is something about
human interaction that inherently requires states, or else those who
profess to see such a need are mistaken.

They may be not only mistaken, however, but biased as well. We
can expect the holders of power to be disposed to spread the doctrine
that states are necessary even if they are not. Government may rest on
error, and the error may even be deliberately fostered by those in
power. Government may, in short, rest essentially on what amounts
to fraud.[9]

If government is unnecessary, though, something else is: a basis of interpersonal agreement regarding the underlying rules to be followed, and moreover, that those rules include essential prohibitions of force and fraud. That is, the fact that someone got something by force or fraud must be accepted by essentially all as constituting a basis for grievance, compensation, and perhaps retribution. Thus it sounds as though there must be what has been called a "natural law" of human association. Especially in view of its historical associations with our project, a few words about it are in order.

Natural Law

Most ways of expounding the idea that some moral rules are "natural" have the notable disadvantage that what they claim appears to be empirically refuted. Obviously it is untrue that people *do* behave strictly in accordance with the tenets of any recognizable version of "natural law." And apparently it is untrue that all human infants emerge into articulate consciousness espousing those rules. Most of them do manage something of the sort, to be sure; but (1) by then they've been exposed to a good deal of social teaching and reinforcement; and (2) unfortunately for the natural law hypothesis, it seems that there is a good deal of variability in what particular individuals end up accepting in the way of general rules of conduct, especially insofar as they are members of differing groups. St. Thomas's dictum that the natural law is "written on our hearts" evidently needs to be taken with quite a few grains of salt. What, then, are we to replace it with?

There is, I think, a fairly short and quite reasonable answer to this, supplied in essentials by Thomas Hobbes, whose Laws of Nature are claimed by him to be "theorems" of prudence. People concerned about their own well-being, he thinks, will have to accept these rules as being rationally called for by a combination of four things: (1) their interests; (2) their powers; (3) the proclivities and capabilities of their fellows; and, of course, (4) the characteristics of the nonhuman environment. People wishing to do well will see the benefits of association with their fellows and will see the need for such association to be along peaceful and cooperative lines rather than the reverse. The need in question will be perceived, in Hobbes's account, as arising from the evident rough equality of the human capacity for destruction and violence and the evident impossibility of getting on if others are free to use those destructive capacities. In short, Hobbes argues that the general shape of the rules of human interaction are not self-evident and certainly not matters of some special sort of "intuition," but rather, pretty straightforward inferences of common sense about the four factors mentioned.

Yet Hobbes, as we know, was also the champion of the state, of "Sovereignty" as an essential device for securing the actual benefits of the rule of natural law. Natural law, he thinks, will rule only if *somebody* rules. But—fortunately for the would-be anarchist— Hobbes's argument is flawed, and fatally. It is important to see where he went wrong in order to understand which way is right.

Hobbes's argument makes use of an idea that is still regarded as virtually a theorem of decision theory. A familiar type of human interaction exemplifies the general structure known as Prisoners' Dilemma. In such a structure, each participant chooses freely between two alternatives whose payoffs are a function of what others choose as well. If all choose x, then everybody is better off than if all choose y; yet each individual is best off if he chooses y while the others choose x. Since he will then be better off than in any alternative outcome, that is the one he will prefer. So Hobbes held, and most modern decision theorists join him in holding, that the rational actor will indeed choose y in such situations. All making this individually best choice in a condition in which there are absolutely no rules about *anything* leads to the famous "war of all against all," in which everybody is enormously worse off.

In order to head off this unfortunate result, thinks Hobbes, situations with such structures need to be fundamentally altered. Those who choose y must not be *able* to do so without entailing some further disutility not included in the original picture. This disutility is a penalty. In the Hobbesian scenario, it is to be wielded by a state. Why a state? Because, Hobbes reasoned, only a state has the necessary power to force any and all miscreants into line.

There are several questions to ask. First, is the state of nature—the situation we would have in the absence of government—indeed of broadly Prisoners' Dilemma type? Second, is the proposed inference to the individual superiority of the noncooperative strategy sound? And third, even if it is, would there be means of dealing with it other than Hobbes's proposed sovereign?

Regarding the first question, most theorists who have considered the question at all have, in effect if not on the verbal face of it, accepted Hobbes's characterization. We should perhaps take note of a possible description of society according to which the situation facing humans is not even a Prisoners' Dilemma, but instead a *zero-sum* game—a situation in which one person's gain is another's loss. Of course, if nobody can improve his own situation without worsening that of someone else, there is no hope of cooperation, and the general advancement of society is simply out of the question. Fortunately, the zero-sum thesis is simply wrong.[10] (The modern version of it invokes claims about limited resources and the like. Those versions are also wrong, but the point cannot be argued here.[11])

A situation in which all are free to resort to violence at will is dominated by one in which no one is: every single individual will do better than that very individual will have done if everyone, including himself, takes on a reliable commitment to refrain from violence (and the other vices detailed in Hobbes's list—all of which, of course, Hobbes claims, I think correctly, to follow from the fundamental vice,[12] which is the disposition to resort to violence in the promotion of one's various ends). Is there any real reason to doubt this thesis?

This, it turns out, is a rather tricky question. The short answer is "No": of course everyone will do better to take that alternative than to take the single alternative of having no commitments *at all*. But is that really the only other option? It seems not. In real life, people are often reliable but sometimes not. A selective mix of cooperation and defection will at least seem to pay and is certainly what almost all individuals actually do exemplify in any considerable stretch of social life.[13]

Matters get considerably more complicated when we consider the possibility that human interactions might have the structure known as "Chicken" rather than Prisoners' Dilemma (henceforth PD, for short). In both games, the participants have a common second-best; but in the Chicken game, they have a common worst outcome, in contrast to the PD, in which both parties have a common third-best outcome. In PD, therefore, one player's best is the others' worst: A's best response to B's threat of aggression is defense—A can't do better by knuckling under. But in Chicken, unfortunately, he can. If he insists on resisting, and the other does not back down, then both will lose; if, instead, A knuckles under, then A may be enslaved, but at least he is still alive. Faced with the choice between being the chicken and being the hawk, A may prefer being the chicken, nor is A clearly irrational in so choosing, as Peter Danielson[14] so cogently points out.

This problem is clearly not an easy one, but certain general comments are in order. One is that if it is possible to prevent social

Chicken games from developing, then it is plausible to say that we should do so, and plausible for the same reasons that recommend cooperation in PD. It is not at all surprising that it is a theorem of commonsense morality that we ought not to employ coercion, just as we ought to refrain from violence. This response may be lame, for the question then is whether social rules of that kind have the clout necessary to achieve their purpose. But then, the very same question can be asked about PD; and certainly the answer, in a vast range of real-life cases, is that it certainly does. Social life is generally not a fracas, despite the many temptations for the unscrupulous or the sociopathic. That we have much to gain by cooperation and much to lose without it, as a general observation about our situations vis-á-vis our natural environment and each other, seems too obvious to need more than a mere mention.

Nevertheless, Danielson's challenge does seem to me to be right in one very important respect: it probably accounts for the existence and survival of the state. We shall return to that later.

The second of our three questions is whether the Hobbesian deduction from the premise of individual rationality is correct. Now on this, it seems to me, there is room for another view. That other view has been interestingly expounded by David Gauthier in recent times. Gauthier holds that the disposition to choose the "defect" option in PD is a mistake. We should instead adopt a disposition to cooperate, provided that the person with whom we are dealing is also disposed to do so, and to defect only if it looks as though that's how he is disposed. This Gauthier calls "constrained maximization," in contrast to the strategy of "straight maximization," which calls for defection no matter what the other person does.

Gauthier's solution has seemed to many to smack of moralism. And it is undoubtedly more complicated than the game theorist's response. Instead of adopting a simple, unconditional "nasty" strategy, the rational individual, according to Gauthier, sees the need in such situations to operate on a more complex strategy. Now, the complexity of this strategy is seen to be especially deep when we ask how we could know that the other person has the similar disposition—and above all when we reflect that that disposition is a disposition to cooperate if I am disposed to cooperate, so that part of my solving my problem about him is that he has to have solved the same problem about me.[15]

Even so, though, it looks as though there must be some kind of empirical solution to this problem, for we in fact do successfully cooperate, without depending on coercive enforcement agencies, in countless cases; and we all think that people should keep their agreements and that people who do not are on that account to be criticized. Is this last fact to be shrugged off as irrelevant? In accepting it, after all, I move from the rationality of actually doing the cooperative thing to the rationality of certain types of reactions to those who do not.

But this, I insist, is actually sufficient for our purposes. It is rational for me to insist on your keeping your agreements with me and for you to insist on my keeping my agreements with you. The perception that this is so, as well as lively awareness of the likelihood of followup reinforcement, seems to be extensively motivating in human affairs, and for good reason. Other theorists have pointed out that if we turn from the *one-shot* PD to the *iterated* dilemma, in which we face, time and again, the same general structure with the same people, then the rationality of a rule to treat the other this time as he has treated you previously is very plausible indeed.[16] People with a continuing tendency to defect will certainly do worse than people with the tendency to cooperate as long as the other person has done so. It is obvious that they will and easy to demonstrate to them. Iteration, indeed, seems to be a context in which we have the kind of evidence regarding dispositions that the Gauthieran cooperator requires.

I shall therefore propose that we settle for something very close to the Gauthieran conclusion. It *is* rational to be disposed to cooperate where cooperation looks to be likely; it is rational to insist on cooperation wherever cooperation is possible—as it generally is; and it is irrational, in real life, to behave the way a Hobbesian state-of-nature maximizer is alleged to behave.

This brings us to the third question: even if we were to accept the miserable view of the standard game theorist, would there be means of dealing with it other than Hobbes's proposed sovereign? It is here that the anarchist's case is the strongest, since the answer is so obviously in the affirmative. The topic, we should be careful to recognize, takes in a great deal of terrain. Hobbes's sovereign is intentionally totalitarian, the scope of his power essentially unlimited. No one should want to defend such an institution. Those who think that the state is justified insist that a state must be very much less nearly omnipotent than Hobbes's argument would have it. In particular, virtually all theorists since, including his successor John Locke, insist that a state must be, broadly speaking, democratic *and* must operate in an environment of constitutional restrictions. The point is, then, that there seem to be many alternative sorts of sovereigns alongside the anarchist's alternative of no sovereign at all and that none of them accepts the fundamental argument of Hobbes. It is an important question whether this is somehow a pipe dream, but facts must be faced. Contemporary states do frequently refrain from various policies because it would be evidently in violation of their constitutions, and governments are, every now and then, chucked out of office by electoral processes.

What should we do in the face of this apparent plethora of possibilities? The anarchist's answer is that we must find out what is wrong with the state *as such*, so that even as minimal a state as we can imagine will still suffer from that defect. In addition, the would-be anarchist must show that no state has compensating advantages such that it is nevertheless preferable to anarchy. Even if we can do that, there remains the daunting question of whether anarchy is really feasible in the world we live in. It may be that for some reason it is not—some reason other than any having to do with the virtues of states, if there are any. That would be a dismal result, indeed; even so, one might learn something from it.

The Case against the State

Why think that there is anything inherently and necessarily wrong with the state? To see the answer to this, we need to attend carefully to the distinction between states and associations. The bridge club, the gardening society, even the philosophical association can decide to set up a governing board, hold elections, subject themselves to the resulting rules, and so on. The individual may join some organization ruled, for all practical purposes, by an absolute monarch. What distinguishes the state from all these is that those subject to it don't *join* and that its authority extends to all, in respects that have nothing to do with any reasons why those, if any, who do join did so. Given that many are certain not to share the purposes proposed as justifying what the state imposes, it is highly probable that they will be badly done by.

Is it certain, though? Let's think about that one. We may here propose a general formula for acceptable law. What is needed is that *each individual* subject to it is better off, *in his own terms*, from being so subjected than he would be if not so subjected to it. Bear in mind that this recipe applies not only to the general idea of law but also to its *application* and does so in *each individual case*. Officer O'Malley rightly applies the law to Jones at time t only if subjecting Jones to this penalty at this time is such as to bring it about that Jones is better off on the whole, in his own view, than he would have been had he not been subject to the law in such a way that this penalty is called for by persons doing just what Jones does at t in the circumstances prevailing then.

It is logically possible that this criterion could be met. But it is incredibly unlikely. State officials are paid to administer some or other laws. Making their pay contingent on the right administration of those laws is exceedingly difficult—to the point of being humanly impossible. This probability is enormously increased if the people who administer the rules are hired by Jones to do so, and moreover to administer precisely the rule now being administered. (Enthusiasts for the state sometimes argue that that is the situation with the state. In order to make that stick, they must stretch the sense of "hired" beyond recognition.) From the point of view of institutional design, an institution that incorporated the distinctive feature of the market, that the consumer is boss—"consumer sovereignty"—has a far better chance of success than any recognizable state.

Democracy, to be sure, is widely advertised as incorporating this feature. If you find that idea compelling, just imagine a supermarket that advertised that you would, upon entering the store, enter a vote for a "buyer" who would buy whatever he thought was likely to get him more votes from all the customers than either of two other candidates for this position, and he would then give you whatever share of the goods he felt like, and there was nothing you could do about this until the next such election, four years hence. Only someone with remarkably dim perceptions of the functioning of the state, or with a bizarre sense of humor, could regard democracy as providing anything much resembling market services. For the rest, the track record of actual democracies in providing genuine services to their citizens is sufficiently dismal that what little theoretical support there is for this form of government at the conceptual level is reduced to nil at the empirical level.[17] Lord Acton is too often quoted to the effect that "All power corrupts, and absolute power corrupts absolutely." But those who blithely quote him concentrate only on the evils of the spectacular tyrants of history—the Stalins, the Napoleans, and so on. But the anarchist's real case concerns the little guys—the ones elected by the people in hopes that they will actually do some good. Political power is inherently likely—"certain" is close enough to the truth—to cause more evil than good, and the good that it occasionally does can be better brought about by people who, either because it pays or because they are interested in it, are motivated to do it rather than to bring about the side payments of politics.

Prospects for Anarchism: Not Good

There remains the question of why anarchy is not more popular than it is. With proper perspective, of course, it is in fact enormously popular, in the sense that the functionally anarchic parts of our societies, such as the markets for most consumer goods (despite the limits imposed by taxes and the welter of regulations hovering over everything), not only work superbly but also are perceived by all concerned to do so in practice. Nevertheless, anarchy in the sense of the total absence of government is so far from popular as to be almost entirely ignored, and treated with derision insofar as not ignored. Why should this be so, one wonders?

There are, I think, three kinds of answers, not entirely unrelated.

1. Throughout this essay I have ignored the nonrational aspects of government. Six million Britons volunteered to fight for their country in the First World War, even those who knew what was in store for them at the front. The first Canada-Russia hockey series culminated in a closely fought game that was televised around the world; in Canada itself, the country essentially came to a halt during that game. (This author recalls being at Stratford at a production of Shakespeare when, during the third act, suddenly the action on stage came to a temporary halt, and one actor stepped to center stage to inform the audience that Canada had just won the series by virtue of a heart-stopping goal in the last seconds of the final game. The audience broke into a five-minute ovation before Shakespeare could be resumed.) It is fair to say that things like this cannot be readily factored into my arguments above. Is the state justified because otherwise we would not have Canada-Russia games? Because the Olympics would never be the same? Because if the state goes, so does its pomp and majesty and suchlike? And a lot of what has been most interesting about history along with it? We'll leave the reader to ponder that one, but I do not want to underrate that factor. The question is whether the entertainment value of the state is really worth the costs. Frankly, I doubt it, and I doubt that most ordinary people would think so either.

2. There is no such thing as a free lunch—but there is such a thing as a boondoggle. Modern government encourages 90 percent of the populace to think it's getting something for nothing. The great majority

of citizens belong to at least one group or other that has managed to induce legislators to do something for its own particular special interest. What it does is to provide a service that is virtually free to many people in its constituency—free in the sense that its (highly inflated) price is paid for by *others*. Each beneficiary group throws a cost onto the rest. This would not matter if everyone was a member of enough beneficiary groups and the service provided was sufficiently efficient that it would be worth it, from the point of view of each person, to pay as much as he is in fact paying in taxes for what he gets. But this is very far from being the case—a fact that much too rarely comes home to the clueless or bemused taxpayer.

3. Why is the taxpayer so clueless and bemused? Here we come to the most important reason of all: the self-interest of the governing class, which with big government is very large. The bureaucrats, policemen, secretaries, parliamentarians, and so on are interested in jobs: in keeping them and in their being secure. The power of government enables them to be fairly secure—in many cases *very* secure. It is also attractive on its own, enabling the office holder to wield authority over underlings and power over ordinary citizens.

To this, unfortunately, we can add the interests of considerable segments of modern populations who perceive that their careers or other interests are forwarded by the continued power of government. Not only popular media but also most of what we might call the intellectual upper-middle class support the welfare state, the art-subsidizing state, the medical state, and the rest. All this effectively acts, in the end, to keep the lower orders down rather than to provide the help that well-meaning and intelligent people supposed they could provide by all these means. But that is not a message that easily gets through to such people—who, after all, forearmed with the meaningless but effective epithets of today's politics, stand ready to dismiss analysis as "right wing," after which who needs to read farther?

Good government is government in the interest of the governed, not of the governors. But, as we are coming more and more to appreciate, under the impetus of public choice analysts as well as common sense, the law is predominantly driven by the interests of the *governors*, not of the *governed*. And part of the package is that government has the power to induce people to believe that what it does for people is both necessary and useful.

Why does government remain in power? Why, in fact, are there still governments? The short answer is that governments command powers to which the ordinary citizen is utterly unequal. When an individual tries to defy the authorities—to "fight city hall"—he will be met by resistance. The ordinary citizen invariably pays his speeding fines instead of fighting them in court: the probability of losing is high, and even if he wins he has paid so much in time, trouble, and money that the gain is scarcely worth it to him. Multiply this by virtually the entire population, and the point becomes clear.

It is true that most laws are evaded or ignored much of the time and indeed, in a great many significant cases, most of the time. One may speculate that if the population suddenly were to "work to rule" and obey all the laws, society would come fairly close to grinding to a halt. The cost of this would likewise be terrific. How does all this happen? The secret lies in the Chicken game. When both parties resist, they both come out worse than if one or the other had knuckled under—but the cost to the individual of knuckling under is characteristically lower than the cost to the state. It's an unequal competition, and the individual generally loses.

Only at the polls does the citizen exercise real power—but that power is also minuscule, as we know. Moreover, the differences among candidates are generally trivial, so far as the citizen is concerned. None of the candidates is about to run on a platform of disbanding the government, nor would they get many votes if they did. Citizens are firmly, though not rationally, convinced that their government is a good and necessary thing, however poor its track record in detail. All candidates continue the time-honored tradition of promising what they know perfectly well cannot be delivered, and what they do deliver is at costs the citizen either doesn't understand or believes will be largely paid by others.

Despite its brilliant track record and the abysmal track record of governments, the market has, therefore, little chance of expanding into domains taken over by the public. Superior force has a way of winning the battles. Government, indeed, depends on the market: if there is no income and wealth to tax, government goes out of business. This imposes a limit on the destructiveness of government activity, indeed, but that limit is very high, and government's capacity to keep us near that limit is immense. Prospects for anarchy, then, are not good. We will not soon see the end of government.

It is, however, unnecessary to talk, globally, of "the end of government." Privatization in this, that, or the other domain is in principle possible and occasionally even happens. Many governments are about at the limit of their capacity to increase borrowing, after years of irresponsibly promising voters what others will pay for. They must, perforce, reduce spending at last. Here and there government programs will be virtually or completely suspended, and the beneficent influence of anarchy will be reinstated. The most that the anarchist can realistically hope for is an occasional small victory of that kind. At the practical level, his best hope is to chip away at small things. For the rest, patient labors expended in demonstrating, to the few who will read, that government provision of services is a bad idea in domain after domain are about the best anarchists can do for the foreseeable future. A certain amount of intellectual satisfaction is the reward for that, no doubt, even if its immediate gain for the typical citizen is small.

But as for a general dismantling of Leviathan—don't hold your breath.

Notes

1. See David Friedman, "Anarchy and Efficient Law," this volume, 235–253.

2. See A. John Simmons, "Philosophical Anarchism," this volume, 19–39, and Leslie Green, "Who Believes in Political Obligation?" this volume, 1–17.

3. We cannot here go into the important distinctions among preemption, punishment, and exacted compensation.

4. See Jan Clifford Lester, "Market-Anarchy, Liberty, and Pluralism," this volume, 63–79.

5. See Peter Danielson, "The Rights of Chickens," this volume, 171–93.

6. It might be wondered why fraud is ruled out. The answer is straightforward. To communicate successfully, parties A and B require a common system of language sufficient to get the message in question across. These messages concern the way things are around them. If A intentionally misleads B, A utilizes this common system effectively to bring it about that B believes Q rather than P, where P is, so far as A knows, true. Now, when B acts on Q rather than P, B expects to bring about a result, R, which B supposes will occur if and only if Q. Since P is what is true, however, B's action will not result in the intended R. A has thus effectively brought it about, by action for which A is responsible, that B does not do what B wants. This, by definition, infringes B's freedom.

7. See Green, "Who Believes in Political Obligation?"

8. Again, it is too large a subject to go into here how a rule of property flows from the general rule against violating liberty. See Narveson, *The Libertarian Idea* (Philadelphia: Temple University Press, 1988), chaps. 6–8. An unpublished paper by the author, "The Justification of Private Property by First-Comers," is available on request.

9. This thought is developed in the author's "Toward a Liberal Theory of

Ideology: A Quasi-marxian Exploration,'' a paper presented at the meetings of the Canadian Philosophical Association, 1992.

10. I am assuming that the zero-sum claim is a general claim about humans. There perhaps are some few who get their kicks from seeing other people suffer, but to suppose that this is the dominant motive of typical human beings is to suppose what flies in the face of the evidence, if evidence is allowed.

11. Among the many valuable books rejecting the current versions, the most amusing is P. J. O'Rourke's light-hearted but incisive *All the Trouble in the World* (New York: Atlantic Monthly Press, 1994). There are many others. See the author's ''Resources and Environmental Policy,'' *Philosophic Exchange* 24–25 (1993-94): 39–62.

12. R. E. Ewin, in *Virtues and Rights*, argues that the Hobbesian moral rules are, as Hobbes at some places says, virtues and not ''laws,'' despite their title of ''Laws of Nature.'' In one sense, he is certainly right: morality has to be a matter of the internal disposition of the soul. But in another sense, the claim is wrong, or at least very misleading, for these laws may certainly be appealed to as the basis for settling claims and, if need be, settling them by force.

13. A fascinating study by Jeffrey Olen, *Moral Freedom* (Philadelphia: Temple University Press, 1988), makes this point very effectively.

14. Peter Danielson, ''The Rights of Chickens.''

15. Peter Vallentyne, ed., *Contractarianism and Rational Choice* (New York: Cambridge, 1991), has a number of critical essays on the work of Gauthier and a response by him that readers somewhat versed in game theory will find extremely interesting and helpful.

16. See John T. Sanders, ''The State of Statelessness,'' this volume, 255–88.

17. A footnote referring the reader to detailed support would run to several volumes, but a good start is provided by William C. Mitchell and Randy T. Simmons, *Beyond Politics* (Boulder, Colo.: Westview Press, 1994).

11

The State and War Making

Cheyney Ryan

War made the state, and the state made war.
—Charles Tilly
*The Formation of National States
in Western Europe*

There is a long history of complaint about the extent to which the state has required individuals to sacrifice their material possessions, but surely the more extreme sacrifice that states have required of individuals is the sacrifice of their bodily persons for the purposes of warfare. "Religion and philosophy have claimed their martyrs, as have family, friendship, and office," Michael Walzer has written in one of the more trenchant essays on this topic. "But surely there has never been a more successful claimant of human life than the state."[1]

A central concern of much recent political sociology has been the extent to which these two forms of sacrifice are connected.[2] States, of course, cannot engage in wars without making claims on both the material possessions and bodily persons of their citizens, but recent research has advanced the larger and more historical claim that the steady expansion of welfare state institutions (and other forms of state involvement in the economy) in the modern era has been largely because of the state's increasing involvement in the actions and arrangements of warfare.[3] This view has been offered as a corrective to both liberal and marxist social theories, which have tended to regard the state's war-making activities as secondary, and largely subservient, to its economic activities. The new view does not entirely reverse this perspective, but it does suggest that the state's penchant for violence is something to be understood in its own right and something that itself helps explain, say, the (re)distributive policies of the state.[4]

The authority of the state to make claims on its citizens' lives for the purposes of warfare would seem to be deeply problematic from the standpoint of liberal individualism.[5] Indeed, one would think that a political view that has voiced such fundamental doubts about the state's authority to dispose of our material possessions would voice even greater doubts about its authority to dispose of our bodily persons in times of warfare; yet, as George Kateb has recently observed in his *The Inner Ocean*, a notable (I should say remarkable) fact about the classical thinkers of the social contract tradition is how little attention they devoted to the state's war-making claims on the individual and how unsatisfactory their discussion of those claims was—when they devoted any attention at all to them.[6] The same could be said for contemporary social contract theorists or theorists of liberal individualism in general, as Kateb himself points out. John Rawls, for example, devotes only one page to the topic in *A Theory of Justice*.[7] The debate between Rawls and Robert Nozick that has so preoccupied Anglo-American philosophy in recent years would lead one to conclude that the most serious questions about the state pertain to its (re)distributive dimensions rather than to what I would term its strictly destructive dimensions.

During the 1960s and early 1970s there was significant (though not extensive) discussion of the state's war-making claims, most notably in the discussions of conscription—and the extent to which conscription seems to presume what Michael Walzer has termed "the obligation to die for the state."[8] That such discussion has almost totally subsided since that time can probably be explained by the fact that in the United States the draft was ended in the early 1970s. There are, however, a number of reasons why the end of the draft hardly justifies today's relative silence about the status of the state's war-making claims. To begin with, though the state may have suspended the draft for the moment, it certainly maintains (and proclaims) the right to reinstitute that practice whenever it sees fit. The state's reservation of that right harkens to the fact that, as all the evidence suggests, warfare in its modern form requires conscription. Volunteer armies work fine, as long as the army is not required to do what it is meant to do—engage in fighting for any length of time.[9] A state without the power to conscript is a state without the power to engage in warfare, in any meaningful sense; so as long as the state (or any collective entity, for that matter) is accorded the authority to engage in warfare, the state's authority to engage in conscription will remain a significant theoretical problem.

The most immediate problem raised by conscription is whether it requires individuals to become soldiers without their consent. This problem might presumably be resolved if military service were placed on an all-volunteer basis,[10] but there would remain the problem, addressed in some of the past discussions of conscription, of whether the status of soldier is one that individuals can intelligibly be conceived as choosing or whether the sacrifices that individuals are required to make as soldiers involve, say, the alienation of that which simply cannot be alienated (in the eyes of liberal individualism), for if the sacrifices required of soldiers necessarily do involve such alienation, then the military per se would seem to be illegitimate—regardless of how it is constituted. This possibility is one that has long been entertained by the traditions of pacifism and nonviolence, traditions that have had a deep impact on my own thinking and that I shall return to briefly at the end of this essay. These traditions are committed to a kind of anarchism, insofar as they believe that a legitimate state requires a legitimate military—and no military can be legitimate.

What follows is part of a larger endeavor of rethinking political philosophy from the standpoint of violence in general and warfare in particular. I have remarked on how both liberal and marxist social theory have accorded insufficient importance to the state's war-making function. The same could be said for liberal and marxist political theory and the accounts they have provided of the logic and legitimacy of the state.[11] In this essay, my chief reference point will be the liberalism of the classical social contract tradition, the tradition of Thomas Hobbes, John Locke, and Rawls. I have spoken of the apparent reluctance of this tradition to address the problems around the state's war-making claims on the individual. My discussion will suggest that this is more than just a casual omission, that it harkens to the depth of the problem posed by those claims and to the possibility that the state's war-making claims (those claims implicit in conscription and in the disciplinary requirements of military organization) are simply incompatible with the commitments of liberal individualism. This is a big suggestion, one I cannot possibly confirm with any thoroughness in the pages that follow. I shall try to motivate it though, by discussing in the section titled "The Right of Self-Preservation" below the relation between the state's war-making claims and the right of self-preservation. My reference point here will be Hobbes and some of the commentaries to which his views have given rise. In the next section, I shall extend the discussion to more contemporary figures and issues, with particular reference to the debate between Rawls and Michael Sandel. In the last section I conclude with some brief remarks on the place of these concerns in the history of liberalism and the importance of those anarchist thinkers associated with the tradition of nonviolence.

The Right of Self-Preservation

The claim that liberal individualism in general and classical social contract theory in particular face deep if not insurmountable problems in accounting for the state's war-making claims on the individual is one that has traditionally been advanced by idealist thinkers. F. H. Bradley states in his anti-individualist essay "My Station and Its Duties" that no social contract theory can explain "except by the most palpable fictions" the right of the state to compel self-sacrifice.[12] The young G. W. F. Hegel put the point even more sharply, suggesting that if the state existed solely for the protection of life and property, then for a citizen to expose himself to death in defense of the state would be to do something absurd, since the means would annul the end that it served.[13] Now, Bradley and Hegel raise this problem from a standpoint almost diametrically opposed to mine. They take it for granted that the state is a positive good—indeed, they take it for granted that sacrificing oneself for the state is a positive good; so for them the fact that social contract theory cannot account for these goods amounts to a reductio ad absurdum of that approach. I assume none of this, but I do assume that liberal individualists who approve of the state must provide an account of the state's war-making claims if their commitment to the state is to be sustained. I shall suggest that the problem they face in so doing is evoked by Hegel's rather dismissive remarks.

As noted, it is beyond my powers here to demonstrate that liberal individualism cannot account for the state's war-making claims, but I do want to explore some of its difficulties in doing so by focusing on the views of Thomas Hobbes.

On the whole, Hobbes says rather little about the state's war-making authority—though he does say more about that authority, and conscription in particular, than any other classical liberal thinker.

(Deborah Baumgold attributes this to the fact that noncooperation, or resistance to participation in the military, was a serious problem in the English Civil War.[14]) Hobbes's reserve on these matters is continued by his commentators. Most recently, for example, Jean Hampton's much admired *Hobbes and the Social Contract Tradition* says almost nothing on the topic.[15] Baumgold does speak to the issue in her *Hobbes's Political Theory*, as does the late Gregory Kavka in his *Hobbesian Moral and Political Theory*.[16] These commentators (like every other that I have encountered who remarks on the matter) begin by acknowledging that the state's war-making authority constitutes a substantial problem for Hobbes's approach and for any approach like his. Kavka provides a succinct statement of the general problem: "How are we to reconcile the individual's right of self-preservation with the State's authority to control its citizens' conduct for its own protection and the promotion of the common good?"[17]

Hobbes maintains that "everyone is obliged" to bear arms in defense of the state when needed, "because otherwise the institution of the commonwealth . . . was in vain."[18] Hobbes's point would seem to be that if the state cannot defend itself, then it cannot possibly be relied on to carry out the purpose for which it is instituted (in the Hobbesian view): to defend us. So there is something absurd in constructing a state that does not have the right and means to its own self-defense. The question remains, however—and it is a question implicit in Kavka's query above—whether the state's right to self-defense might not infringe on the individual's right to self-defense.

The natural response to this problem is to insist that the state's war-making claims on the individual are ones that individuals grant to the state in the interest of self-preservation. Hobbes insists that "no man can transfer or lay down his right to save himself from death"; but the war-making claims of the state, and the institutions (of soldiering and the military) that they animate, do not represent any alienation of that right. They represent, rather, an assertion of the right to self-preservation—in constituting a collective means to its defense. On this view, then, the obligation to die for the state, which many have seen as at the heart of military service, is simply a chimera. When soldiers defend the state, they are really defending themselves, and if they die in the process, they are not really dying for the state, but dying in defense of their own lives.

Can the matter really be this simple? Let us consider two problems that arise in this context.

(1) The first might be termed the personal retreat problem. It

arises when your status as a soldier requires you to continue fighting alongside your fellow soldiers, but your self-preservation is much more effectively served by your personal retreat. Now, an effective military requires that individuals not retreat in such circumstances. Even more, an (even minimally) effective military requires that every soldier be assured in the knowledge that his fellow soldiers may not and will not retreat, for otherwise there is a massive reason for all soldiers to run when the going gets difficult. It is because the military must be confident (and be confident that everyone will be confident) that soldiers will not retreat to save themselves that it invariably imposes the ultimate sanction on soldiers who desert. (General Dwight D. Eisenhower, in approving the execution of Private Eddie Slovik for desertion in World War II, asserted that the action was necessary to maintaining an "effective fighting force."[19])

An interest in self-preservation certainly provides a reason for constituting a military force and consenting to become a soldier. In so doing, it may even provide a reason for binding oneself not to retreat in the circumstances described. The problem, though, is whether these considerations (and the obligations they imply) can possibly override the reason for retreating when one actually finds oneself in such circumstances, for if they cannot, then it would seem that individuals in becoming soldiers necessarily maintain a certain right to be "cowards," a right that undercuts an essential requirement of military discipline (and a basis of soldiers' confidence in one another). Hobbes, it should be noted, suggests that conscripted soldiers do maintain a reason for retreating and the right to do so in such circumstances, but he also suggests that the state reserves the right to punish them with death if they do so, all of which leads to the very interesting conclusion that soldier and military in such circumstances have entered into a state of war with one another![20]

Some have suggested that the problem here might be resolved by appealing to the element of risk that is involved in constituting a military and consenting to be a soldier.[21] One might think of the soldier who has been proven wrong in his judgment as to the value of the military for his own self-preservation as no different from the investor who loses money on his investment because his financial intuitions proved wrong. The fact that an investment does not pan out does not show that one was necessarily irrational in committing oneself to the investment in the first place. Similarly, the fact that soldiering does not turn out to be the most effective means to one's self-preservation does not show that one was irrational in committing oneself to it in the first place. It is all part of the risk we must take, if we are to have a military at all. The cases are really quite dissimilar, though: a soldier who confronts the choice between fighting or retreating is not like an investor whose financial commitments have simply failed to pan out. He is more like an investor who must decide whether to maintain his financial commitments in the face of the fact that they will fail to pan out. Rationality in both cases requires that you cut and run.

Hobbes suggests that individuals may rightfully retreat in such circumstances because "no man can transfer or lay down his right to save himself from death, wounds, or imprisonment."[22] Now, a soldier who continues fighting is not renouncing any and every action in his own defense, of course, but he still renounces his right to self-defense, insofar as that right is not just the right to take some action in defense of one's life, but the right to take the most effective available action in defense of one's life. A further point is that, in suggesting that it is irrational for soldiers not to retreat in such circumstances, I am not suggesting that it is always irrational for persons to fight rather than flee when the latter constitutes the most effective means of self-preservation. At times there are reasons for sacrificing oneself in this way (when doing so might ensure the safety of a loved one, say), but the problem we face with soldiering is not the general one of whether rejecting the option to retreat can ever be rational. The problem is the more specific one of whether it is rational for individuals to reject that option qua soldiers, given the reason for which they become soldiers in the first place—self-preservation.

(2) The second problem might be termed the cannon fodder problem. It arises when your status as a soldier requires you to submit to certain death—in the words of Locke, "to march up to the mouth of a cannon, or stand in a breach, when (you) will surely perish."[23] To some extent this would seem to be but a more extreme version of the previous problem, but it helps illuminate some further issues.

To begin with, the issue here is not really self-defense so much as suicide, for I should think that an order to march "to the mouth of the cannon" would be naturally construed as an order to commit suicide, as distinct from an order not to defend oneself; as one marches to one's doom, one might after all do whatever possible to defend oneself against the cannon one approaches. The right to self-defense and the right to commit suicide are, of course, importantly distinct rights: many religious traditions, and even the Anglo-American legal tradition, have been deeply committed to self-defense while deeply ambivalent about suicide. What is notable about the state's war-making claims is that they seem to infringe on the individual's authority over suicide not only by requiring that individuals do commit suicide at times, but also by requiring that individuals not commit suicide (when they might otherwise wish to do so) so as to remain available as a resource for fighting. (Those claims, Walzer has suggested, require that you not only die for the state but live for the state as well.[24])

Again, the issue posed by the cannon fodder problem is not the general one of whether it can ever be rational to commit suicide. One assumes it clearly can be. The problem is the more specific one of whether it is rational for individuals to consent to suicidal commands qua soldiers, given the reason for which they become soldiers in the first place—self-preservation. If, before, the problem involved the inherent rationality of "cowardice" for the prudent soldier, the problem now would seem to involve the inherent irrationality of "heroism"—conceived (as it has tended to be conceived) as the capacity for certain sorts of suicidal acts, all of which suggests the element of truth in Hegel's suggestion that ultimate sacrifice is rendered absurd by an individualist account of these matters.

Writes Walzer, any theory

> which begins with the absolute independence of freely willing individuals and goes on to treat politics and the state as instrumental to the achievement of individual purposes would seem by its very nature incapable of describing ultimate obligation. This is certainly true when individual purposes reach no further than bodily safety or the appropriation and enjoyment of physical objects.[25]

Now, I have spoken in quite general terms of the state's war-making claims on the individual as manifested in what is required of individuals qua soldiers. I have articulated the requirements implicit in the latter status by appealing to what the military requires of soldiers in conditions of battle; but these requirements, it might be pointed out, have a certain plasticity to them. After all, until recently, in the United States military a captured soldier was forbidden to tell his questioners anything more than his name and rank, but this requirement was substantially altered after the Vietnam War. Perhaps, then, the problems here raised about the compatibility of the military with liberal individualist commitments are not really problems about the military and soldiering per se, but problems about the particular forms that these have tended to take.

On the one hand, I might be ready to grant this point, though I would suggest that the forms that the military and soldiering have taken are not just contingent historical artifacts; rather, at least some of those forms are intimately connected with the requirements of the modern nation-state, so that any radical transformation of those forms would seem problematic without the radical transformation of the nation-state—or its abolition (as we have come to know it). On the other hand, I am still inclined to believe that at least some of the objectionable aspects of the military are ones that we will find in any collective organization oriented to the effective use of violence, in which case we might face a choice between giving up some of our individualist commitments or giving up some of our tolerance of collective violence. I shall say more about this matter below.

Current Thinking on War Making

I now want to place the problem at hand in a more current context by relating it to the work of John Rawls and some contemporary critics of the social contract tradition.

Rawls, as I have noted, devotes but one page of his 587-page *A Theory of Justice* to the problem of conscription (as far as I can determine, he does not mention the problem in his later *Political Liberalism*). He observes that conscription constitutes "a drastic interference with the basic liberties of citizens" but suggests that it is permissible "when demanded for the defense of liberty itself, including here not only the liberties of the citizens of the society in question, but also those of persons in other societies as well."[26] Rawls hardly says enough about this issue to warrant a serious critique of it, but the lines of his account seem clear enough to raise some rather obvious questions about it. The right to self-defense does not play as prominent a role in Rawls's work as it does in Hobbes's, so the problem seems a bit less pressing of how (for Rawls) individuals can intelligibly alienate their right to self-preservation in becoming soldiers.

Within Rawls's framework, there are serious questions about whether persons, employing a "maximin" strategy, would alienate the right to self-preservation as soldiering requires them to do. Kateb asserts flatly that the "drastic interference" with basic liberties implicit in conscription cannot be justified by a maximin strategy.[27] This is a complicated issue, though, if only because in Rawls's recent work the force of his veil-of-ignorance apparatus has become progressively fuzzier. A clearer problem, perhaps, involves the potential difficulties in the sort of trade-off between liberties that Rawls identifies with conscription and military service. What I have in mind is this: Rawls's comments on interfering with liberty for the sake of defending liberty would seem to liken conscription to those limitations on, say, freedom of speech in the name of the greater freedom of all, but the cases are really quite dissimilar, since the interference with liberty involved in conscription and military service is qualitatively so much more severe than any other limitations licensed by liberal institutions, involving as it does the risk and potential sacrifice of life itself. The limitations on liberty that one consents to in submitting to the requirements of military service are ones that can render any other liberties one might enjoy meaningless. (It should also be noted that, as a matter of historical fact, these limitations have had a deep inequity to them, insofar as the criteria according to which some people and not others are chosen to serve in the military have evidenced a consistent class bias. This problem would have to be addressed in the Rawlsian framework for the limitations on liberty to be legitimate.)

Instead of pursuing how such problems might be addressed within the framework of *A Theory of Justice*, though, I want to proceed on a somewhat higher metalevel to consider how the questions I am raising about the state's war-making claims relate to Rawls's more recent and developed conception of what political philosophy in general and political liberalism in particular are all about. In so doing, I hope to begin moving beyond questions about liberal individualism in particular to some considerations of how political philosophy and reflection on the state might be transformed if we took violence and warfare seriously.

A notable fact about Rawls's more recently elaborated conception of political liberalism is how much the aspiration to peace animates his conception of justice. While Rawls's conception, because of its depth, is difficult to summarize, its orientation is something like this: liberal individualism assumes as both inevitable and desirable that individuals or groups will have differing, and potentially competing, conceptions of the good. Because of these multiple conceptions, there is always the prospect of social life collapsing into conflict—there is always the prospect of civil war. The distinctive fact about liberalism, according to Rawls, is that it seeks to address this potential conflict politically, not metaphysically. That is, it does not seek to address it by finding some metaphysical standpoint according to which everyone shares (or should share) the same conception of the good. Rather, it seeks to address it by finding some conception of justice that everyone can share despite the differences in their conceptions of the good, a conception that will provide a standpoint of reconciliation when conflicts between conceptions of the good arise. Such a conception provides us with public reasons for political behavior that are above and beyond the more personal reasons that animate our particular projects and concerns.

Rawls and other liberal thinkers, such as Charles Larmore, make much of the liberal privileging of neutrality.[28] The neutrality of liberal justice rests largely in its not engaging any particular conception of the good, but it seems wrong to say that for liberalism neutrality is the central value, for that value would seem to be peace—the peace that is achieved through that rightful resolution of differences in which all participate and to which all can agree. This attention to the claims of peace takes us back to the initial Hobbesian project, which itself was a response to the social conflicts of its day, but a crucial difference would seem to be that Hobbes's conception basically aspires to what Martin Luther King, Jr., and others have termed "negative peace," the mere absence of violent conflict, whereas Rawls's conception aspires to "positive peace," a peace that is not just pacification, not just the termination of conflict, but the healthy resolution of it.

Rawls, however, is also committed to the state and to the legitimacy of the state in its war-making function; hence, the question we might pose to him is this: if our commitment to the state is not an expression of our personal conception of the good, is that commitment substantial enough to motivate our dying for the state? If my personal conception of the good and the projects that arise from it are what endow my life with its particular meaning, then I can certainly imagine dying for it; but the question here, in some ways similar but in other ways different from that which we encountered with Hobbes, is whether I have sufficient reason to submit to the requirements of soldiering and even to die for a state and its justice when the importance of the state lies primarily in the fact that it allows for the peaceful reconciliation of my conception of the good with that of others—for in dying for the state, I might naturally experience myself as forsaking my conception of the good and the projects that it inspires in defense of the conceptions and projects of others, a prospect that has the same sort of self-defeating dimensions that we have met before.

One might put this point in terms of a certain dilemma that faces Rawlsian-type liberalism: the state is, on the one hand, an agent of internal peace; it and the conception of justice that it embodies seek to achieve a condition of enduring concord among its citizens and to avoid civil war. The state is also, however, an agent of external peace; it is designed to maintain the security of the society against external threats, by organized violence, if need be. Rawls's account suggests that a necessary condition of the state's properly performing its first function is that its guiding principles of justice not engage any particular conception of the good. The concerns that animate our commitment to the state should have neither that comprehensiveness nor that depth, but if they do not, the question arises whether the state can rightfully perform its second function without engaging persons on that deeper level. By this I mean: can it provide persons with anything like adequate reasons for sacrificing their lives and all that goes with it if those reasons are of the purely public character that Rawls conceives them to be?

Posing the problem with Rawls's theory in this way allows us to revisit the debate between Rawls and Michael Sandel and to see elements in the latter's criticism of Rawls that Sandel himself may have missed.[29] The tendency among Rawlsians and like-minded thinkers in recent years has been to regard Sandel's criticisms of Rawls, or what Sandel calls "deontological justice," as basically missing the point of what Rawls is all about.[30] Sandel's criticisms are, of course, not easy to summarize, but at their heart, certainly, is the suggestion that Rawls's conception of justice as fairness rests on a conception of what Sandel terms the "unencumbered" self, a conception that neither acknowledges nor allows for the importance of persons having deep commitments that they regard as defining, in a rather essential sense, who they are. The Rawlsian response to this is that it wrongly construes his project as metaphysical, rather than political. Rawls certainly allows for the deepest of commitments, animated by what he regards as our personal conceptions of the good. His insistence is just that such commitments and conceptions must be held in abeyance for the purposes of constructing a standpoint of civil concord.

Sandel's general ideas about persons and society evoke elements of the idealist tradition, but on the whole his criticism of Rawls tends to be individualist in its thrust, in that it faults Rawls's conception of justice from the standpoint of what individuals require (a type of nonalienated existence, in this case). Sandel suggests, for example, that among those requirements may be participation in a social order that demands more than what justice, or at least Rawlsian justice, requires. The problem that I have raised questions Rawls from the standpoint of what society—specifically, the sort of society that Rawls himself endorses (the society of the nation-state)—requires. In this regard, the problem I have raised is more in keeping with more traditional idealist criticisms of social contract theory, yet Sandel's work helps us fill it out. My basic suggestion is that the war-making claims of the state on the individual, claims that the state requires for its continued existence, are demands that exceed what (Rawlsian) justice either requires or allows. Accordingly, the kind of deep engagement with the self that Sandel envisions for society is something that is necessary to elicit the sort of ultimate commitment that the state requires to defend the just order. At the same time, that deep engagement is seen as incompatible—in the Rawlsian view—with the constitution of that just order.

At the heart of the Rawlsian project is what he calls the stability problem: the search for a social order that is capable of sustaining the support of persons otherwise marked by their vast differences in their conceptions of the good; but as long as that community is organized into a state, we also have what might be termed the security problem: the search for a social order that is capable of eliciting the kind of ultimate sacrifice that a state requires for its survival—the sacrifices that are implicit in the war-making claims of the state. My suggestion (but it is only a suggestion, for one should never underestimate the resources of Rawls or his theory) is that Rawls's solution to the one problem undercuts any solution to the other.

Conclusion

Those familiar with the history of liberalism in this century may now have noted that the kind of problem that I have raised is akin to one that proponents and opponents of liberalism alike have reflected on, particularly in the period immediately preceding World War II. At that moment in history, in the face of the Fascist threat, the question on people's minds was whether the ideals of liberal individualism were sufficient to elicit the sort of passionate self-sacrifice that the conflict with fascism seemed to require.[31] The question of liberalism's capacity to elicit conviction is also one that the late Christopher Lasch raised, most notably in his *The True and Only Heaven* (a work that traces this question back to the Puritans).[32] These thinkers have framed the problem as more of a psychological one, whereas I have framed it as more of a logical one: can liberal individualism (in this essay: classical social contract theory) make sense of the state's war-making claims on the individual, claims that liberal individualism's commitment to the nation-state seems to require?

If it cannot, as I believe it cannot, then it would seem that we have at least two options.

One option is to question liberal individualism, to seek to amend or transcend it to allow for the state's war-making claims, on the assumption that states themselves are a necessary feature of the social order, or at least a necessary feature of the sort of order that liberal individualism otherwise wishes to sustain. I take it that this is the option that certain idealists have wished to pursue in raising the criticisms that I have noted, but not only idealists have taken this approach. Even Kateb, who raises such trenchant criticisms of social contract theory's wafflings on the state's war-making claims and who seems so deeply skeptical of the claims of the state on human life— even Kateb takes it for granted that in the end we must regard as reasonable at least some of those central claims.

A second option is to be more critical of the state's war-making claims and of liberal individualism's traditional acquiescence to those claims. Given traditional liberalism's general commitment to and confidence in the authority of the state, what this will involve is a general rethinking of the liberal tradition as a whole.

Part of this rethinking will involve a rethinking of liberalism's history, or how we have come to construct that history. I have noted that Hobbes's preoccupation with the problem of peace must be placed in the context of his times. Hobbes wrote in a time of social strife, the period of the English Civil War, a period of extraordinary political reflection that has left its mark on all subsequent Anglo-American thought. He has remained the most enduring figure from this period, but his orientation marks only one of the many possibilities that emerged during that time. Another is represented by Gerrard Winstanley and the Levellers, perhaps the most prominent and well-known figures of the generally little-known individuals and groups that constituted what David Petegorsky has called, in one of the earliest studies of this movement, the "Left Wing Democrats" of the English Civil War.[33]

I speak of this movement as little known, yet Kateb has made a convincing case that the Levellers "practically originated the modern theory of rights in almost its entirety" and hence are rightly regarded as (among other things) the sources of the American founding.[34] He also observes that the Levellers alone seem to have employed the social contract model to reject the very notion of conscription in their insistence that "impressing or constraining any of us to serve in the wars is against our freedom."[35] Kateb seems reluctant, however, to regard the Levellers as representing one of liberalism's very viable and yet undeveloped alternatives, perhaps because he assumes that ("to be sure") the Levellers went "too far" in their absolute opposition to conscription and the state's war-making claims.[36] Perhaps the Levellers went where logic took them in the importance that they perceived in warfare for the state and the deep suspicion they maintained of both.

The Levellers may be placed within a tradition of anarchism that regards its opposition to the state as intrinsically linked with its opposition to organized violence in almost any form. More contemporary figures in this tradition include Herbert Read, Dorothy Day, Paul Goodman, and perhaps the later Lewis Mumford.[37] For these thinkers, the state is not an institution that just happens to be involved at times in the abuses of warfare. For these thinkers, the state is an expression of those abuses; indeed, it is one of those abuses. They agree, then, with those political sociologists cited at the outset of this essay who insist that the relation between war and the state is more intimate than is commonly supposed, and from this they conclude that because of this, opposition to one necessarily means opposition to the other, that a viable anarchism necessarily brings with it a certain commitment to nonviolence.

The state presents itself, and not unreasonably so, as one of our most effective mechanisms for securing our self-protection and deterring the spread of individual and social violence. The idea of a world without states raises the specter of crime, confusion, conflict, and chaos. We have good reason to be fearful of these problems, for they are the very problems that the history of states has imposed on us. Truly transcending them may mean rethinking in fundamental ways our attitudes toward states and violence together. It may mean returning not only to Winstanley and the Levellers, but also to the Quakers and George Fox, those contemporaries of Hobbes who believed that the anarchism required by liberty could be realized only if the spirit of nonviolence came to prevail.

Notes

1. Michael Walzer, *Obligations* (Cambridge, Mass.: Harvard University Press, 1970), 77.

2. A general overview of the recent ideas and literature on this subject is Bruce Porter, *War and the Rise of the State* (New York: Free Press, 1994).

3. Michael S. Sherry has argued, in his *In the Shadow of War: The United States since the 1930s* (New Haven, Conn.: Yale University Press, 1995), that almost all the social programs of the last five decades have been determined, in one way or another, by the culture of war. See also Deborah Dwork, *War Is Good for Babies and Other Young Children* (London: Tavistock Publications, 1987); J. M. Winter, *The Great War and the British People* (Cambridge, Mass.: Harvard University Press, 1986); and R. Titmuss, "War and Social Policy," in his *Essays on the Welfare State* (London: Unwin, 1958). This view provides a certain tonic to those libertarians, such as Robert Nozick, who regard the state's (re)distributive policies as more the reflection of ideals such as equality or impulses such as envy.

4. See Anthony Giddens, *The Nation State and Violence* (Berkeley, Calif.: University of California Press, 1987). On the historical importance of war in our time and the failure of both liberal and Marxist traditions to appreciate it, see Gabriel Kolko, *A Century of War* (New York: The New Press, 1994).

5. By "liberal individualism" I mean, as noted, primarily the classical social contract theorists, but also such utilitarian thinkers as John Stuart Mill, all of whom have been committed to the legitimacy of the state. I thus distinguish this tradition from libertarian anarchism, but only for the purposes of this discussion.

6. See George Kateb, "The Liberal Contract: Individualism, War, and the Constitution," chap. 7 of *The Inner Ocean* (Ithaca, N.Y.: Cornell University Press, 1992).

7. John Rawls, *A Theory of Justice* (Cambridge, Mass.: Harvard University Press, 1971), 380. He does discuss civil disobedience and conscientious objection in sections 56 and 58.

8. See the essay of that title in Walzer, *Obligations*, 77–97.

9. Only two wars in American history have not required conscription of some sort—the war against the Philippines (the Spanish American War) and the Gulf War (Desert Shield/Storm). Both were essentially short police actions against opponents who were heavily outnumbered and outgunned. On the role of the draft in American wars and the persistent (to the point of violent) resistance to it, see Geoffrey Perret, *A Country Made by War* (New York: Random House, 1990).

10. I say "might" because there remain serious questions as to whether a volunteer army does not constitute a kind of economic draft, imposing unfair (and coercive) burdens on the poor.

11. In his most recent work, Giddens writes, "Neither socialist thought nor liberalism have established perspectives or concepts that are relevant to producing a normative political theory of violence, while rightist thought has tended to think of violence as a necessary and endemic feature of human life." *Beyond Left and Right* (Stanford, Calif.: Stanford University Press, 1994), 18.

12. See F. H. Bradley, "My Station and Its Duties," in *Ethical Studies*, 2d ed. (Oxford: Clarendon Press, 1927), 164–65.

13. The reference to Hegel is in Walzer, *Obligations*, 89.

14. Deborah Baumgold, *Hobbes's Political Theory* (Cambridge: Cambridge University Press, 1988), 88. See Ronald Hutton, *The Royalist War Effort 1642–1646* (London: Longman, 1982), chaps. 15–18, and J. S. Morrill, *The Revolt of the Provinces: Conservatives and Radicals in the English Civil War 1630–1650* (London: Allen and Unwin, 1976), 98–111.

15. Jean Hampton, *Hobbes and the Social Contract Tradition* (New York: Cambridge University Press, 1986).

16. Gregory Kavka, *Hobbesian Moral and Political Theory* (Princeton, N.J.: Princeton University Press, 1986). See also the reference to these matters in Howard Warrender, *The Political Philosophy of Hobbes: His Theory of Obligation* (Oxford: Clarendon Press, 1957).

17. Kavka, *Hobbesian Moral and Political Theory*, 425

18. Thomas Hobbes, *Leviathan* (London: Collier-MacMillan, 1962), 165.

19. Eisenhower was responding to the fact that more than 20,000 American soldiers had already deserted in the European war, and their numbers were increasing.

20. Hobbes, *Leviathan*, 164–65.

21. This line of reasoning is suggested by Kavka, *Hobbesian Moral and Political Theory*, 431. It has also been suggested to me by Jan Narveson in personal communication.

22. Hobbes, *Leviathan*, 105.

23. John Locke, *Second Treatise on Government* (Chicago: Henry Regnery, 1955), para. 139.

24. Walzer, *Obligations*, chap. 8.

25. Ibid., 89.

26. Rawls, *A Theory of Justice*, 380.

27. Kateb, *The Inner Ocean*, 186.

28. See Charles Larmore, *Patterns of Moral Complexity* (Cambridge: Cambridge University Press, 1987).

29. See Michael Sandel, *Liberalism and the Limits of Justice* (Cambridge: Cambridge University Press, 1982).

30. See Thomas Pogge, *Realizing Rawls* (Ithaca, N.Y.: Cornell University Press, 1989), a work whose defense of Rawls against Sandel is cited approvingly by Rawls himself. Pogge has some very interesting points to make on Rawls's treatment of conscription (see p. 246).

31. A prominent and representative figure in this debate is Lewis Mumford, a political thinker now almost totally forgotten in mainstream political philosophy. For an introduction to his views, see Casey Blake, *Beloved Community* (Bloomington: Indiana University Press, 1986).

32. Christopher Lasch, *The True and Only Heaven* (New York: Norton, 1991).

33. See David Petegorsky, *Left-Wing Democracy and the English Civil War* (London: V. Gollancz, 1940). See the seminal discussions of Christopher Hill,

The World Turned Upside Down (New York: Viking, 1972), especially 313–19, where the views of Hobbes and Winstanley are contrasted, and Hill, *The Experience of Defeat* (New York: Viking, 1984). Winstanley and the Levellers are central figures in what might be termed the prophetic tradition of politics, a tradition that also includes John Milton and William Blake and which accords primacy to the problems of war and violence and does not easily fit into any of our received political categories.

34. Kateb, *The Inner Ocean*, 9.

35. "An Agreement of the People," in A. Woodhouse, ed., *Puritanism and Liberty* (Chicago: University of Chicago Press, 1951), 444. I owe this reference to Kateb.

36. Kateb, *The Inner Ocean*, 187.

37. See Herbert Read, *Anarchy and Order* (Boston: Beacon Press, 1971), and (about Read) George Woodcock, *Herbert Read: The Stream and the Source* (London: Faber and Faber, 1972). On Dorothy Day, see *Selected Writings* (New York: Orbis Books, 1983), and my discussion of her views in "The One Who Burns Herself for Peace," *Hypatia*, vol. 9, no. 2 (Spring 1994). On Paul Goodman, see *New Reformation: Notes of a Neolithic Conservative* (New York: Random House, 1971). On Mumford, see Lewis Mumford, *In the Name of Sanity* (New York: Harcourt, Brace, 1954).

12

Anarchy and Efficient Law

David Friedman

More than twenty years ago, Professor (now Judge) Richard Posner suggested that many features of the common law could be explained by the conjecture that it was a set of legal rules that maximized economic efficiency.[1] To what degree the conjecture is correct is still a matter of debate, but, true or false, it has played a major role in the development of the economic analysis of law.

One weakness in Posner's argument was and is the absence of a plausible mechanism to generate efficient common law.[2] What he and his supporters offer instead is extensive analysis of the common law as it actually exists, designed to show that its rules are close to the rules that would have been chosen by an economist attempting to maximize economic efficiency. Lacking a compelling theory, they offer empirical evidence—although one must combine the evidence with quite a lot of economic theory in order to argue that the rules observed to exist are the efficient ones.

My project in this essay is the mirror image of Posner's. The legal system I describe does not exist, so I cannot observe its rules.[3] What I propose is a theoretical analysis of why that legal system, if it existed, could be expected to generate efficient rules.[4]

Law as a Private Good

Imagine a society with no government. Individuals purchase law enforcement from private firms. Each such firm faces possible conflicts with other firms. Private policemen working for the enforcement agency that I employ may track down the burglar who stole my property only to discover, when they try to arrest him, that he too employs an enforcement agency.

There are three ways in which such conflicts might be dealt with. The most obvious and least likely is direct violence—a miniwar between my agency in its attempt to arrest the burglar and his agency in its attempt to defend him from arrest. A somewhat more plausible scenario is negotiation. Since warfare is expensive, agencies might include in the contracts they offer their customers a provision under which they are not obliged to defend customers against legitimate punishment for their actual crimes. When a conflict occurred, it would then be up to the two agencies to determine whether the accused customer of one would be deemed guilty and turned over to the other.

A still more attractive and more likely solution is advance contracting between the agencies. Under this scenario, any two agencies that faced a significant probability of such clashes would agree on an arbitration agency to settle them—a private court. Implicit or explicit in their agreement would be the legal rules under which such disputes were to be settled.

Under these circumstances, both law enforcement and law are private goods produced on a private market. Law enforcement is produced by enforcement agencies and sold directly to their customers. Law is produced by arbitration agencies and sold to the enforcement agencies, who resell it to their customers as one characteristic of the bundle of services they provide.[5]

The resulting legal system might contain many different law codes. The rules governing a particular conflict will depend on the arbitration agency that the enforcement agencies employed by the parties to the conflict have agreed on. While there will be some market pressure for uniformity, it is logically possible for every pair of enforcement agencies to agree on a different arbitration agency with a different set of legal rules.[6]

Indeed, one could have more diversity than that. Suppose there is some small group within the population with specialized legal requirements. An example might be members of a religious sect that forbade the taking of oaths. Such a group might have its own enforcement agency and let that agency negotiate appropriate legal rules on its behalf. Alternatively, an agency might produce a specialized product for members of the group by negotiating agreements under which those customers, if involved in litigation, were not required to swear the usual oaths.

As this example suggests, the potential legal diversity of such a system is very large; in principle, a different set of legal rules might apply with respect to every pair of persons. In practice, such diversity would be constrained by costs of negotiation and by costs of legal diversity. The transaction costs of separately negotiating a different law code for every pair of persons would be prohibitively high, so it is likely that each pair of enforcement agencies would agree on a single law code interpreted by a single arbitration agency, with provisions for occasional variances of the sort described above.

Legal diversity has substantial costs. If, for example, contract terms enforceable against customers of agency A may be unenforceable against customers of agency B, that makes it more difficult and expensive for firms to draw up satisfactory contracts. Such costs will provide an incentive for arbitration agencies to adopt more uniform law, to be balanced against the incentive for nonuniform law provided by the differing desires of different customers.

Generating Efficient Law

Suppose a set of law codes of the sort I have described exists and that there is some potential change in the legal rules prevailing between two enforcement agencies that would yield net benefits to their customers. If the change benefits both sets of customers, it is in the interest of the enforcement agencies either to persuade their arbitration agency to make the change or to shift to one that follows the superior set of rules. If it benefits the customers of one agency but imposes costs on the customers of the other, with net costs smaller then net benefits, it is in the interest of the two agencies to agree to the change, with the loser compensated either directly or by some other change elsewhere in the legal rules. In practice, since it is the arbitration agencies that specialize in legal rules, we would expect them to try to identify all such improvements and include them in the legal codes they offer to their customers.

This argument suggests that any change in the existing set of codes that would produce a net improvement will occur. The result should be a set of legal codes that is economically efficient in the conventional sense.[7]

That result must be qualified in several ways. To begin with, in a world of nonzero information and transaction costs, an enforcement agency does not perfectly internalize the welfare of its customers, since it cannot engage in perfect discriminatory pricing. Furthermore, negotiations between enforcement agencies are not costless, so some opportunities for mutual gain may go unexploited. For these reasons, what we would expect is not a perfectly efficient set of legal rules, but a set of legal rules with tendencies toward efficiency. Where a legal change benefits almost everyone, we would expect to see it, but where it generates both substantial benefits and substantial costs, we would expect the system to do an imperfect job of balancing costs and benefits and thus to at least occasionally get the wrong answer. One additional reason why the result will fall short of complete efficiency will be discussed later in this essay.

Competition or Monopoly

Readers familiar with the economic literature on efficiency may notice that my argument owes more to Coase than to Marshall. I have relied on the idea that parties will negotiate toward efficient contracts, rather than on the conventional analysis of a competitive industry. The reason for that choice is that this marketplace, despite the very large number of buyers and sellers, is not competitive in the sense necessary for the standard economic proofs of efficiency.

To see why, let us eliminate from our analysis the intermediaries, the enforcement and arbitration agencies, and consider the market for legal agreement in terms of the individual producers and consumers of that good. Each individual wishes to buy the assent of every other individual to some legal code or codes, in order that future disputes between them, if they occur, may be peacefully resolved. Each individual is thus both a buyer and a seller of legal assent, buying from and selling to every other individual.

The reason that the large number of buyers and sellers does not produce a competitive market is that the goods they are selling are not substitutes for each other. I desire legal agreement with both A and B; if I am equally likely to be involved in a dispute with either, I may have the same value for legal agreement with each; however, getting A's agreement to apply some legal rule in disputes with him does not eliminate the value to me of B's agreement with regard to disputes with him, so the two are not substitutes. Unlike the case of an ordinary good, I cannot simply agree with A on a price and then buy all the agreement I want from him. It follows that despite the large number of participants, the interaction is essentially one of bilateral monopoly. Only A can sell me his assent to legal rules between me and him, and only I want to buy it.

Because of this, a conventional analysis of a uniform good sold at a single price by all sellers and to all buyers does not work for this market. One way of seeing this is to try to construct such an analysis.

Consider a particular legal change, a shift from strict liability to negligence for some class of cases. The shift benefits defendants at the expense of plaintiffs. If total benefits are larger than total costs, summed over all plaintiffs and defendants and including not only direct costs and benefits when litigation occurs but also all of the associated indirect benefits and costs,[8] then the change increases economic efficiency.

When A and B agree to a negligence rule for disputes between them, they are agreeing to two things: that A's liability will depend on A's negligence when A is the defendant and that B's liability will depend on B's negligence when B is the defendant. For purposes of analysis, those are separate agreements; one could imagine one without the other.[9] We may think of A buying from B (at a positive price) B's assent to the rule for cases in which A is the defendant and B the plaintiff, and B buying from A (at a positive price) A's assent to the rule for cases in which B is the defendant and A the plaintiff.

Assume, for simplicity, that every pair of individuals is equally likely to become involved in a dispute[10] and that the nature of the potential disputes is the same across individuals, so that the value to A of legal assent from B is the same as the value to him of legal assent from C, D, and so on. Parties differ, however, in their value for consuming and cost of producing legal assent. A thus may be willing to pay, if necessary, up to $2 each to buy agreement from B, C, D, and so on, to a negligence rule that will apply when A is the defendant. B may be similarly willing to pay up to $3 to each of the others. Meanwhile, A may be willing to sell his assent, to agree to a negligence rule in cases where he is the plaintiff, for any price above $1, and B similarly for any price above $3. Following the analogy to an ordinary good, we would say that A values the assent of others at $2 per person, and B values it at $3 per person. A's cost of producing assent is $1 per person, B's cost is $3 per person. The efficient rule is for each party to sell his assent to anyone who values it at more than its cost, thus maximizing the gains from trade. If B values assent at more than its cost to A (as he does: $3 > $1), it is efficient for A to agree to accept a negligence rule if he sues B. If A values assent at less than its cost to B (as he does: $2 < $3), it is efficient for B not to agree to accept a negligence rule if he sues A.

Suppose, in analogy to an ordinary market, that each seller specifies a price at which he will sell assent to anyone willing to pay and that each buyer then buys assent from anyone selling it at a price less than the buyer's value. Will this produce the efficient result?

It will not. Consider the situation from the standpoint of A. If he offers to sell his assent at $1 to any buyer, the result will be efficient, since any buyer who values it at more than $1 (A's cost) will buy it. But A will get no benefit from the transaction, since he is selling the good for its cost to him; all of the gain from trade is going to the buyer. If A raises his price to $2, some potential sales (to buyers with a value between $1 and $2) will be lost, but the remaining sales (to buyers with a value greater than $2) will be made at a gain for A of $1 each. Exactly what price maximizes A's net gain will depend on the distribution of values among the other sellers, but it will be more than $1. The result, therefore, will be inefficient: buyers who value A's assent at more than its cost but less than its price will not buy.

This is the familiar deadweight problem of a single-price monopoly. A monopolist maximizes his profit at a price above his cost, eliminating some efficient transactions. It seems out of place here because we seem to be dealing with a market of many buyers and many sellers, but one seller cannot substitute for another, so it is really a market with a very large number of bilateral monopolies.

One could reverse the form of the transaction by having buyers offer a price and sellers decide whether to accept it. The result would be essentially the same. Buyers would state a price below their real value, giving up some (efficient) transactions in order to increase their gain on the remaining transactions. This time we would call the situation monopsony instead of monopoly.

If this analysis is correct, and I believe it is, conventional models of perfect competition do not apply to the market for legal agreement. It is more appropriately modeled as bargaining among the parties buying and selling legal assent, as in the previous section. Such a model implies an efficient outcome subject to the limits imposed by bargaining costs.

In practice, a number of features of the situation are likely to hold down those costs. In many cases, the optimal rules (ex ante, before an actual dispute has occurred) are the same for almost everyone. This is particularly likely to be the case if the bargaining is over symmetrical rules. My agreement to accept a court that operates under negligence rules makes me worse off when I am the plaintiff, but better off when I am the defendant. If negligence is a significantly more efficient rule, it is likely that most people will prefer it.

A second reason is that I must pay for the advantages of a favorable legal rule not only in the process of negotiating it but also in the price of transactions with others who will be bound by it. Suppose, for example, I manage to get a "favorable" legal rule for conflicts between me and any attorneys I hire: if they advise against settling and I lose the case, I can sue them for malpractice with a good chance of winning. One consequence of that rule will be to raise the cost to me of hiring a lawyer. In this and in many other cases, a "favorable" legal rule, like a "favorable" term in a contract, must be paid for in every transaction it applies to, and if it is inefficient, the price is likely to be more than it is worth. That is part of the reason why, as Judge Posner and others have argued,[11] the legal system is a poor instrument for income redistribution.

These arguments suggest that the bargaining problems implied by the bilateral monopoly nature of the market for legal assent should not be insuperable, that bargaining among enforcement agencies representing groups of customers ought to be able to produce something close to an efficient outcome. Absent some theoretical structure more powerful than Coasian bargaining, it is hard to be more precise than that.

The Baseline Problem

In my discussion so far I have assumed the existence of some baseline, some initial set of law codes from which bargaining begins. While the location of that baseline does not affect the argument for the efficiency of the eventual equilibrium legal rules, it does affect what that equilibrium looks like. Many steps in the process of bargaining toward efficiency will involve some parties agreeing to a legal change that makes them worse off, in exchange for some balancing benefit. If we start with a rule of strict liability, to take the example above, a shift to negligence may require individuals who prefer the latter rule[12] to pay individuals who do not for their assent. If we start with a rule of negligence, a shift in the other direction will require payments the other way. So although the baseline does not determine the efficiency of the outcome, it may well affect the associated distribution of income.[13]

It is not immediately obvious what that baseline is.[14] If two enforcement agencies fail to agree on a mutually acceptable arbitrator to settle their dispute, after all, the result is not that the dispute is resolved according to the Uniform Commercial Code or the Delaware Commercial Code, but that it is resolved by force.

This suggests that the ultimate baseline is the solution to a bilateral monopoly bargaining game among the agencies. Each agency can threaten to refuse to agree to any arbitrator, subjecting both to the costs of occasional violence, or at least of ad hoc negotiation to avoid violence. Each knows that the other would prefer even a rather unfavorable set of legal rules to no agreement at all. Each knows that if no agreement is reached, they are both at risk of losing their customers to other agencies that have been more successful in negotiating agreements.

The situation is analogous to a union/management negotiation or the negotiations determining borders, trade policies, and the like between neighboring countries. While there is no good theoretical account of exactly what determines the outcome of bilateral monopoly bargaining, experience suggests that some tolerably stable equilibrium usually exists. Most unionized firms manage to settle their differences without lengthy strikes, and most nations are at peace with most of their neighbors most of the time.[15]

We may thus imagine the market for law as starting out with a set of default rules between each pair of protection agencies, representing the result of bargaining backed by threats of refusal to agree on an arbitrator. From there, the agencies bargain to an efficient set of rules. The distributional outcome is the result of an implicit threat game between the agencies; the allocational outcome is the result of a (logically subsequent) bargaining game to move the agencies (and their customers) from the starting point to the Pareto frontier.

Experience suggests that there is enormous inertia in mutual threat games of this sort. National boundaries do not move half a mile one way or the other each time one nation becomes a little richer or a little more powerful. In practice, an anarchocapitalist society will probably be built not so much on an ongoing mutual threat game as on a mutual threat game played out in the distant past. That suggests that, once the initial equilibrium has been established, the success of a protection agency will be based mainly on its ability to produce protection for its customers, not on its ability to defeat rivals in open warfare.

While it is always possible for one firm to threaten to withdraw from its arbitration agreement with another unless the terms are renegotiated de novo, such threats are unlikely to be either common or successful. Other agencies have a strong incentive to insist on basing their bargaining on the existing rules in order to prevent the costs both of continual renegotiation and of violence when negotiations break down.

The stability of a status quo in part reflects the influence of Schelling points, outcomes recognized by both parties as unique, on the outcome of bargaining.[16] Where the alternative to agreement is costly, almost any agreement is better than none, so both parties have an incentive to look for alternatives that they can converge on. This suggests the possibility that if anarchocapitalist institutions evolve out of an existing state-run legal system, the rules of that legal system might function as the status quo from which further bargaining proceeded. Whether or not such rules are efficient, they are familiar to the parties and they specify answers to most of the relevant questions. They therefore provide a potential point of initial agreement from which to conduct further bargaining.

Market Failure in the Market for Law

I have argued that the market will tend to generate efficient law for much the same sort of reasons that markets in general tend to generate efficient outcomes, although the argument depends on Coasian bargaining rather than perfect competition. Even if markets tend toward efficiency, however, that tendency is limited by various forms of market failure. Are there forms of market failure to which this market is particularly vulnerable, and, if so, what are their implications?

The answer, I think, is that there is a special sort of market failure relevant to this market. It is plausible to imagine a pair of enforcement agencies bargaining to an outcome close to the set of rules that maximizes the net welfare of their customers. It is not, I think, plausible to imagine a set of a hundred enforcement agencies bargaining together to a single outcome maximizing the welfare of all of their customers. So we can expect the legal rules between A and B to maximize their joint welfare, even to maximize the joint welfare of all of the clients of their enforcement agencies, but we cannot expect the rules applying between A and B to maximize the joint welfare of everyone, including customers of other enforcement agencies.

It follows that the rules will be optimal only when the legal rule between A and B produces no net third-party effect on C, C being a customer of some other agency. In many cases this seems plausible, at least as a reasonable approximation. The rule that determines what happens if A breaks his contract with B or breaks into B's house or breaks B's arm should have relatively little effect on C.[17]

Consider, however, intellectual property law. When B agrees to respect A's intellectual property, the result is an increased incentive for A to produce such property, which may benefit others who use it. Such benefits will not be taken into account in the negotiations that determine whether B makes such an agreement. The result will be a lower than optimal level of intellectual property law.

Indeed, the result may well be no protection for intellectual property at all. To see why, imagine that A, a producer of intellectual property, is bargaining with B, a consumer, for protection. If they agree on protection, B will be liable to pay A $10 for each copy of A's computer program that B makes. What are the cost and benefits of such an agreement?

The most obvious benefit is that A will receive $10 per copy. This, however, is exactly balanced by the cost to B of paying $10 per copy. If these were the only costs and benefits, agreement and disagreement would be equally efficient.

There are at least two other costs and one other benefit. One cost is that B will make fewer copies of the program than if copying were free—perhaps he will put a copy on his desktop machine but not on his portable. Perhaps he will buy copies of two of A's programs, but not a third, since the third one is worth only $5 to him. This cost is the familiar deadweight cost of copyright—the inefficiency due to the difference between the (positive) price of making an additional copy to the user and the (zero) marginal cost of permitting an additional copy to the copyright owner, resulting in an inefficiently low number of copies.

A second cost is the cost of enforcing the agreement. Keeping track of what copies B has made will be costly, perhaps impossible, and any resulting dispute will lead to expensive litigation.

To balance these costs, there is an important benefit: the incentive that A has to write computer programs if he will be paid for them and does not have if he will not. If we were considering the question of requiring or not requiring all consumers of A's intellectual property to pay for using it, that benefit might well outweigh the costs we have described, making copyright protection for programs economically efficient. After all, if A does not write any programs, there will be nothing for B to copy.

We are considering the question, however, not with regard to the whole world, but with regard only to B. The additional revenue A will receive as a result of B being covered by his copyright is very small and will produce only a very small increase in output. That increase will benefit everyone who uses A's programs, but only the small part of that benefit that goes to B will be relevant to the negotiation between them. It follows that the benefit is vanishingly small, implying net costs, hence no protection.

The result is similar but less extreme if we consider negotiation, not between individuals, but between enforcement agencies. The agency will take into account, not merely the benefit to B from the increased output because of B being bound by A's copyright, but also the benefit to all of its customers because of the increased output from all of them being bound by A's copyright. The result is still only a small fraction of the total benefit—assuming that there are many enforcement agencies, each serving only a small fraction of the population—but a larger fraction than in the case of individual negotiation. The fraction becomes larger still if we allow for the possibility of copyright negotiations among groups of enforcement agencies, with each agreeing to recognize the copyrights of the customers of all of the others if they will all agree similarly. Such negotiations would be analogous to the negotiations among nations by which international intellectual property rights are now established.

Even allowing for the possibility of such multiparty negotiations, our result, although weaker, still remains; we would expect an inefficiently low level of protection for intellectual property. We might well get no protection at all. This raises two questions, both outside the range of this essay. One, whether intellectual property protection is desirable, and if so, how desirable, has been discussed at some length in the intellectual property literature.[18] The other, whether the equivalent of intellectual property protection could be provided in other ways, for instance, by contract, is discussed (in the context of computer networks and encryption) in a forthcoming article of mine.[19]

Similar problems will arise with pollution law, where A's right to sue B for polluting A's air results in a reduction of B's emissions and thus an external benefit for A's neighbor C. Such problems may well arise in other important contexts as well. In all of these cases, we would expect the legal rules generated by the private market to be inefficient. It does not follow that they will be worse than the rules

currently generated by courts and legislatures. *Pace* Posner, we have
no good theoretical reason to expect those legal rules to be efficient
either.

The Evidence

While there are no modern anarchocapitalist societies with legal systems to be analyzed, there are a number of real-world institutions, past
and present, that are in some ways analogous. Evidence on the
working of such institutions may help us answer two related questions
about the private market for law: whether conflicts would be settled by
law rather than violence and whether the resulting legal rules would
be efficient.

Consider the settlement of legal claims between insurance companies at present. Company A's client runs into and injures Company
B's client, giving the latter a possible tort claim against the former.
The two companies can resolve the dispute at a low cost by settling
out of court, provided they can agree on an outcome (or an arbitrator),
or they can settle it at a high cost in court.

Their situation is analogous to the "arbitrate or fight" decision faced
by a private enforcement agency every time one of its clients has a
legal conflict with a client of another agency. There, too, there is a
low-cost solution (arbitration) that depends on an agreement between
the two agencies and an alternative (violence) with high costs for
both parties. In both cases, the parties (insurance companies and
enforcement agencies) can expect to have many such conflicts with
each other, so they are engaged in a repeated game in which considerations such as reputation will play a large role.

The argument is not, of course, limited to auto accidents. It applies
wherever parties are faced with the decision to settle or litigate, since
that is a bilateral monopoly problem of the same sort I have been
describing. The evidence suggests that the overwhelming majority of
parties in such cases settle.[20]

Evidence on settlement rates provides some reason to believe that,
under the institutions I have described, almost all disputes would be
settled peacefully, but it does not tell us what the rules under which
disputes were settled would be like. The literature on norms as a
private substitute for law suggests that such institutions might produce
a reasonably efficient set of rules.

In his book *Order Without Law*, Robert Ellickson described his investigations into how conflicts were settled in modern-day Shasta County, California.[21] He found that interactions between neighbors, with regard to straying cattle and many other things, were controlled, not by law, but by a system of norms, a private law code having no connection to courts, legislatures, or any other agency of state power. When a rancher was informed that one of his animals was trespassing, he was expected to apologize, retrieve the animal, and take reasonable precautions to keep it from happening again. If significant damage had been done, the rancher was expected to make up for the damage.

The system was self-enforcing. If a rancher consistently let his animals stray or failed to offer to make up for significant damages, the victim would respond by initiating true negative gossip, spreading the word that that particular rancher was not behaving in a proper neighborly fashion. If that failed to work, straying animals could be transported far from the victim's (and owner's) property, imposing significant costs on the owner, who had to retrieve them. In extreme cases trespassing animals might even be deliberately injured. The one thing good neighbors did not do, even under severe provocation, was go to court.

Straying cattle were not the only things to which legal rules were irrelevant. California has quite detailed laws specifying under what circumstance one of two adjoining landowners can build a fence between their properties and charge part of the cost to his neighbor. Landowners in Shasta County build fences, and their neighbors sometimes end up paying for them, but what fences get built and who pays for how much of the cost are unaffected by what ought to be the relevant law. Nor do such norms apply only in modern-day Shasta County. Ellickson's examples of societies with such norms included orchard owners in the Pacific Northwest, whalers in the nineteenth century, and modern American academics.

Ellickson's central thesis was that close-knit groups tend to develop efficient norms. He concluded that while formal law is important and useful in human affairs, it is less important and less useful than generally believed. In a wide variety of situations, not only do people succeed in resolving their conflicts without recourse to law, but they also do it by mechanisms that work considerably better than the legal system.

I have discussed elsewhere the reasons why I believe that Ellickson's thesis is a plausible one and offered some evidence that the norms he describes are in fact efficient.[22] The relevance of that discussion to this essay is that the system of norms and norm enforcement that he describes is a simpler version of the sort of private market for law discussed in this essay. There are no middlemen or arbitrators, everyone is his own enforcement agency, and the only available court is the court of (local) public opinion; but the structure of the market for norms is the same as the structure of the market for law. Each person can choose whether to act in a neighborly fashion toward each other person, and each pair of persons must in some way reach agreement on what that implies. If individuals fail to agree (or violate their agreements), the result is costly conflict. If, as Ellickson argues, such a structure tends to generate efficient norms, that is at least some evidence that a similar structure would tend to generate efficient laws.

Efficiency, Justice, and Liberty

The attentive reader, and especially the attentive libertarian reader, will have noticed that I have said nothing about what the laws generated by the market will be, other than efficient. In particular, I have said nothing about whether those laws will be consistent with either justice or liberty. That omission was deliberate. My purpose here is to discuss what outcomes we can expect a competitive market for law to produce, not what outcomes we want it to produce. This is an essay in economics, not moral philosophy.

Whether these outcomes will be consistent with either justice or liberty depends on whether either justice or liberty is economically efficient. In the case of liberty, I think there is good reason to believe that, as a general rule, it is. A considerable part of libertarian writing, my own included,[23] as well as a good deal of economic theory from Adam Smith on, defends the thesis that, on the whole, leaving people free to run their own lives maximizes total human happiness—for which economic efficiency may be considered a rough proxy.[24]

Whether justice is efficient is a harder problem and comes in two parts. The first is the question of whether the rules implied by justice are themselves efficient rules; to that I have no answer, since I have no theory of justice to offer other than that implied by individual liberty. The second is the relation between individuals' beliefs about justice and their preferences for law.

Suppose that almost everyone in a society shares certain beliefs about justice—perhaps that the conviction of innocents is a very bad thing, to be avoided even at high cost, or that murderers should be executed, or that children should not be executed, even for murder.

Those beliefs will affect but not determine what laws the people in that society demand. Justice is only one of the things people value—an individual might favor a legal rule he considers unjust if he thinks it benefits him—so we would expect the efficient set of legal rules that the market generates to represent some compromise between the legal rules that would be efficient absent specific beliefs about justice and the rules implied by those beliefs. To put it differently, beliefs about justice affect the value to individuals of being under particular legal rules, which affects what legal rules are efficient, which affects what legal rules the market will produce.

Anarchy, Efficiency, and the Common Law

I have argued that there is reason to expect a system in which legal rules are generated by firms competing in a private market to produce efficient rules. Richard Posner has argued that there is considerable empirical evidence to suggest that the actual rules of Anglo-American common law are efficient. This raises an obvious and interesting question: can the mechanisms I have been describing explain the observed efficiency of the common law?

I do not know the answer to that question. Certainly some forms of competitive law have contributed to the creation and development of the common law. The common law had its origin in the legal system of Anglo-Saxon England, the early form of which involved a large element of private enforcement and private arbitration.[25] It evolved in an environment of multiple court systems—church, royal, and local— where litigants had at least some control over where their disputes were resolved. Some common law rules originated as private norms, and I have argued that norms are produced on something like a competitive market. Some rules may have been borrowed from the medieval fair courts, which had some of the characteristics of the system I have described.

It is thus possible that what Posner observes in present day common law is fossilized efficiency, produced by institutions that no longer exist[26] and preserved by the conservative nature of the common law. That conjecture is consistent with the observation that the efficiency of the common law seems to have decreased over time, at least in this century, with the long retreat from freedom of contract providing the most striking example. It is also consistent with Posner's claim that it is common law, not legislated law, that tends to be efficient. But it would require a much more extensive knowledge of the history and content of the common law than I have to say whether such a conjecture provides a plausible account of such efficiency as modern common law possesses.[27]

In any case, the principal purpose of this essay is not to offer a solution to the puzzle of why the common law is efficient, supposing that it is. My purpose is to show why the law generated by the institutions of private property anarchy would tend to be efficient and to explore some of the limitations of that tendency. Although the arguments I offer do not imply anything like a perfectly efficient legal system, they may provide better reasons to expect efficient law under anarchy than we have to expect efficient law under other forms of legal system, including the sort we now have.

Notes

1. The work in question was the first (1972) edition of *The Economic Analysis of Law*. As far as I know, this was the first appearance in print of the conjecture. In the current (1992) edition Posner writes, "The theory is that the common law is best (not perfectly) explained as a system for maximizing the wealth of society." Posner prefers the term "wealth maximization" but uses it in a sense corresponding to conventional ideas of economic efficiency. For a more detailed discussion of such ideas, see David Friedman, *Price Theory: An Intermediate Text*, 2d ed. (Cincinnati: South-Western Publishing, 1990), chap. 15, and Richard Posner, *Economic Analysis of Law*, 4th ed. (Boston: Little Brown, 1992), especially 13–16.

2. Some arguments for such a mechanism can be found in Paul H. Rubin, "Why Is the Common Law Efficient?" *Journal of Legal Studies* 6 (1977): 51–63; in George L. Priest, "The Common Law Process and the Selection of Efficient Rules," *Journal of Legal Studies* 6 (1977): 65–82; and in Posner, *Economic Analysis of Law*, 254–55, 535–36. For arguments on the other side, see Paul H. Rubin and Martin J. Bailey, "The Role of Lawyers in Changing the Law," *Journal of Legal Studies* 23 (1994): 807.

3. I will offer some evidence based on existing markets with a similar economic structure.

4. The original form of this argument appeared in David Friedman, *The Machinery of Freedom, Guide to a Radical Capitalism*, 1st ed. (New York: Harper and Row, 1973), 159–64. Interested readers will also find there, and in the current edition (La Salle, Ill.: Open Court, 1989), discussions of other problems raised by an anarchocapitalist society, including defense against foreign states and stability against the reintroduction of the state. See also Tyler Cowen, "Law as a Public Good: The Economics of Anarchy," *Econom-*

ics and Philosophy 8 (1992): 249–67, for a criticism of anarchocapitalist institutions, and Friedman, "Law as a Private Good," *Economics and Philosophy* 10 (1994): 319–27, for a reply.

5. Economists are accustomed to the idea that the principal justification for government is as a producer of public goods. Law enforcement, although it has some public-good elements, is both crowdable—it costs a police force more to protect all the citizens of a town than to protect half of them—and excludable. Arbitration is an ordinary private good, although one of its outputs and inputs, information in the form of precedents, shares the public-good characteristics of other forms of information. See William Landes and Richard Posner, "Legal Precedent: A Theoretical and Empirical Analysis," *Journal of Law and Economics*, vol. 19, no. 249 (1976), and Landes and Posner, "Adjudication as a Private Good," *Journal of Legal Studies* 8 (1979): 235.

6. A single arbitration agency might supply different law codes to different customers, so the number of law codes could be greater than the number of arbitration agencies. If, on the other hand, customers valued the simplicity and predictability of uniform law, many arbitration agencies might choose to adopt identical, or at least very similar, law codes.

7. For one explanation of economic efficiency, see Friedman, *Price Theory*, chap. 15.

8. Such costs and benefits include costs of precautions taken by parties to avoid liability and benefits due to accidents prevented by such precautions.

9. In many legal systems, legal rules are not symmetrical between parties. Even in our legal system, that is true if one of the parties is a government protected by sovereign immunity, or a minor, or some other party with special status.

10. If one wanted to drop this assumption, one could do so by introducing a "quantity" π_{ij}, representing the probability of a dispute between i and j. A uniform price P for legal assent would then be per unit, making the price at which i bought assent from j $P\pi_{ij}$.

11. Posner, *Economic Analysis of Law*, 474.

12. Perhaps something about their circumstances makes them particularly likely to be accidental (but not negligent) tortfeasors.

13. Imagine, for example, the baseline rules with regard to race that we might expect if an anarchocapitalist society had somehow been established in the American South in the 1840s. Even if the system succeeded in bargaining its way to the (efficient) outcome of freedom for slaves, it would presumably be freedom on very unfavorable terms.

14. This problem was first called to my attention by James Buchanan, in a perceptive review of the first edition of Friedman, *The Machinery of Freedom*. See James M. Buchanan, "Review of *The Machinery of Freedom: Guide to a Radical Capitalism* by David D. Friedman," *Journal of Economic Literature*, vol. 12, no. 3 (September 1974): 914–15.

15. For one approach to understanding how the solution to such conflicts is

determined and maintained, see Friedman, "A Positive Account of Property Rights," *Social Philosophy and Policy*, vol. 11, no. 2 (Summer 1994): 1–16.

16. See Friedman, "A Positive Account of Property Rights," and Thomas C. Schelling, *The Strategy of Conflict* (Oxford: Oxford University Press, 1960).

17. Little, but not none. A might not bother to ascertain B's enforcement agency before deciding whether to break his arm. If so, the fact that C's enforcement agency has obtained severe penalties for assault in its negotiations with A's agency may provide some protection to B.

18. For discussions of whether intellectual property protection is desirable, see S. Breyer, "The Uneasy Case for Copyright: A Study of Copyright in Books, Photocopies, and Computer Programs," *Harvard Law Review*, vol. 84, no. 281 (1970): 292–301, and F. Machlup, "An Economic Review of the Patent System," Study no. 15, Subcommittee on Patents, Trademarks, and Copyrights, Senate Committee on the Judiciary, 85th Cong., 2d Sess. (1958).

19. David Friedman, "A World of Strong Privacy: Promises and Perils of Encryption," forthcoming in *Social Philosophy and Policy*, also available from the author.

20. Patricia Danzon and Lee Lilliard found that fewer than 10 percent of malpractice claims were tried (Patricia Munch Danzon and Lee A. Lilliard, "Settlement Out of Court: The Disposition of Medical Malpractice Claims," *Journal of Legal Studies* 12 [1983]: 345–75); Kip Viscuzi found that 95 percent of product liability claims that were not dropped were settled either before or during trial (W. Kip Viscuzi, "The Determinants of the Disposition of Product Liability Claims and Compensation for Bodily Injury," *Journal of Legal Studies* 15 [1986]: 321–46). Department of Transportation research on bodily injury and uninsured motorist claims found that "less than 1% of all claimants went all the way to a verdict" (Marshall S. Shapo, reporter, "Towards a Jurisprudence of Injury: The Continuing Creation of a System of Substantive Justice in American Tort Law," Report to the American Bar Association, 1984, quoting from 1 Department of Transportation, Automobile Personal Injury Claims 121 [1970]). Hammitt reported that, of the bodily injury cases in their study, only about 1 percent were tried to a verdict; about an additional .5 percent of the cases settled during trial (James K. Hammitt, *Automobile Accident Compensation, Volume 2: Payments by Auto Insurers* [Santa Monica: RAND, 1985]). I do not know what fraction of the cases in any of these studies was conducted by insurance companies against insurance companies. I conjecture that, if one could separate out such cases, the settlement rates would be even higher, because of the discipline imposed by repeat dealing.

21. Robert C. Ellickson, *Order Without Law* (Cambridge, Mass.: Harvard University Press, 1991).

22. Friedman, "Less Law than Meets the Eye," a review of *Order Without Law*, by Robert Ellickson, *The Michigan Law Review*, vol. 90, no. 6 (May 1992): 1444–52. In this review I suggest limitations to the efficiency of norms corresponding to those offered here with regard to the efficiency of privately generated law.

23. Specifically, large parts of Friedman, *The Machinery of Freedom*. See also Friedman, *Price Theory*, chap. 15, 455–65.

24. Friedman, *Price Theory*, chap. 15, 434–54.

25. See David Friedman, "Private Creation and Enforcement of Law—A Historical Case," *Journal of Legal Studies* 8 (March 1979): 399–415, for a discussion of similar legal institutions in Saga period Iceland.

26. This is not entirely true; the common law still imports some rules from commercial practice and thus may continue to be influenced by private systems of norms.

27. Readers interested in this subject may want to look at Bruce Benson, *The Enterprise of Law* (San Francisco: Pacific Research Institute for Public Policy, 1990).

13

The State of Statelessness[1]

John T. Sanders

The appearance of Robert Paul Wolff's 1970 book, *In Defense of Anarchism*,[2] represented something unusual in twentieth-century Western philosophy: an argument *sympathetic* to anarchism from a well-regarded philosopher in the (relative) mainstream of the profession. When Robert Nozick's *Anarchy, State, and Utopia*[3] became something of a hit later in the 1970s, it offered something even more unusual: an argument that actually took *market* anarchism seriously, written by a member of one of the most prestigious departments of philosophy in the world. Since that time, arguments supporting anarchism have met with somewhat less incredulity and have been offered at least the kind of minimally respectful academic attention once given by Gaunilo's fellow monks to his attempts at refuting Anselm's "proof" of God's existence.

Discussion about the legitimacy and propriety of the state has been remarkably wide ranging over the centuries, though, and anarchists can be found on the political left, on the right, and even—surprising to some, perhaps—in the center. Philosophical anarchism is perfectly compatible with pragmatic gradualism, as will become apparent in due course.

All anarchist arguments appear to depend on at least these two presumptions: first, that government always involves some fundamentally objectionable form of coercion and, second, that this kind of coercion can and should be avoided. Beyond these two presumptions, arguments against the state take a variety of forms and, just as is the case in every other area of philosophical inquiry, contention between proponents of the various forms of anarchism occasionally becomes quite vigorous.

The objective of the present paper is to address a handful of issues that typically get raised in discussions of philosophical anarchism. Some of these issues arise in discussions among partisans of anarchism, and some are more likely to be raised in efforts to defend the state against its opponents. My hope is to focus the argument in such a way as to make clearer the main issues that are at stake from the point of view of at least one version of philosophical anarchism.

The Argument from Autonomy

The problem of resolving the conflict between the nature of government, on the one hand, and the moral necessity of preserving and enhancing human autonomy, on the other, was central to Robert Paul Wolff's defense of anarchism in his 1970 book. As Wolff pointed out, the conflict does have at least one theoretical solution.

> There is, in theory, a solution to the problem . . . and this fact is in itself quite important. However, the solution requires the imposition of impossibly restrictive conditions which make it applicable only to a rather bizarre variety of actual situations. The solution is a direct democracy—that is, a political community in which every person votes on every issue—governed by a rule of unanimity. Under unanimous direct democracy, every member of the society wills freely every law which is actually passed. Hence, he is only confronted as a citizen with laws to which he has consented. Since a man who is constrained only by the dictates of his own will is autonomous, it follows that under the directions of unanimous direct democracy, men can harmonize the duty of autonomy with the commands of authority.[4]

Unanimous direct democracies are noncoercive. If such societies are to take action on any matter at all, they require the consent of every society member. If even one member fails to consent, then nothing is done. Unanimous direct democracies are held almost universally to be hopelessly impractical.[5]

They are not quite so hopeless, however, if one frees one's conception of community organization from its traditional close link with geography. It is a community of *people*, after all, that we hope to coordinate, and their ties to the land they are on are peripheral.

It is important to see that voluntary organizations of people, whether accomplished through mutual self-help or through the hiring of agents or subscription to services, are noncoercive in precisely the sense offered up as "merely theoretical" in Wolff's picture of unanimous direct democracy. If a person is dissatisfied with the actions taken by her cooperative group or agency, she does not have to continue to support them. Such a person "is only confronted as a citizen with laws to which [s]he has consented"; but where unanimous direct democracies of the kind envisioned by Wolff seem to *collapse* when one member fails to consent, this is only because of the conceptual links between communities and geography. Once that conceptual link is relaxed, it may be seen that communities can survive the withholding of assent of even large numbers of their "citizens": voluntary cooperative arrangements and private protection agency schemes survive even when membership shifts dramatically.

Under this kind of conception, "societies" are common interest groups. Since there is no requirement that free market societies establish unanimous consent within a given geographic area, they are not subject to the same restrictions that govern unanimous direct democracies as conceived by Wolff. They serve as focal points for societal organization, but they do not violate the demands of human autonomy. This "free market" society thus resolves what Wolff has called "the fundamental problem of political philosophy" (p. vii) by questioning the need for *geographically* bound provision of the social services that governments have tried to provide; that is, it does this by breaking the conceptual links between society and geography.[6] The human need for social cooperation is met, and human autonomy is not sacrificed.

Rawlsian "Social Contract"

Just what *kind* of agreement would be reached by ideally autonomous individuals acting rationally in behalf of their own interests? Would they ever choose to subject themselves to a state? It is the primary concern of social contract theory to address such questions. In particular, in all of its best-known forms, social contract theory functions as follows: from the sorts of things that more or less ideal people did or would decide on as the social conditions of their lives, under a set of real or hypothetical constraining circumstances, conclusions are drawn as to how society *should* be arranged (or at least as to how society may permissibly be arranged).

Contemporary social contract theory comes in two distinctive flavors: Hobbesian and Rousseauian. The former has led to quasi-mathematical treatment via game and decision theory, while the latter has led, through Kant, to the extremely influential work of John Rawls.

Now, it has not always been completely clear, in the works of social contractarians, why the contract argument should be at all convincing. It has virtually no merit as a historical argument, since (1) it is extremely unlikely that existing societies have contractual agreements of the kind envisioned as their foundations, and (2) even if they did, it is difficult to see why that should influence conclusions about what society *should* be like. More importantly, since the historical claim has never really been made or taken very seriously, the contract argument has been troublesome because it has not always been clear why normative conclusions about society should be warranted by decisions made collectively in even a hypothetical contract: no matter how the parties to the contract are viewed—no matter what constraints they are placed under—why should their decision influence anyone else's? One of the primary apparent virtues of the Rawlsian version of contract theory is that it has seemed, at least partially, to clear up some of these problems.

Not only is contract theory not to be interpreted as making any historical claims about how societies came to be, but, for Rawlsian versions anyway, it also is not even important for the contractarian argument that separate individuals be involved in making the social decision. Although Rawls characterizes his "original position" as involving several "representative" persons, this aspect of the theory appears not to be essential. Since the hypothetical parties to the social contract are viewed as being equally rational and as being unaware of individual differences that would cause them to make use of their rationality in different ways (i.e., in pursuit of different ends), each of them will come to the same conclusion about the proper social arrangements. Since this is the case, it is possible to ignore the fact that there are several parties to the hypothetical contract and to concentrate on the considerations of any one of them, as each deliberates on the problem of how society should be arranged. Normative conclusions in Rawls's theory are held to follow, *not* from the fact that several people in a certain situation would draw them, but from the fact that they are the conclusions that *reason itself* would yield when suitably constrained.[7]

The contractarian terminology is useful for Rawls's framework because it highlights some of the problems that must be faced in developing a rational ethical or political theory and because it suggests solutions to these problems. It emphasizes the fact that real people, rational though they may be, may have interests that are different enough that their common rationality alone will not suffice to tell them how, collectively, they should arrange their social lives. It also emphasizes, though, the fact that individual differences need not be irreconcilable, and lays the groundwork for taking first steps toward understanding which constraints it is appropriate to place on reason in attempting to arrive at the best social arrangements (pp. 16, 140, 185).

The Rawlsian theory thus relies, for its argument, not so much on agreement or contract between different people, but on reason. Reason is thus the foundation on which the methodological framework is to be built, and it is not likely that this choice will instigate much controversy, so long as it be stipulated that no *particular* conception of reason is envisioned. Particular conceptions of reason will comprise part of the content of a fleshed-out theory.[8]

The problem of how society should be organized is therefore, for Rawls, a problem of rational choice. Now, such problems have unique solutions only in case the circumstances in which the choice is to be made can be spelled out in some detail. In general, one must know the beliefs and interests (the goals) of the party or parties making the choice, one must know the alternatives from which the choice is to be made, and so on (pp. 17–18). One must, that is, be able to give content to what Rawls refers to as the "initial situation." With a reasonably filled-out initial situation, one should be able to determine the sorts of organizational principles that reason dictates be chosen for society.

Now, giving content to the initial situation is itself clearly a problem of rational choice. The problem is to list the restrictions that may reasonably be imposed on arguments for one or another set of social principles. Once any such choice of restrictions is made, the initial situation will have been given a certain content and will thus amount to a choice among the many possible initial situations.

What is plain, though, is that any such choices will be controversial; indeed, it is precisely such choices that are frequently the *central* item of contention among conflicting political or social theories. Rawls certainly was aware of this; indeed, it is a main contention of his that the methodological framework to be found in *A Theory of Justice*—considered apart from the liberal choices Rawls favors in filling out the framework—is no more than an extremely suggestive device for portraying ethical and social arguments. The framework includes the idea of the "initial situation," in which some constraints are placed on the procedure of deciding on principles of justice that should guide society; it includes the idea of the "veil of ignorance," which serves to separate appropriate from inappropriate considerations; and it includes the idea of the "constitutional convention," in which the decision as to whether to adopt government is made, again under constraints provided by some positioning of the veil of ignorance. The framework may be filled out in a variety of ways, depending on the decisions made as to which constraints to place on the decision procedure, as to which considerations are to be obscured by the veil of ignorance, and as to which adjustments are to be made for the constitutional convention. As such, it is truly neutral with respect to particular ethical and political theories. It offers "a general analytic method for the comparative study of conceptions of justice" (p. 121).[9]

Rawls's book does more, however, than merely set up a "general analytic method." The great bulk of *A Theory of Justice* is devoted to presenting a specific theory, as the title suggests. It is, then, the liberal theory, rather than the methodological framework, that has been the target of Rawls's critics.[10] The tone of all of these criticisms is neatly captured by Joseph Margolis.

> In a word, what Rawls has provided is an impressively articulated statement of which "equilibrium" best suits certain intuitions about man's condition and the nature of justice: it is a philosophically informed *ideology*, not a demonstration of the validity of the thesis of justice as fairness against the claims of its competitors.[11]

All of the criticisms—whatever their merit—seem actually to be directed at the content of Rawls's theory and not at the framework. As a matter of fact, each of them is formulated from within the framework. There seems to be no good reason to contend that the framework itself is ideologically tainted (unless, of course, one *identifies* as part of the framework some of Rawls's liberal filler).[12]

By the same token, however, there is no reason to presume that the framework—and thus the Rawlsian social contract methodology—privileges liberalism in any way. Liberalism is just one of the ideological standpoints that may be exhibited within the framework. The question about which standpoint is best remains to be debated. Once again: the advantage of the Rawlsian analytic framework is just that it offers an elegant mechanism for comparing and contrasting the similarities and differences between different ideological approaches at the level of their various decisions about which constraints, if any, are appropriate at the various levels of social choice that are met with in the framework.

In particular, since decisions about whether it is reasonable to establish a state will be made in what Rawls calls the level of the "constitutional convention," the framework can highlight just what specific differences there may be among different political and socio-logical ideologies concerning what is reasonable to consider (and what is reasonable to place behind the veil of ignorance) not only at the level of the constitutional convention but also all the way down. There are likely to be differences about choices "reasonably" to be made in the initial situation and in the original position, in particular. But there may well also be differences about whether all of these different levels really need to be distinct; or perhaps some ideologies would require *additional* levels in order adequately to display their characteristic reasoning about principles of justice, about the reasonableness of this or that constraint on decision making, and so on.

The point here, though, is simple. The Rawlsian framework is radically distinct from Rawlsian (or any other) interpretations of it. There is nothing about the *framework*, in particular—therefore nothing about the general constraint that social structure be understood as a matter of rational social choice—that either favors or rules out the state. Even if all parties to the discussion were to agree that the Rawlsian framework is useful for organizing political and social argu-mentation, therefore, the substantive issues would all be left open. And it is *certainly* possible, in particular, to argue, within a rationally constrained Rawlsian constitutional convention, that the state is more trouble than it is worth.[13] Rawlsian versions of social contract theory thus cannot possibly be predisposed to affirmations of the state unless they beg the question that is at issue by confusing framework with substantive ideological *interpretation* of the framework.

The Prisoners' Dilemma and Other Diversions

The other main flavor of social contract theory may appear, at first glance at least, to be less idealized and thus more realistic. As should become apparent fairly quickly, this appearance is dangerously mis-leading, but just because the appearance of realism has been so seductive, it must not be ignored. In Hobbesian-style approaches to social contract theory, attempts are made to understand what people really *would* do in making choices under various more or less social circumstances. While Rawlsian approaches are not particularly concerned with genuine interactions among separate individuals in choice situations, Hobbesian approaches focus on exactly this factor, albeit in a manner that is just as idealized, in the end, as is the Rawlsian framework.

For example: let's say that you have been caught and thrown into prison after participating in your special crime. Now you are faced with a dilemma. Your accomplice, for whom you have no concern at all, has also been caught. Both of you have the same dilemma, and you are aware of that fact.

The problem is this. You are not able to communicate with your accomplice, and the prosecutor has been trying to get both of you to confess. The prosecutor has offered you freedom in exchange for information that will lead to the conviction of the accomplice. If your information turns out not to be needed, however—in particular, if the accomplice also confesses—then you will get the normal (neither maximal nor minimal) sentence.

You have every reason to believe that the prosecutor has offered the same deal to you both, but you also have reason to believe that in the absence of a confession from either of you, the prosecutor's case will not be strong enough to get more than a very minimal sentence.

So what do you do? If neither of you confesses, then both of you will get minimal sentences. If both of you confess, then both will get normal (neither minimal nor maximal) sentences. If one confesses and the other one keeps silent, the first will go free while the second gets the maximum sentence.

Not only don't you have any concern for what happens to your accomplice, the two of you are not even sufficiently acquainted to make it possible for either of you to feel confident in guessing what the other will do.[14]

Finally, there's one more thing: no matter what you decide, you will never be interacting in the future with either your accomplice or with anyone who cares one way or another what you do in this case.

That's the Prisoners' Dilemma.[15]

With what seems to be increasing frequency over the years, this fascinating problem has exercised both mathematically and philosophically inclined minds ever since 1950, when it was discovered by Melvin Dresher and Merrill Flood of the RAND Corporation. When the problem is carefully constrained with all the provisos that appear above, a similarly constrained prediction has emerged: when faced with such situations, those who are motivated primarily by the desire to maximize their own gain will end up choosing a course of action that *fails* to maximize their own gain. That's why the problem is so much fun.

Since it may seem reasonable to think that real people, when making real decisions that affect their real lives, are motivated in much the same way as are the rational maximizers in the Prisoners' Dilemma (PD) scenario, it has seemed reasonable to apply the conclusion derived within the PD setup to real-world questions concerning human cooperation in a "state of nature." This is why the problem has taken on such a vigorous life in recent discussion of the state and its rationale. The state of nature would offer frequent analogs to the Prisoners' Dilemma, it is thought. People would not find it possible to achieve their goals in the absence of some means of enforcing agreements. In general, why would *anyone* follow through with an agreement? If noncompliance is an option, every rational maximizer would reason as follows: If I can persuade my partner in this agreement to comply first, then I will be better off not complying myself than I would be if I fulfilled my part of the bargain. If *I* must somehow go first, then I surely won't comply, for if I do, then my partner will reason exactly like I just did and won't follow through. So *whoever* goes first, my wisest policy is not to comply.

Rational maximizers thus will not comply—or so the argument goes—unless there is something that prevents the option of noncompliance; thus, we all wind up consigning ourselves to normal sentences instead of gaining the reduced sentences we could have had if we had kept faith with our partners.

Now, the suggestion is made surprisingly often that this problem can somehow be overcome if we all agree to establish the state, the purpose of which is precisely to prevent welshing on agreements. This is surprising, of course, because it is not terribly easy to see how we could manage to come to this agreement in an environment wherein no agreements are possible. But perhaps the state comes about in some other way than via agreement,[16] and we somehow manage to swing it to this purpose—perhaps gradually, over time, via some other more or less rational dynamic. In any case, whether the state is to be defended as having arisen because of the need for enforcement of agreements or whether it is to be defended as having been co-opted or seized in some way, the Prisoners' Dilemma defense of the state comes down to this: the state is necessary in order to avoid a problem in rational decision making. Without it, rationality yields irrational results.

The main problem with all of this is that Prisoners' Dilemma games are really *so* constrained as to make it quite impossible to draw conclusions about what real people would do (or would be able to do) in the absence of government. In order to get the result that rational decisions yield results that are not Pareto-optimal, the players must be in a situation where it is reasonable to presume that they will never play with this particular opponent again, that their performance in this particular transaction will have no effect on any other transactions that they plan or that they are engaged in presently, and that the players have absolutely no concern whatsoever for one another.

Finally, "rationality" must be understood as strictly a matter of egoistic maximization. Whereas such an assumption is not particularly problematic in most decision-making contexts, since the "egoistic" desires that a decision maker hopes to fulfill might be as other-oriented as you please, it plays havoc with one's intuitions in connection with Prisoners' Dilemma games, since these depend on explicit renunciation of such altruistic personal values, at least as regards the opponent in particular.[17]

Collectively, these conditions are so restrictive that it is not at all clear what one can reasonably conclude about real decision making and about the state from the Prisoners' Dilemma.[18] It is often said that there is something counterintuitive about the idea that rationality should lead to dominant strategies that are so inferior to a cooperative alternative. Surely, though, the sense of paradox is *really* fed by a failure to appreciate fully just how peculiar, and how restrictive, the conditions of the game are. If one really was in a situation like the one characterized in Prisoners' Dilemma, and provided that one really does mean by rationality nothing but pure egoistic maximizing, unsullied by any concern—even by egoistic concern—for the opponent, then surely noncooperation *is* rational. But so what?

Relaxation of even the slightest of the constraints, of course, yields far different results. Where partners can anticipate that further games might be played with the same partner—that is, where the Prisoners' Dilemma game is "iterated"—it is well known that the strategies that tend to dominate play over time are cooperative strategies, such as Anatol Rapoport's tit-for-tat strategy. Robert Axelrod has shown that cooperative strategies do tend to dominate "mean" strategies whenever they are also *clear*, *provocable*, and *forgiving*.[19] That is, the best strategies are ones that are always inclined to cooperate but that respond immediately and consistently to noncooperation on the part of others with noncooperation of their own. In short, the lesson is that

Prisoners' Dilemma games yield *cooperation* among players if only one condition is relaxed: that the games be part of a series of games in which the players can expect that their opponents will formulate their strategies on the basis of their experience of previous play. Since that is really much more like the situation that real people are likely to face even in the most adverse state-of-nature sorts of situation, it is hard to take Prisoners' Dilemma seriously as an argument for the state.[20]

There are other games than Prisoners' Dilemma, of course. Some analysts appear to think that games such as Chicken—where the conditions of play give some players reason to prefer being exploited by their opponents over refusing to cooperate—offer models of possible state-of-nature scenarios that would make government necessary—or at least very desirable—in securing payoffs that all rational players would want; but this result is not at all so clear.

Chicken is the game-theoretic analog of a perhaps mythological rite of passage, thought by some to have been practiced among tribes of American teenagers during the 1950s. Typically, the game is supposed to have pitted two lost "Young Ones"—and their hot rods—against one another. They were to start at opposite ends of a drag strip or lonely road and drive pell-mell toward one another. The first to swerve was a "chicken." The basic difference between Chicken and the Prisoners' Dilemma involves the ranking of the several payoffs. In PD the payoff for mutual defectors is superior to the payoff for suckers, so mutual defection is likely. In Chicken, mutual defection (no one swerves) is worse than chickening out, so mutual defection is less likely. In the latter game, though, the terms of cooperation seem likely, at least on the surface, to foster bullying.

Games of Chicken are, thus, different from Prisoners' Dilemma. In particular, it is not quite as obvious in Chicken as it is in Prisoners' Dilemma that desirable cooperative strategies would come to dominate iterated play; but even in Chicken, the tendency toward some form of cooperation is extremely strong and, in general, domination by cooperative strategies is more likely than not.[21]

Whether the game is Prisoners' Dilemma or Chicken, though, these are still two-person games that are severely constrained. The constraints are the price of the precision one gets in game theory. Loosening the constraints further leads one closer to the real world—and thus closer to being truly apt for political philosophy—but makes the analysis considerably less certain. One way of loosening the constraints yields a slightly more sophisticated and considerably more realistic objection to anarchism: the public-goods problem.

Coercion, Public Goods, and the Free Market

John Dewey once said that "the political and governmental phase of democracy is . . . the best means so far found for realizing ends that lie in the wide domain of human relationships and the development of human personality."[22] Apart from potential argument concerning what the "political and governmental phase of democracy" specifically comes down to, this assertion is clear enough. It offers a challenge to the claims of anarchists that can be met in the courts of argument and experimentation.

Critics of anarchism, however, are rarely so clear. They often seem to base their opposition to anarchism on a commitment to the quite general idea that political means are required for the achievement of vital human goals. Different reactions to this idea may arise in part because of different understandings of what is meant by the expression "political means." At least two interpretations are possible. One might mean only some form of cooperation or another. On this interpretation, the general idea in question would come to nothing more than the thesis that the best means yet found for accomplishing community ends is cooperation. Anarchists would surely have no trouble with this claim, although it does not seem to be particularly informative. One thus suspects that political means must be a bit more substantial if the general idea is to be saved from vacuity.

Franz Oppenheimer once distinguished between political means and economic means for achieving community ends. The mark of the first, according to Oppenheimer, is the readiness to resort to coercion in achieving desired ends.[23] Max Weber is well known for having described states as "human associations that successfully claim the monopoly of legitimate use of physical force within a given territory."[24] It is precisely because "political means," "government," "the state," and various other relevant terms are almost universally understood in terms of force or coercion that the philosophical anarchist is opposed to them.

It is not anarchists, in particular, who have defined these terms and concepts in this way, and it is, of course, possible to define them in terms that do not involve coercion at all.[25] But if the intended institutions (and means of community action) really *are* coercive in the way envisioned by Oppenheimer and Weber (however one contrives to define the relevant terms), then matters will not have been altered at all. The philosophical anarchist will continue to insist that, precisely because of this element of coercion or force, governmental institutions are at least prima facie undesirable. Whether they are desirable all things considered will depend on how the prima facie undesirable (and, for that matter, prima facie desirable) characteristics of government stack up against the pros and cons of alternatives.[26]

But it is absolutely vital to understand that, if one has in mind a *non*coercive arrangement when one thinks of "government," "the state," or "political means," then one is not thinking of anything that the anarchist opposes. Indeed, anarchists often work very hard at coming up with cooperative schemes that, they hope, will efficiently (and ethically) accomplish community ends; thus they can hardly be charged with being opposed to such schemes in principle.

As to the general idea that political means are the best means yet found for accomplishing community ends, anarchists are inclined to point out that, where political means (i.e., coercive means) are used, it is plain that, at the very least, one community is forcing its will on another. It may very well be that majority rule is generally superior to minority rule, but the philosophical anarchist is committed to the thesis that it is rule as such that ought to be avoided. After all, "majority rule" is just the principle that whoever has the biggest gang gets to force those in the minority to do what they want.

Societies that append a list of restrictions on majority rule—lists, for example, of "inalienable" human rights—take a step in the right direction. They thereby carve out an area in which force is not to be permitted, even when the majority will conflicts with minority interest. But if *any* area remains in which majorities rule, there we have an area of activity that is, to put it in the plainest possible terms, ipso facto dominated by the principle that might makes right. The philosophical anarchist argues that this is to be avoided, even if a case could be made out for the greater "efficiency" of such means in accomplishing "community" ends.

What is really going on, at least in most cases, is that one community simply requires another one to support *its* (the first community's) interests. To say that political means are *efficient*, in this context, is literally to praise the virtues of theft over honest toil.

But again: if defenders of the state do not mean to praise theft and the use of force in achieving the ends of those who rule (whether the majority or not) at the expense of those who are ruled, then it may be that philosophical anarchists are not at all opposed to such "states." Since coercion has traditionally been part of the concept of the state, however, it would be useful to clarify the lines of this redefinition.

Crucial special questions are raised, of course, in considering what have come to be called "public goods." For this reason a great deal of the emphasis in arguments for and against the state has traditionally been placed on the question about whether public goods could be provided without government (even when authors do not explicitly refer to "public goods" as such).[27]

A common, collective, or public good, according to a particularly clear definition offered by Mancur Olson, is "any good such that, if any person x_i in a group $x_1, \ldots , x_i, \ldots , x_n$ consumes it, it cannot feasibly be withheld from the others in that group."[28] The important fact to note about public goods is that *if* the good is created or provided by some members of the group, there is no feasible way of excluding or preventing those members who have *not* contributed from sharing in the consumption of the good (pp. 14–15). It is not necessary, in the definition of public goods, that it be technically *impossible* to prevent noncontributors from partaking in what others have provided: it must only be infeasible or uneconomic (p. 14).

Public goods are thus defined with respect to specific groups of people. To avoid certain complications, it helps to limit attention only to those public goods that require that someone make some sort of investment—whether it be of labor, cash, or whatever—if they are to become available. For similar reasons, it is best to worry about only those situations in which the members of the group with respect to which some public good is defined are unanimous in their desire for that good. This restriction is justified by the fact that even in cases where all of the members of a very large group are unanimous in desiring a public good, it appears that that good will not be provided, given that the members can choose whether they will help in providing the good and that they make this choice rationally.

As Olson argued especially plausibly, provision or nonprovision of public goods within a group depends in an important way on certain fundamental characteristics of the group itself. To understand his argument, it is necessary to examine briefly his "taxonomy of groups" and his analysis of the varying potentials that different kinds of groups have of providing public goods in general.

In the first place, Olson distinguished between what he calls "exclusive" and "inclusive" groups.

An exclusive group is best characterized as that sort of group whose members hope to keep membership restricted as much as possible. Within such groups, competition or rivalry is the characteristic relationship holding between members. In general, the character of an exclusive group is determined by the fact that the particular public good sought is such that it is fixed in supply—that is, it is such that the more benefit one member gets, the less others get (p. 37).

For a characteristic *in*clusive group, on the other hand, the larger the membership, the happier the individual members. In such groups increasing the membership hurts no one and, in fact, typically leads to a reduced cost burden on each member. For inclusive groups, the benefit from a public good is *not* fixed in supply: if one member gets more, others need not get less. It is the inclusive group that is most interesting in connection with public goods.

There are three kinds of inclusive groups: "privileged" groups, "intermediate" groups, and "latent" groups. With respect to the provision of any one public good, the distinction among the three kinds of groups is merely one of size.

For the sake of understanding this taxonomy, consider a public good with a net cost that rises linearly in relation to the number of people in the group. Privileged groups are groups that are small enough that the cost of providing the public good is so low that at least one member would be willing to pay the whole cost if that were the only way to secure it.

Intermediate groups are groups that are large enough that the cost of providing the public good is too large for any one member to be willing to pay it, even if that were the only way to get the good. Intermediate groups are still small enough, though, that failure of any one member to pay his share will have a noticeable effect on the burdens of the other members.

Latent groups, finally, are groups that are large enough that no one member would pay the whole cost of the public good, and are *so* large that failure of any one member to pay his share will have no significant effect on the shares of other members (pp. 49–50).

Now, a privileged group defined with respect to one public good may be larger than a privileged group defined with respect to a different good. Much depends on the cost of providing the good and the value that individuals place on having it provided.[29] But the three kinds of groups are defined by Olson in such a way that interesting results may be obtained even when particular costs and particular values are ignored. Attention is focused, instead, on the different courses of action that a rational person would take as a member of each of the three kinds of inclusive groups and on the differences this would make regarding provision of the public good.

Olson, in a singularly precise analysis of a notoriously vague problem area, concludes that public goods are not likely to be provided in any community that meets the following three conditions: (1) the community is a latent group; (2) the members of the community have the option to abstain from supporting the effort to secure the public good; and (3) the members behave "rationally," once again on the understanding that rationality involves egoistic maximization.[30]

It is absolutely vital to note, however, that there are at least five plausible ways of defending a noncoercive social order—the state of statelessness—even while acknowledging Olson's argument. They are as follows:

(1) It might be argued—and often is—that it is wrong to think that helping to provide a public good in a latent group is irrational. One might think that the careful reasoning of Olson's argument would be taken into consideration by a rational person in a latent group. In considering whether to help pay for the good, a rational person might think: "But if everybody avoids paying, the good won't get provided." It is difficult to feel comfortable with calling a decision to pay on the grounds of this kind of consideration irrational. Olsonian rationality, applied to decisions in latent groups, seems to violate what might as well be acknowledged as Kant's categorical imperative; and it seems a bit strong to call that principle irrational in such situations, especially since it seems to be supported by Olson's conclusion that, if people were to act as he thinks rationality dictates, they would fail to get what they wanted.

Such an argument may not be too helpful, however, even if it could be made to work. Olson's line of reasoning may be reformulated in such a way that instead of dealing with what it is *rational* for people to do as members of latent groups, it deals with what people *in fact* do, or with what people may reasonably be expected to do, as members of such groups. Olson lists several historical examples of latent groups and their behavior in his book. These examples seem to support, with certain important qualifications (see below, option 4), the thesis that latent groups don't manage to provide themselves with public goods. This first option is thus less attractive than it may at first seem. In order to make effective use of it in defending the state of statelessness, one would have to be able to argue plausibly that the particular goods being considered are such that people could be expected to help in providing them, even as members of latent groups.[31]

(2) It might be argued that there is a noncoercive means of ensuring that the particular goods that are being considered would be demanded only by privileged groups. Since there is a presumption that public goods would be provided in privileged groups, this option would be a very attractive one if it could be utilized plausibly.

(3) It might be argued that there is a noncoercive means of ensuring that the particular goods that are being considered would be demanded only by (at the largest) intermediate groups. This option is obviously much less attractive than the last, since whether intermediate groups will be able to provide themselves with public goods is, in general, indeterminate. It might be, however, that knowing which goods were in question would allow one to have a better idea about the likelihoods involved. If this option were to be effective, it would have to make it plausible that these particular goods would be provided even by intermediate groups.

(4) It might be argued that public goods could be provided to latent groups by a provision of nonpublic goods to those who pay or by some sort of noncoercive disincentives to those who fail to pay. This option is suggested by Olson himself, and he lists several examples of latent groups that do seem to manage to provide themselves with public goods in this way. As he notes, though, there is a hidden trap to this option. If this option were the only one available, then it seems likely that the model would fail.[32] This option might be useful in conjunction with one or more of the others, however.

(5) It might be argued that the goods being considered were private goods, rather than public goods. That is, it might be argued that there *is* a feasible way of withholding the goods in question from those who fail to help in providing them. This option would be very powerful if, in addition, it could be argued that one could *expect* the goods to be provided privately in a noncoercive society.

While the public-goods problem really is worth examining, in other words, it does not necessarily rule out the very real possibility that people might actually manage to provide themselves with such things.[33] But when all is said and done, it is perfectly possible that even those who agree in principle with the anarchist's theoretical arguments against the state will be reluctant to agree with the anarchist that governments should be abolished. The reasons might appear to such people to be *practical* rather than theoretical. Since I cannot possibly imagine how a theory that is not useful in practice can be any good at all, I turn now to some of these more pragmatic considerations.

The Consequences of Instant Anarchism

If governments were allowed to collapse this morning, we would see widespread rioting, murder, impoverishment, and other horrors by this afternoon. So, anyway, runs what surely is the most visceral reaction to the idea of statelessness. There is nervousness about this even among those who find anarchy desirable in principle. For a variety of reasons, people often reach the conclusion that philosophical anarchism is impractical. Some of the better reasons for worrying about this will be addressed in this section.

Because of the way governments work, people become dependent on them. They come to need government even in areas in which they would not have needed government had government not created the dependency in question. An illustrative situation—one that is extremely vivid in my own mind as I write this—is the situation in Russia in the early 1990s.[34] On the breakup of the Soviet Union and the effort to establish something like a Western economy, there functioned in Russia, side-by-side and intertwined, at least four major economies.

At the most impoverished level there were large numbers of people who had worked their entire lives under a system in which they had come to believe that they would be taken care of. It is to be presumed that some worked harder than others in this system, but that is neither here nor there. No one had a choice; the rewards and punishments of this system were fairly clear to all concerned, and one had to participate in it whether or not one liked it. When that system collapsed, many people found themselves unable for one reason or another to succeed in the new one (the very young, the very old, the ill, and the otherwise disabled were among the most poignant cases). This portion of the population continued to depend on the state, and the state had simply abandoned them. They lived extraordinarily poorly, unable to afford even the tiny sums (minuscule by Western standards—a kilo of tomatoes for ten cents, subway tokens costing a small fraction of a cent, etc.) charged for services on the growing ruble economy. They had had the floor ripped out from under them, and their plight is what many critics of anarchism fear would be the general upshot of statelessness.

A second economy, however—also a ruble economy—seemed to be growing by leaps and bounds. At some subway stops in Moscow it was almost impossible to move from the station to the street, since the way was blocked by curb-to-curb kiosks, stands, and purveyors of this and that. Anyone who was able to bring anything at all to market appeared to be free to do so, with little regulation at all of such small business undertakings, and very good livings were earned by large numbers of people who had the ingenuity and the ability to bring things to this market. The situation was very much like the way things must have been at the turn of the century in New York City or Chicago, with very few regulatory mechanisms available to restrict people from participating in the market.

There were lots of people in Moscow who were able to afford to buy the newly available products, so there was a growing economy that produced not only wealth but also something of a middle-class housing boom in the area surrounding Moscow.[35] It is important to note, however, that the people who lived on the first economy, described above, were by and large not able to buy and sell in this second economy. They were dependent on the state, and the state as caregiver had simply vanished, for all intents and purposes.

There were two more economies that bear mentioning: there was a legitimate hard currency economy, which produced in Moscow an increasing number of millionaires (and a tourist economy that was among the most expensive in the world) and there was an illegitimate underground economy that was to a large extent run—or at least successfully manipulated—by the Russian mafia. It was in some locales not easy to tell where the mafia left off and where legitimate business (or government) began, and where government was corrupt, both old line and new line politicians were well represented in the corrupt activities.

Now, proponents of anarchism dwell most frequently on the extent to which creativity, imagination, and productivity can be liberated once restrictions and regulations are lifted from people. They focus on analogs of the second Russian economy discussed above. Critics of anarchism, on the other hand, focus attention on the hardships that will be caused by lifting restrictions: they dwell on analogs of the first economy, where people who had become dependent on government were simply abandoned; worse, they think of analogs of the mafia economy and imagine that *it* would dominate an anarchist society.

Anarchists argue that people who are dependent on government should never have been made dependent in this way—that whatever resources they might have had otherwise were robbed from them and that this is what must be stopped. But this does not lessen the pain of those thus robbed. Anarchists argue that the opportunity for mafia-type activity is largely provided by government regulation and would not exist in the absence of government. Even if this were to be conceded, though, it would not lessen the damage to victims of the mafia once government is relaxed or abandoned.

The question thus arises: even if statelessness is a worthy goal, how can one do away with the state without, at least in the short run, creating great harm? And since the short-term harm is so likely to be great, what reason would free people, acting voluntarily, have to continue to pursue the anarchist ideal? Would it not be much more rational to establish and preserve government, evil though it may be in some prima facie philosopher's sense?

The answer, it seems to me, is not very difficult at all. That it is not seen clearly by those who think about the prospects of anarchism is caused, I think, by a not altogether irrational hysteria that befalls anyone who reflects on the prospects of trying to make one's life in the Sarajevos and Gaza Strips of the early 1990s—but the answer is this: anarchism is an ideal. It should serve as a goal. As long as it seems that it is a worthy goal, even if just in principle, it is reasonable to try to achieve it, but nothing about the goal yields any reason at all to think that its immediate or early achievement is worth any and all costs that may be encountered along the way. Where proceeding toward the goal of statelessness seems plainly to entail suffering—especially when it is the suffering of innocents—then we should stop and reconsider. Perhaps detours must be taken, perhaps the ground must be prepared in one way or another before further progress can be made.

Anarchism's desirability does not go without saying, and it is reasonable to test it as a goal at every step of the way. But as long as it retains its desirability, it retains its value as a goal.

The short answer to the challenge presented to anarchists by the fact that some innocent persons have become dependent on government (all of us have, to be frank about it) and would certainly be harmed by the immediate abandonment of government is this: government should, for this reason, not be abandoned immediately. Its abandonment should be accomplished in such a way as to take care not only to avoid doing more harm than good but also to ensure that anarchism will not lose its attractiveness by virtue of being tainted by the consequences of the too-hasty collapse of the governmental apparatus. The important empirical rule of trial and error should be respected. It is in no one's interest to embark on a political course that seems beautiful from some philosophical perspective but that destroys people's lives.

The Argument from Gullibility

People who are to some extent sympathetic with anarchism as an ideal have nevertheless argued that, even though the abandonment of government would be a good thing, it will never happen because people can be too easily bamboozled by various interested parties into thinking that government is good for them.[36] This argument might be formulated in such a way as to emphasize the obstacles and diversions placed in the way of clearer understanding of the nature of political rule by these interested parties, or it might be formulated in terms of an allegedly inevitable lack of political savvy on the part of the ruled.

While there can be no doubt that those who owe their positions of relative economic or political power to the existence of government do wield a great deal of influence in modern societies, I am not convinced that the situation is as bleak as is suggested by either of these two related lines of thought.

For one thing, people have not been fooled quite as much as might be thought. There is widespread dissatisfaction with government among regular citizens. While it is true that most of this dissatisfaction is directed toward particular political players and parties, with an accompanying tacit hope, anyway, that some other player or party might solve the problems, this is not anywhere near the whole story. In the United States, at least, there is widespread dissatisfaction with government as such, and this has been documented in poll after poll, over an impressively long period of time and over a fairly representative geographic area. What is most impressive is the extent to which this dissatisfaction is expressed in terms of a loss of faith that endemic social problems can be solved by *any* government.

This belief appears to be growing more widespread, although it would be impossible to predict what will happen even next year. The problem is usually reported along with hopeful discussion about how this belief trend might be reversed. The position of the anarchist, of course, is that this belief trend reflects a growing political sophistication and that the early resolution of whatever problems are created by this growing lack of faith requires abandonment of the governmental fetish.

It is unreasonable, however, for either the partisans of anarchism or for anyone else to place great hope or trust in shifting opinions about the usefulness of government. If governments can accomplish their assigned tasks without unwarranted coercion, then this needs to be demonstrated. If nongovernmental alternatives can do the same jobs either as well or better with less coercion, then that needs to be shown. One can expect that such demonstrations would be a powerful force in *directing* public opinion, and these are therefore the tasks that confront partisans on both sides.

Anarchists argue that social affairs can be successfully directed through voluntary arrangements of some kind. They argue, further, that the reason this is not apparent is that governments have made such voluntary arrangements either impossible or extremely costly in terms of the investment of time, energy, and resources. The task before those who think that governments are more trouble than they are worth is therefore to work at the removal of obstacles to voluntary provision of goods and services, to make such alternatives available, and to improve first efforts that do not accomplish their ends. As alternatives become available to people in one area of social cooperation after another, the argument that government is necessary will seem increasingly less convincing.

This is a strategy far superior to the one more often adopted by anarchists, which primarily involves waiting for governmental attempts to solve problems to fail, pointing to the failure, and then wailing in despair when people respond to such failure with yet another attempted governmental solution. If there are noncoercive alternative institutional arrangements that could do the job as well or better, then surely anarchists can think them up and work to make them available.

It is also crucial to note that such efforts can be made on a piecemeal, service-by-service basis and in such a way that the principle of trial and error, mentioned earlier, is respected.

The Capitalist/Socialist Argument

Some of those who argue against the state call themselves "capitalist anarchists." Others contend that this is a contradiction in terms, since capitalism institutionally requires the state. Curiously enough, the capitalist anarchists frequently say the same thing about the socialists. Such arguments recapitulate, within the ranks of those who oppose the idea of some people ruling others as such, the more general arguments that we are familiar with in the broader political arena.[37]

At least as regards the arguments that arise among anarchists, and to a considerable extent also as regards the more general argument, this conflict rests largely on terminological ambiguity. Beyond this ambiguity, there is also an empirical question that is too frequently avoided in favor of a perhaps more comfortable assumption, made by interlocutors on both sides, that their opponents simply have their values upside down.

The terminological issue is this: the term "capitalism," as it has been understood by most proponents and opponents alike, has virtually never referred exclusively to the pristine workings of market forces alone. Karl Marx's critique of capitalism certainly presumed that what he was criticizing was thoroughly political. As Marx envisioned capitalism, it is a politicoeconomic system that succeeds by manipulating economic power (and, in passing, by manipulating ideology) to gain political power, which is then wielded to rearrange the economic playing field. Marx did not always blame capitalists for this—indeed, it seems to be a vital piece of the overall marxian argument that this be more or less inevitable for those who are capitalists—but blameworthy or not, capitalists were, *by virtue* of being capitalists, major actors in the political and ideological realm. They were political manipulators.

Now, the people who call themselves capitalist anarchists are not any happier about this kind of use of political power than marxists are, so a confusion has been generated. Capitalist anarchists favor reliance on market processes alone, yet their choice of name leads more traditional anarchists—in the spirit of M. A. Bakunin and P. A. Kropotkin—to suspect that they are mere apologists or dupes of a *political* system that they don't understand.

That this is merely a terminological issue on at least one level is revealed by the fact that attacks on the abuse of political power to build and maintain economic dominance are as large a part of the literature in the capitalist anarchist tradition as they are in the socialist anarchist tradition, and the traditional sources cited in both bodies of work are largely the same. This terminological issue can be resolved fairly easily. One way to do it is for capitalist anarchists simply to begin to refer to themselves as "market anarchists." This would at least avoid the nearly pointless arguments, endemic between the two groups, about whether capitalism really is driven by markets. If it isn't, then market anarchists are no happier with capitalism than socialist anarchists are.

The more substantive issue that remains, then, in this argument among anarchists involves just what it is that reliance on markets may actually be expected to lead to. This is an empirical question, although it is not an easy empirical question to resolve. My own claim is just that markets—when understood as the locus of *all* voluntary exchange and cooperative undertakings—are at least a fairly clear mechanism for instantiating noncoercive anarchist ideals. And it seems that many of the shortcomings attributed to markets are actually caused by political distortions of market process, rather than by the markets themselves.

Anarchism as Too Demanding an Ideal

Finally, while many people are sympathetic with the ideal of voluntary human cooperation emphasized by anarchist political thought, it is frequently objected that this idea is really practical, if at all, only for small groups, since normal fellow-feeling does not extend very far. This objection often shifts naturally to the complaint that anarchism cannot work until and unless people become angels.[38]

Anarchists are not only *sympathetic* to the view that the idea of natural human community cannot be stretched indefinitely to include all members of the human species, this is often a central part of their case against government, although it is rare that anarchists put the matter precisely like this.

The ideal of natural community, or the general positive idea of moral or other authority, clearly must not and cannot be extended beyond its natural limits.[39] The state—especially the grand modern nation-state—is, according to anarchists, precisely the reflection of an attempt to make such an extension. Anarchism typically calls attention to the artificiality of such attempts, and especially to the *coercion* required to sustain them. Anarchist literature also points to many ways in which reliance on *government* makes unreasonable assumptions about how wise, how competent, and how just political office holders and citizens can be expected to be. The state, according to the anarchist, is the archetypical utopian dream gone awry.

Contrary to the idea that reliance on voluntary arrangements must inevitably lead to *small* communities, however, it seems reasonable to urge that such questions are surely empirical ones. How widespread a particular cooperative venture might be will surely vary from issue to issue, and there is no reason to prevent such variation. One of the key contributions of market anarchists is the suggestion that there is no need to imagine that all social problems should be taken care of by one single monolithic cooperative organization. The tasks may be separated—even should be separated—so as to enhance the prospects of widespread agreement. People who may agree about how one social issue should be resolved may disagree on others, and there is no need to lump them all together into one bag.

Conclusion

The arguments usually urged in defense of the state are, no doubt, passionately felt. They are not by any stretch of the imagination unreasonable. It really is hard to imagine what the world would be like without governments, and, as urged above, it is perfectly reasonable to demand something more than just abstract theoretical musings from anarchists.[40]

By the same token, though, when theoretical considerations seem so very friendly to the thesis that the state of statelessness has every chance of working quite nicely, when the advantages of the state seem so dubious and so freighted with risk, and when the dangers of states are everywhere apparent, whether in historical or contemporary perspective, it is reasonable to insist that anarchic alternatives be considered seriously.

A human situation in which autonomy is increased, in which cooperation is encouraged, and in which coercion is minimized is certainly an unequivocally good end. Both proponents of the state and of the state of statelessness should surely be able to agree to this proposition. The whole argument depends for its resolution, then, on what can be expected to result from state-of-nature arrangements, as compared to what can be expected to result from the state. This is no light question.

However government first arose, it has become a bad habit. We have come to be too dependent on it. So whether in the end it seems wisest to shake it off altogether or not, it seems hardly debatable that good must inevitably come from continuing reconsideration of the legitimacy and propriety of the state. If we do *not* take such reconsideration seriously, after all, we commit ourselves to continuing participation in and support of institutions that are, at their very foundations, coercive. If that could be avoided, it would be a very good thing indeed.

Notes

1. I received support from Fulbright Scholar Award no. 95-65079, from a Rotary International Grant, from the Rochester Institute of Technology, and from the Graduate School for Social Research at the Polish Academy of Sciences while preparing the final drafts of this article. Many of the thoughts presented in it arose in response to a panel discussion on anarchism that I organized in August of 1993 for the meetings of the International Society of Value Inquiry in Helsinki. I am grateful for inspiration both to the participants

in that panel discussion—Guy Axtell, Jan Narveson, Kirill Thompson, Aviezer Tucker, and Naomi Zack—and to the audience. A version of the paper was then read and discussed at the Annual Conference of the Northern New England Philosophy Association, Plymouth State College, New Hampshire, October 1993. I am especially grateful to Robert Paul Wolff for his helpful commentary on that occasion and to Richard Orr and Victoria Varga for helpful suggestions and thought-provoking conversation on other occasions. Finally, I owe thanks to Barton Lipman for his generous help to an almost anonymous stranger on a personally vexing point.

2. Robert Paul Wolff, *In Defense of Anarchism* (New York: Harper Colophon Books, 1970).

3. Robert Nozick, *Anarchy, State, and Utopia* (New York: Basic Books, 1974).

4. Wolff, *In Defense of Anarchism*, 27. The problem may also be addressed through an examination of the legitimacy of the very concept of political or social authority. For such an examination, see John T. Sanders, "Political Authority," *The Monist*, vol. 66, no. 4 (October 1983): 545–56.

5. Something like the principles of unanimous direct democracy were actually put into practice from the sixteenth through the seventeenth centuries in Poland. The Polish Sejm, which during this period held most real legislative power, followed a rule called the *Liberum Veto*, according to which any single member could halt all proceedings by the simple expression of dissent. See Norman Davies, *God's Playground: A History of Poland in Two Volumes* (New York: Columbia University Press, 1982), especially 345–48. "Such was the strength of feeling about the need for unanimity, that it was considered quite improper to continue when a single voice was raised with the words *Veto* (I deny), or *Nie pozwalam* (I do not allow it)" (vol. 1, 345). The inability of the government to accomplish much of anything under this rule became quite notorious in Europe. When the entire system became the object of a thorough attempt at reform, during the Four Years Sejm of 1788–1792, the threat of a more effective (and considerably more radical) Polish state on its western border led imperial Russia to invade Poland and crush all resistance (mostly by frightening the Polish king, rather than through decisive military action).

6. It is the Aristotelian ideal of community that inspires this distinction, of course. Aristotle emphasizes that a state (in his sense) is determined *not only* by geographic characteristics, but also by common views regarding the good life. Wilhelm Hennis agonizes over this problem in his "Ende der Politik? Zur Krisis der Politik in der Neuzeit," *Merkur* 25 (1971): 509–26 (see especially p. 516). The free-market model of social organization tries to ease the problem by questioning the importance of the geographic considerations. Tibor Machan has argued, interestingly, that the nature of *protective* services, in particular, is such that protectors need to be able to reach protectees, and thus that there has to be some assurance of access that transcends the individual property rights of individual owners. This leads him to conclude that "the only moral

means by which people could delegate to others the authority to protect and preserve their human rights is by uniting into homogeneous human communities, with one legal system per community, administered by a given 'firm' or government.'' See Machan, *Human Rights and Human Liberties* (Chicago: Nelson Hall, 1975), 149–50. The conclusion is unwarranted. What one needs is some reasonable assurance of the kind of access that is in question. Whether one needs government (or monopoly of any kind at all) to get this—or, indeed, whether governments and other monopolies are even good ways to get this—is precisely the question at issue. For what is probably the most detailed attempt to establish a thesis similar to Machan's, see Robert Nozick, *Anarchy, State, and Utopia*, especially the first section. For a critical response to this attempt, see John T. Sanders, ''The Free Market Model Versus Government: A Reply to Nozick,'' *Journal of Libertarian Studies*, vol. 1, no. 1 (Winter 1977): 35–44, included in a slightly revised form as chap. 10 of Sanders, *The Ethical Argument against Government* (Washington: University Press of America, 1980).

7. John Rawls, *A Theory of Justice* (1971; reprinted, Cambridge, Mass.: Belknap Press, 1973), especially 139.

8. It is true, as Kai Nielsen reminds us, that we cannot stand outside our concept of rationality ''to see what rationality really is.'' What we can do, however, is to try to arrange a completely general format, within which various understandings of reason may be displayed and contrasted. It seems to me that this is one of the virtues of the Rawlsian methodological framework. See Nielsen, ''Distrusting Reason,'' *Ethics* 87 (1976/77): 49–60.

9. Robert Nozick argues that ''Rawls' construction is incapable of yielding an entitlement or historical conception of distributive justice,'' although it ''might be used in an attempt to *derive*, when conjoined with factual information, historical-entitlement principles, as derivative principles falling under a nonentitlement conception of justice.'' Even if it *is* used in this way, Nozick thinks that the derived historical-entitlement principles can, at best, be only approximations of the principles of acquisition, transfer, and rectification that he favors; thus, Nozick thinks that his theory of justice could not be adequately reconstructed using the Rawlsian framework: ''it will produce the wrong sorts of reasons for them [the Nozickean principles], and its derived results sometimes will conflict with the precisely correct principles'' (*Anarchy, State, and Utopia*, 202). But what are the *right* sorts of reasons for Nozick's principles? He tells us (p. 51) that he hopes to grapple with this issue on another occasion, but all of his clues seem to amount either to factual considerations or to notions that, Nozick thinks, might ''straddle'' the is-ought gap (pp. 49–51). From what Nozick tells us about candidates for the latter category, it is not easy to see why they, along with other factual information, could not be used in an original position to derive Nozickean principles. Why couldn't these highly idealized rational persons do what Nozick hopes to do? If there are any reasons *at all* for Nozick's theory of justice, they would surely

be considered by the parties to the original position, the only qualification being that these reasons may not themselves rely on Nozickean justice. If there are *no* reasons, then either the theory is not rationally defensible or the principles of justice are just brute facts. Even in the latter case, though, it is hard to see why such facts could not be considered in an original position (they aren't just brute facts for Rawls, of course). It is hard to see how Nozick can be so circumspect about the basis of the constraints he recommends and yet so confident that Rawls's framework could not be used to exhibit that basis.

10. Although it has been suggested by some authors that Rawls's liberalism infects even the idea of reflective equilibrium, most critics have accepted this notion and have objected only to Rawls's specific use of it. For a good example of the former concern, see Edward F. McClennan's review of Brian Barry, *The Liberal Theory of Justice*, in *Social Theory and Practice* 3 (1974): 117–22; also Peter Singer, "Philosophers are Back on the Job," *New York Times Magazine* (7 July 1974): 6–7 and 17–20. Singer's concern may not be quite the same as McClennan's, but it is clear that he is uncomfortable about the idea of reflective equilibrium as a tool for discovering or revealing principles of justice. For a response to such suspicions about reflective equilibrium, see Marcus G. Singer, "Justice, Theory, and a Theory of Justice," *Philosophy of Science* 44 (1977): 594–618, especially 608–09. For an extremely suggestive general defense of the "method of wide reflective equilibrium," see Norman Daniels, "Wide Reflective Equilibrium and Theory Acceptance in Ethics," *Journal of Philosophy* 76 (1979): 256–82. For critique of Rawls's liberal *interpretation* of his framework, on the other hand, here is a motley array of articles that approach the issue from a variety of different political perspectives: Adina Schwartz, "Moral Neutrality and Primary Goods," *Ethics* 83 (1972/73): 294–307; Richard Miller, "Rawls and marxism," *Philosophy & Public Affairs* 3 (1973/74): 167–91; David Gauthier, "Justice and Natural Endowment: Toward a Critique of Rawls' Ideological Framework," *Social Theory and Practice* 3 (1974): 3–26; David Gauthier, "Rational Cooperation," *Nous* 8 (1974): 53–65; Kenneth J. Arrow, "Some Ordinalist-Utilitarian Notes on Rawls' Theory of Justice," *Journal of Philosophy* 70 (1973): 245–63; Douglas B. Rasmussen, "A Critique of Rawls' *Theory of Justice*," *Personalist* 55 (1974): 303–18; David Lewis Schaefer, "The 'Sense' and Non-sense of Justice," *Political Science Reviewer* 3 (1973): 1–41.

11. Joseph Margolis, "Justice as Fairness," *Humanist*, vol. 33, no. 3 (1973): 36–37, 37.

12. It seems to me that the Rawls literature is burdened by confusions over what is framework and what is content. See, for example, Kai Nielsen's "On Philosophic Method," *International Philosophical Quarterly* 16 (1976): 349–68, especially pp. 358–68, for some typical confusion. The distinction is, admittedly, difficult to sort out. One of the best early critiques of the framework, however, seems to be David Keyt's "The Social Contract as an Analytic, Justificatory, and Polemic Device," *Canadian Journal of Philosophy* 4

(1974/75): 241–52. Keyt argues that the "analytic" use of the framework may not expose derived principles of justice to refutation, since there would be, for any set of such principles, an indefinite number of initial situations from which they might be derived. Keyt cites evidence that Rawls would want special attention directed to the "most reasonable" initial situation for any conception of justice, and he argues persuasively that there is no such animal, short of an initial situation that is specified in such a way as to be logically equivalent to the principles to be derived. If Keyt is right, then the methodological framework cannot refute "isms" in one fell swoop. Whether Rawls thought it could is, I think, open to question. Whatever the answer may be to this question, though, the Rawlsian framework is still helpful in criticizing *particular* attempts to elaborate a conception of justice or a social philosophy.

13. For an extended argument of this kind, see Sanders, *The Ethical Argument against Government.*

14. Prisoners' Dilemma games are sometimes conceived as real interactive games, played in real time, where one party goes first and the other must then respond. This changes the game conceptually, but still leaves the same problems at the door of the first player—or, for that matter, of each player—as consideration is given, before play begins, to questions of strategy.

15. Quite generally, decision problems with Prisoners' Dilemma structure arise when (1) players are constrained to making one of two mutually exclusive choices (usually between "cooperation," on the one hand, and "noncooperation" or "defection," on the other); (2) the payoff matrix is such that (a) the highest payoff comes to players who defect in conjunction with cooperation on the part of their opponent, (b) the next highest payoff comes to players who jointly cooperate, (c) the next highest payoff comes to players who jointly defect, and (d) the lowest payoff comes to players who cooperate in conjunction with defection on the part of their opponent (players covered under type (d) are called "suckers"); (3) the relation among these several payoff amounts is (at least by some authors—such as Robert Axelrod, "The Emergence of Cooperation among Egoists," *American Political Science Review* 75 [1981]: 306–18, and Barton L. Lipman, "Cooperation among Egoists in Prisoners' Dilemma and Chicken Games," *Public Choice* 51 [1986]: 315–31) further constrained such that when one adds together the payoff to type (a) players and the payoff to type (d) players, the result is less than twice the payoff to type (b) players (this ensures that mutual cooperation is Pareto-preferred to alternating between the two single-defection situations); (4) play is strictly "self-interested" in the sense of attempting to maximize payoff (neither player has any interest *other* than maximization of expected payoff); (5) there is no opportunity for communication among the players; (6) the game will be played precisely once, so that no questions can arise concerning either information about what strategy players have used in the past or what strategy may be expected in the future; and (7) the game is played without the benefit of any information at all about how the opposing players have played, are playing, or

will play similar games with other opponents. All these constraints are required in order to generate a proper Prisoners' Dilemma situation. While lip service is almost always paid to this fact in literature that attempts to apply game theory to real social situations, the degree to which these constraints make such application dubious is not always sufficiently appreciated, as will become clearer below.

16. For discussion of related matters, see Sanders, "Political Authority."

17. One could construct a Prisoners' Dilemma situation in such a way that the players were understood not as being egoistical in any *normal* sense, but still as being egoistical maximizers in the economic and game-theoretic sense. For example, one can imagine two philanthropists—each trying to maximize the benefits to others, all things considered—engaging in a Prisoners' Dilemma game. That they are philanthropists means that the relevant payoffs will be measured in terms of benefits to others, rather than benefits to the players themselves. All that is necessary to produce the Prisoners' Dilemma situation is that these payoffs—whatever their metric—be ranked in the way indicated in note 15 above (as well as satisfying the other conditions mentioned there) and that these payoffs really do reflect what the players want to accomplish. It is only in this latter sense—the sense in which the values expressed in the payoffs really are the values of the players—that the game needs to be "egoistical." *Whatever* the goals and values of the players—provided only that these not make specific reference to benefits to the opponent, in particular—players will find cooperation to be irrational when the decision situation is structured as in note 15. Finally, it has been suggested—notably by David Gauthier (*Morals by Agreement* [New York: Oxford University Press, 1986], chap. 6), and Jan Narveson (*The Libertarian Idea* [Philadelphia: Temple University Press, 1988], 140–47, and "The Anarchist's Case," this volume, 195–216)—that since egoistical maximizers would not be able to cooperate in PD situations, they must (rationally) rearrange their personal dispositions in such a way as to make cooperation possible. This seems to me to "solve" the PD problem simply by ignoring it. Even if I am mistaken about this, though, the fact that cooperation becomes rational for egoistical maximizers as soon as the entirely unrealistic presumptions about communication and information are relaxed (see the text, above and below) seems to make this rather radical step quite unnecessary.

18. It would really be peculiar if agreement required very *much* in the way of statelike constraint, since it is notorious that even the rankest criminals manage to forge working agreements with one another in order to achieve their ends. For discussion of this issue in a rather different context, see John T. Sanders, "Honor among Thieves: Some Reflections on Professional Codes of Ethics," *Professional Ethics*, vol. 2, nos. 3–4 (Spring/Summer 1993): 83–103.

19. Robert Axelrod, *The Evolution of Cooperation* (New York: Basic Books, 1984). For a theoretical rather than empirical argument in favor of the individual rationality of something like a tit-for-tat strategy in iterated play,

see Anthony de Jasay, "Self-Contradictory Contractarianism," this volume, 137–169. See also Michael Taylor, *Anarchy and Cooperation* (London: John Wiley & Son, 1976), and Taylor, *The Possibility of Cooperation* (Cambridge: Cambridge University Press, 1987). Tit-for-tat also strongly resembles the "avenging angel" strategy discussed in Gregory Kavka, "Why Even Morally Perfect People Would Need Government," this volume, 41–61. Kavka's discussion seems most relevant, however, to games such as Chicken rather than to games like Prisoners' Dilemma. For more on Chicken, see below.

20. As David Schmidtz points out, real life state-of-nature situations are likely not only to be ones in which iterated play is the rule, but ones in which *concatenated* play is most likely. That is, players will not just be playing with a single player, over and over again, but simultaneously with many others, who will revise their play on the basis of the reputation that any given potential player acquires through past play with others. See Schmidtz, *The Limits of Government: An Essay on the Public Goods Argument* (Boulder: Westview Press, 1991), 101–02. See also de Jasay, "Self-Contradictory Contractarianism," and Howard H. Harriott, "Games, Anarchy, and the Nonnecessity of the State," this volume, 119–136.

21. See especially Lipman, "Cooperation among Egoists in Prisoners' Dilemma and Chicken Games." It is the *terms* of the cooperation that are likely in real social situations that properly concern writers such as Peter Danielson ("The Rights of Chickens: Rational Foundations for Libertarianism?" this volume, 171–193). This issue deserves serious independent attention. The availability of mixed strategies embodying varying forms of cooperation offers some hope for a successful anarchist response to Danielson's objections, but such a response has yet to be worked out in substantive detail. For an interesting discussion of attempts to apply game theory (and "metagame theory," which considers strategic games as embedded in broader and more dynamic decision settings) to real situations, with specific comparison of PD games and Chicken games, see Steven J. Brams, *Game Theory and Politics* (New York: The Free Press, 1975), especially 39–50. Questions about which strategies are stable in games of Chicken can be answered, of course, only when details about payoffs—among other things—are known. For an exceptionally helpful discussion of attempts to model biological conflict via "evolutionary game theory," again with special reference to Chicken, see Karl Sigmund, *Games of Life: Explorations in Ecology, Evolution, and Behaviour* (Oxford: Oxford University Press, 1993), especially 161–79. It is instructive (and important) to keep in mind, when considering which strategies might be likely in real-world situations that are supposedly modeled by theoretical tools like the game of Chicken, that in nature it is within populations of doves—and similarly ill-armed beasts—that one finds relatively unconstrained escalation of conflicts. More dangerously equipped animals—like hawks, for example— turn to posture and ritual a great deal more than doves do and are much less likely to escalate conflicts with competitors of their own species. The details

of the situation that will determine which strategies are stable for any real-world situation are thus likely to be extraordinarily complex, and will need also to take into account the fact that all human real-world applications of game and metagame theories will invariably involve asymmetries—hawks and doves interacting with one another, not just each with similarly equipped partners—that are not well modeled in simple games like Chicken. Finally, for a short overview of just how powerful evolutionary game theory can be, even as a predictive tool rather that just as an explanatory tool, see Robert Pool, "Putting Game Theory to the Test," *Science* 267 (17 March 1995).

22. John Dewey, "Democracy and Educational Administration," 57–58.

23. Franz Oppenheimer, *The State* (Indianapolis: Bobbs-Merrill, 1914), 25.

24. Max Weber, *Economy and Society*, vol. 1, ed. by G. Roth and C. Wittich (New York: Bedminster Press, 1968).

25. There is an important ambiguity, inherent in the understanding of government as necessarily coercive, that must be addressed. While almost everyone—fans and foes of government alike—would agree that one central task of government is to use coercive force to achieve the ends of citizens (such as protection against aggression, for example), not everyone agrees that governments necessarily must coerce innocent citizens in the performance of these tasks. Tibor Machan, for example, has argued against philosophical anarchism on the basis of an understanding of "government" that imagines that citizens' choice of "government" could be voluntary, that secession might be perfectly permissible, even that "governments" might compete with one another for clientele. See Machan, *Human Rights and Human Liberties*, especially 150–51 (although it is interesting that Machan also describes himself, on p. 157, as having "some reluctance" in choosing the term "government" to refer to such service providers). Such "governments," functioning precisely in the way that anarchists typically suggest that voluntary cooperative *alternatives* to government might function, are plainly not objectionable to anarchists. Nor are they governments. For reasons against adopting an overly liberal definition of "government" of the kind apparently envisioned by Machan, see Sanders, *The Ethical Argument against Government*, especially the introduction. Finally, Machan has more recently made it clear that he thinks of the price of "seceding" from "government" as being withdrawal from human society altogether and that (while he apparently shares at least some anarchic concerns about the risks of an overrich construal of tacit consent) participating in normal human interactions with others implies consent to government. See Machan, *Individuals and Their Rights* (La Salle, Ill.: Open Court, 1989), 171–82. This goes way too far, even on the logic of Machan's own argument. Deliberately engaging in human interaction could reasonably imply consent only, at most, to *some* state of affairs that would make that particular interaction possible (even this goes too far, since people might actually prefer alternatives to the forms of interaction that they are forced to choose under presently existing institutional arrangements). It manifestly does not imply

consent to the particular state of affairs that happen, in this instance, to support the interaction in question. Seceders thus need not imply that they want no part of human interaction (although they might mean this), only instead that they want no part of the particular arrangements for such interaction provided by the system they secede from.

26. In *The Ethical Argument against Government*, I have argued that the case against government is quite strong when one gives adequate attention to all the relevant factors.

27. See, for example, *The Ethical Argument against Government*, especially chap. 6, from which much of the remainder of this section has been taken.

28. Mancur Olson, *The Logic of Collective Action: Public Goods and the Theory of Groups* (Cambridge, Mass.: Harvard University Press, 1965), 14.

29. Where the cost per unit decreases as the size of the group increases, it may very well be difficult to predict that increasing group size will invariably lead to a decreasing willingness (or capacity) to supply the public good. This will, I think, be the *general* tendency of increasing group size, but some increases may have opposite local effects on the curve. See William H. Riker and Peter C. Ordeshook, *An Introduction to Positive Political Theory* (Englewood Cliffs, N.J.: Prentice-Hall, 1973), 73–74, footnote 31. Similar complications may arise if the value that individuals place on the good changes as group size increases. But both of these issues seem to cause trouble only for a *dynamic* theory of the effects of increasing group size. If the various groups are defined as in the three paragraphs immediately preceding this one in the text and if one deals with them without asking what happens dynamically as an intermediate group gets larger and larger (for example), the problems seem not to be raised.

30. In this context, as mentioned above, the ideal of egoistic rationality is much more benign than in connection with the Prisoners' Dilemma, since the personal desires that agents are trying to maximize can be as other-oriented as you please. All that counts is that the desires are the *agent's* desires.

31. Olson does qualify the potential value of his theory by noting that it may not be of much (or any) use as regards "nonrational" or "irrational" groups (pp. 159–65). Among such groups, it seems, he would include those characterized by "ideologically oriented behavior" (p. 162). Karen Johnson, in "A Note on the Inapplicability of Olson's Logic of Collective Action to the State," *Ethics* 85 (1974/75): 170–74, has argued, along the lines of this first option of ours, to the conclusion that the *state* is just the sort of group not covered successfully by Olson's analysis. Her notion of the state is considerably broader than the one being considered here, however. For discussion of some experimental evidence that bears on Olsonian option 1 and for some hope that this option really could serve successfully in defending the state of statelessness against public-goods arguments, see Harriott, "Games, Anarchy, and the Nonnecessity of the State."

32. For discussion of some of the problems with this option, see Sanders, *The Ethical Argument against Government*, 171.

33. See *The Ethical Argument against Government* for an attempt to provide just such an argument, with the public-goods issue held constantly in view.

34. The text of this part of the paper was composed in the Helsinki International Airport at the end of August 1993, during a long wait between flights. I had just left Moscow, where I had spent ten days living on the economy (or economies). My visit was not long, but I was left with remarkably vivid—sometimes surreal—impressions.

35. This same effect is quite astonishingly evident in the suburbs of Warsaw, as well, as I note in the fall of 1995 as this volume goes to press. Indeed, it is not clear that the houses going up at this particular moment in time are at all well described as "middle-class," given the prevalence of indoor swimming pools, towers with turrets, and large tracts of land. Newly affluent Poles seem for all the world to be reinvigorating, at the close of the twentieth century, their nation's historical predilection for castle construction.

36. Jan Narveson has argued this way in "Prospects for Anarchism," a short paper prepared for the Helsinki panel referred to above. A revised version of this earlier paper is included in the closing pages of "The Anarchist's Case." See also A. John Simmons, "Philosophical Anarchism," this volume, 19–39.

37. The recent hard times among the more severe "socialist" states has led to great enthusiasm among "capitalists" of all kinds. The claim that "socialism is dead"—or at least that *communism* is dead—has frequently been made by politicians, by journalists, and by academics. Now, I'm one of those who think that ideological socialism is an inadequate tool for social analysis, both for empirical and axiological reasons, but it seems far from likely that socialism is dead as an ideology, just because a few states have collapsed. For one thing, committed ideological socialists were never particularly fond of the regimes that have recently fallen. For another, as "capitalism" attempts to address the problems of the states recently governed by centralized "socialists," the inevitable disappointment in nasty side effects of "capitalization" will just as inevitably give birth to nostalgia for "socialism," as has been shown in the mid-1990s in election results all over Central and Eastern Europe. The scare quotes in this note are surrogates for critical analysis of the aptness of the terms thus quoted, some of which is to be found back in the text.

38. For an argument to the effect that even angels would need government, see Gregory S. Kavka, "Why Even Morally Perfect People Would Need Government."

39. See Sanders, "Political Authority."

40. Not that there is anything intrinsically wrong with abstract theoretical musings—indeed, there are few things in the world that are more fun—but being taken seriously requires more.

Index

About the Contributors

Peter Danielson is professor of philosophy and senior research fellow at the Centre for Applied Ethics, University of British Columbia. Research interests include ethics and evolution, cognitive and social science, and ethics and information technology. Recent publications include *Artificial Morality* (Routledge, 1992) and *Modeling Rationality, Morality, and Evolution* (Oxford University Press, forthcoming). For current research projects, consult his WEB page: http://www.eth-ics.ubc.cã /pad.

David Friedman wrote his first book, *The Machinery of Freedom*—in which he explored, among other things, the possibility of a society with private property and without government—while working on a Ph.D. in physics and then as a post-doc at the University of Chicago. He then switched fields to economics and has taught at Virginia Polytechnic Institute, the University of California branches at Los Angeles and Irvine, Tulane, the University of Chicago, and Cornell, and is currently a professor of law at the law school of Santa Clara University. His current interests are in economic analysis of law and computer law. He has published articles on a wide variety of topics and is also the author of a price theory textbook. His hobbies include cooking from medieval cookbooks.

Leslie Green teaches at the Osgoode Hall Law School and in the Department of Philosophy at York University, Toronto. He is author of *The Authority of the State* (Oxford: Clarendon Press, 1990) and coeditor (with Allan Hutchinson) of *Law and the Community* (Toronto: Carswell, 1989) and writes widely in jurisprudence and political theory.

295

Howard H. Harriott teaches and researches in political philosophy and inductive logic at the University of South Carolina, where he is assistant professor of philosophy. His articles have appeared in such journals as *International Philosophical Quarterly*, *Journal of Peace Research*, and *Ethical Perspectives*.

Anthony de Jasay is a Hungarian-born economist and political philosopher. His professional career took place in Oxford and Paris. He lives, retired, in France. His published work includes *The State* (Oxford: Blackwell, 1985), *Social Contract, Free Ride: A Study of the Public Goods Problem* (Oxford: Clarendon Press, 1989), and *Choice, Contract, Consent: A Restatement of Liberalism* (London: Institute of Economic Affairs, 1991), some of which has been translated into German, French, and Spanish.

Gregory S. Kavka served as professor of philosophy and social science at the University of California, Irvine, where he taught moral and political philosophy. His books include *Hobbesian Moral and Political Theory* (Princeton, N.J.: Princeton University Press, 1986) and *Moral Paradoxes of Nuclear Deterrence* (Cambridge: Cambridge University Press, 1987).

Jan Clifford Lester is the director of the Liberty Institute and teaches philosophy at Middlesex University (London). He specializes in contemporary political philosophy with particular reference to liberty and the market, in which area he has published articles and reviews. His *Liberty, Welfare, and Market-Anarchy* is forthcoming.

Jan Narveson is professor of philosophy at the University of Waterloo in Ontario, Canada. He is the author of many papers in philosophical periodicals and anthologies, mainly on moral and political theory and practice, and of *Morality and Utility* (Baltimore, Md.: Johns Hopkins University Press, 1967), *The Libertarian Idea* (Philadelphia: Temple University Press, 1989), *Moral Matters* (Peterborough, Ontario: Broadview Press, 1993), and, with Marilyn Friedman, *Political Correctness* (Lanham, Md.: Rowman & Littlefield, 1995). He is also the editor of *Moral Issues* (Oxford: Oxford University Press, 1983) and is on the editorial boards of several philosophic journals. He is also a fellow of the Royal Society of Canada.

Cheyney Ryan is professor of philosophy at the University of Oregon, where he has also been involved in the Peace and Conflict Studies

Program. He has published widely in the areas of political and moral philosophy, philosophy of law, and philosophy of economics. In recent years, his work has focused increasingly on issues of violence and nonviolence. His most recent article (in *Hypatia*), "The One Who Burns Herself for Peace," explores the pacifist anarchism of Dorothy Day.

John T. Sanders is visiting professor of philosophy at the Graduate School for Social Research at the Institute of Philosophy and Sociology of the Polish Academy of Sciences and professor of philosophy at the Rochester Institute of Technology. His work is included in several recent and forthcoming anthologies, and his articles have appeared in such journals as *Philosophy & Public Affairs*, *The Harvard Journal of Law and Public Policy*, and others. He is the author of *The Ethical Argument against Government* (Washington, D.C.: University Press of America, 1980) and *Contra Leviathan: On the Legitimacy and Propriety of the State* (Amsterdam and Atlanta: Rodopi, forthcoming 1996). His interests include political and social philosophy, philosophy of science, metaphysics, and ethics.

David Schmidtz is associate professor of philosophy and associate professor of economics at the University of Arizona. His publications include *The Limits of Government* (Boulder, Colo.: Westview Press, 1991) and *Rational Choice and Moral Agency* (Princeton, N.J.: Princeton University Press, 1994). He is now coauthoring with Robert Goodin a book on individual responsibility and the welfare state for Cambridge Press's new *For & Against* series.

A. John Simmons is professor of philosophy at the University of Virginia. He received his A.B. from Princeton University in 1972 and his Ph.D. from Cornell University in 1977. An editor of the journal *Philosophy & Public Affairs*, he is the author of *Moral Principles and Political Obligations* (Princeton, N.J.: Princeton University Press, 1979), *The Lockean Theory of Rights* (Princeton, N.J.: Princeton University Press, 1992), *On the Edge of Anarchy: Locke, Consent, and the Limits of Society* (Princeton, N.J.: Princeton University Press, 1993), and articles on various topics in political, moral, and legal philosophy.

Jonathan Wolff is senior lecturer in philosophy at University College London and the author of *Robert Nozick* (Oxford: Polity Press; and Stanford, Calif.: Stanford University Press, 1991) and *An Introduction to Political Philosophy* (Oxford: Oxford University Press, 1996).